Calistoga 1944

A Small Town
During a Big War

HERB + GRETCHEN
YOU KNOW A LOT OF
THE FOLKS IN HERE.
ENJOY.

Jack Rannells

Calistoga, CA
2012

ISBN-13: 978-0-9856506-0-5
Library of Congress Control Number: 2012909032

Calistoga 1944

A Small Town
During a Big War

Contents

Introduction

This book records events in and about a small town in California's Napa Valley during 1944. It came to mind while I was doing research in the *Weekly Calistogan* newspapers of that year. I was looking for information about Calistoga High School alumni killed or missing in action in World War II. Those stories are there. They are gripping.

But there is so much more: notes from/about local guys and gals serving in the military – some honoring heroism, some describing living conditions in a combat zone, some whooping over their good luck in seeing famous places. There are many details about life on the home front – the pinch of rationing; civil defense activities; war bond drives; the happy, self-absorbed news of local service clubs, lodges, churches, and schools; the drive to create Robert Louis Stevenson State Park on Mount St. Helena; and, oh yes, the *Weekly Calistogan's* nasty opposition to the re-election of our commander in chief, Franklin Delano Roosevelt, to a fourth term in office.

There are 33 chapters in this book. Each covers a different week in 1944. They start with highlights of that week's war news and other major events, then switch to the local scene, as reported in the *Weekly Calistogan*. The first chapter, "January 7," includes bits from 56 articles and advertisements to give you a feeling for both the newspaper and its community. For the other 32 weeks, only selected articles are included. "Notes" with additional information follow a few articles. Some of the notes are based on talk with people who were involved in the stories and now are senior citizens, like me. Others are based on research.

By 1944, America was gaining the initiative in both the European and Pacific theaters of World War II. But it was still tough times – more difficult than anyone who wasn't there can imagine. Fear had been set in concrete on Feb. 23, 1942 – just eleven weeks after the Pearl Harbor attack – when a Japanese submarine surfaced and shelled an oil field north of Santa Barbara. In January 1942, the government required "enemy aliens" (persons of German, Italian, or Japanese nationality) to register for identification cards. Still, anxiety reigned. Then the government moved about 110,000 people of Japanese heritage – 62 percent of them United States citizens – from their homes along the Pacific Coast into "relocation camps" east of the Sierra/Cascade ranges.

The Japanese military stoked anxieties again in November 1944, when it began releasing balloons with firebombs attached, hoping to spread wildfires across the western states. Very few fires occurred – but the tactic increased public uneasiness.

Throughout the war, there were regular test blackouts, when air raid sirens wailed and everyone had to get into rooms in their homes/buildings with special coverings to keep any light from showing outside.

Almost anything worth wanting was rationed – meat, butter, cheese, sugar, canned foods, shoes, gasoline, tires, cigarettes – if it was available at all. Moms and kids did a lot of the farm labor – especially during the extended summer vacation from school. It's all history – quite unimaginable to most folks now.

I have included an index to mentions of 123 service men and women – many of them more than once. It's in the front of the book, not in the usual index space at the end.

On the next pages and at the back of the book are brief articles you might want to scan to help you appreciate the differences between wartime 1944 and the present.

Please let me know of any errors or omissions in case I decide to produce a second edition of the book. Enjoy.

Jack Rannells
1520 Fair Way, Calistoga, CA 94515
jackbeanier@att.net

Calistoga 1944 – So Different

How different? For starters, it had less than one-fourth of today's population, but it was a far more self-contained community. It had a movie theater (the Ritz); a hospital; a mortuary; a cemetery; a lumber yard; a feed store; a tiny Safeway and four even smaller family-owned groceries (Barberis, Evans, Grauss, and Mariani); a full-line bakery; liquor stores; clothing stores; beauty shops; a laundry; a furniture store; a five-and-dime; a bank; a doctor; a dentist; attorneys; insurance offices; service stations; auto repair shops; shoe repairers; a radio repairer; a jeweler; a water bottling plant; daily Southern Pacific freight trains; seven Greyhound bus trips a day to/from San Francisco; a justice of the peace (judge); and a jail. These services had to be close at hand in a world before freeways and with war-time gasoline rationing in force.

Another notable difference – retail stores closed on Sunday.

Calistoga was a seasonal resort town, with plenty of soda fountains, restaurants, and bars (word was that Calistoga had the most bars per capita in the state). The town was surrounded mostly by prune and walnut orchards and dairies. There were only four wineries in the area (today: forty-six). The walnut plant on Washington Street was a major job source in the fall. There were two chicken hatcheries just outside of town, and several families raised rabbits for sale as food.

The historic multi-story, balconied Hotel Calistoga was the *prima donna* of Lincoln Avenue. It's long gone. So is the fire siren at Lincoln and Washington that screamed "It's Noon!" every day and rallied volunteer firefighters from all around town in emergencies. The police and fire departments were based in City Hall.

Calistoga was a lot more social in 1944. Folks saw each other daily when they shopped for food or went to the post office to pick up their mail (only rural residents had mail delivery). Lodges, service clubs, and churches kept people mixing in both traditional and wartime activities. Outside town, the Bennett and Tucker farm centers bustled with activities.

The two major community projects followed by the *Weekly Calistogans* of 1944 were creation of a Hospitality House for visiting servicemen and the founding of Robert Louis Stevenson State Park on the shoulder of Mount St. Helena.

Read on.

The War Effort at Home

Calistoga geared up quickly once the United States entered World War II on December 8, 1941.

Within weeks, it was training teams of air raid wardens. These volunteers manned a small outpost near the walnut plant, working four-hour shifts around the clock as part of a Bay Area network that reported any unusual planes to the Army Air Force in San Francisco.

A defense center was established next to the post office on Lincoln Avenue. Committees trained there to be ready for medical, rescue, evacuation, and shelter needs. Other groups headed war bond drives and helped manage food stamps. Many Calistoga area residents took jobs at Mare Island Naval Shipyard in Vallejo; the Basalt plant at Napa, where small rescue/salvage ships were built; Benicia Arsenal; or other war-linked work.

The government started mandatory rationing in 1942. It had to control supply and demand for a wide variety of food and materials needed for the war effort. Rationing was deemed a way to do it while avoiding public anger over shortages or the rich getting more than their share.

Rationing covered many food items, clothing, shoes, coffee, gasoline, tires, and fuel oil. Each ration coupon book had specifications and deadlines. The allowance for gasoline and tires depended on the distance to one's job. People were urged to drive at 35 mph, deemed the most efficient speed in terms of fuel use.

Rationing did not end until 1946. It had one serious side effect – illegal "black markets," where people could buy rationed items on the sly (usually at high prices). They dealt mainly in meat, sugar, and gasoline.

Few complained publicly about rationing, because people knew those in the military were making greater sacrifices. The Office of War

Information keyed in on this feeling with posters pleading "Do with less so they'll have enough."

The government also urged the conservation and recycling of metal, paper, and rubber. There were regular scrap metal drives.

Food manufacturers keyed products to wartime shortages. Kraft macaroni and cheese dinner gained great popularity as a substitute for meat and dairy products. Only one ration coupon was required for two boxes. Oleo margarine replaced butter. Cottage cheese became a significant substitute for meat.

"Victory gardens" were one of the major home front efforts. By 1945, an estimated 20 million victory gardens produced about 40 percent of America's vegetables. Many families "canned" fruits and vegetables in glass jars for year-round use.

Through this dark, restrictive background of war, Calistoga's churches, lodges, and service clubs seemed to thrive on the togetherness. The community had standout leaders – homegrown Bank of America executives Frank Piner and Ed Molinari at the top; but everyone seemed to ready to help.

Read on.

Lincoln Avenue Businesses

Main Street (now Foothill Blvd.)

Shell Oil station	Union Oil station
	Simic Funeral Home

Myrtle Street

Public Library

Dr. McGreane / Red Cross	Reeder's Creamery / Union Ice

Cedar Street

Fior d'Italia / bar / restaurant

Napa River bridge

Pacific Telephone	Mitchell Feed & grocery
Howard's Garage	I.C. Adams photography
Ritz Theater	Hospitality House
Albright Real Estate	Ding's Grocery
	Weekly Calistogan / Ted Weil insurance
Masonic building	Allen Dry Goods
Safeway	Dr. Stevens dentist/Conrad Weil, atty/
	Odd Fellows & Rebekahs /
Stanley's 5 & 10	Native Sons & Daughters
	Pacific Gas & Electric
Fisher Real Estate	Lommel's Creamery
barber shop	Al's Market
People's Meat Market	Mercer Jewelry
Walker's Coffee Shop	Puritan Bakery
	Walker's Shoe Repair
Silverado Bar / pool hall	Longmire's Sandwich Shop
Good Eats restaurant	Bank of America

Washington Street

Hotel Oaks/Shamrock Tavern	Alm & Ames Hardware/Mariani's Grocery
Calistoga Drugs/Adams Liquors	Funke clothing, cleaning
Silverado Beauty Shop	Johnston's Pharmacy
Hotel Calistoga / Greyhound	Kelly's Village Green
Justice of the Peace	Roberts Clothing
Cole's Barber Shop	barber
Citizen Service Corps	Bank Club
Post Office	Grauss General Merchandise
Sport Club	Bell restaurant
Green Café / hotel	Mount View Hotel
Tedeschi Liquors	shoe repair
Signal Oil station	White Swan bar
Southern Pacific depot /	
Railway Express Agency /	
Western Union	

Railroad tracks

7

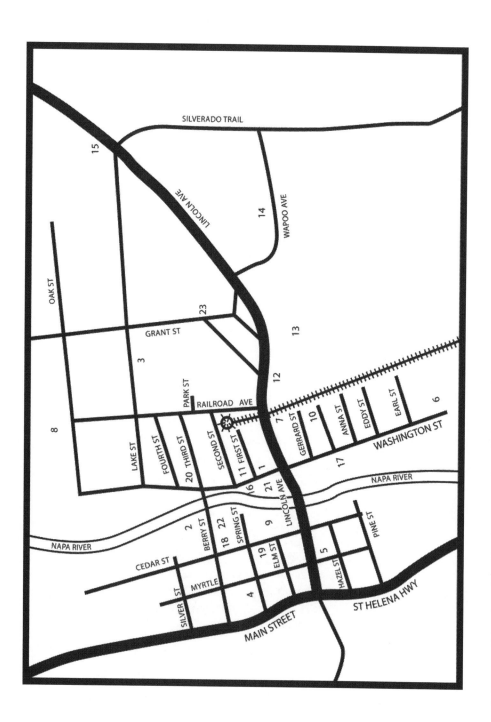

Calistoga Streets, 1944

1. City Hall/police/fire
2. Elementary school
3. High school/tennis courts
4. Hospital
5. Library
6. Walnut plant
7. Railroad depot
8. Fairgroujd
9. Pioneer Park
10. Dr. Aalders Hot Springs
11. Piner's Hot Springs
12. Nance's Mud Baths
13. Pacheteau's Hot Springs
14. Pisa Farm Resort
15. Carvea's fruits/vegetables
16. Hamond Lumber
17. Catholic Church
18. Christian Science Society
19. Methodist Church
20. Presbyterian Church
21. Full Gospel Church
22. Seventh-day Adventist Church
23. Co-op winery

Greater Calistoga Area, 1944

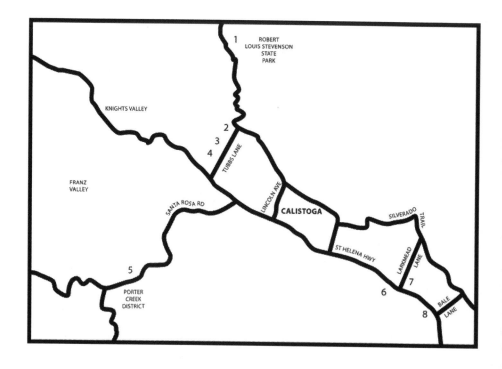

1. Robert Louis Stevenson State Park
(it was farther away than trimmed map suggests)
2. Chateau Montelena Winery
3. Bennett Farm Center
4. Old Faithful Geyser
5. Petrified Forest
6. Tucker Farm Center
7. Larkmead Winery
8. Bothe's Paradise Park

Index to Servicemen / Women

Calistoga 1944

Name	Chapter	Name	Chapter
Ray Leggitt	19	Edward Ottonello	1
Art Leoni	20	Leslie Palmer	1
'Barney' Light	30	Delbert Pearl	28
John Lucas	25	Lauren Procter	33
Bretta Lundell	20		
Riley C. McEuen	20	William C. Richter*	20
Gerald McFall	2	Bill Roberts	20
John McFall	2	Albert Rose	2, 25
William McFall Jr.	2	Doyle Rose	25
John Montelli	21	George Scarfe	5
Kenneth Moran	23	Arnold F. Schade	30
Emily Musante	14, 22	Charles Schmitt	29
Scott Nagel	6	Jack Scott	28
Michael Nagy	6, 8, 9	David Senter*	19
David Newton	13, 17	Jerry Senter	6, 33
Peter Nolasco	15	Richard H. Senter	33
		David Sharp	1, 17

* Died   ** Missing   *** Prisoner

Seven veterans listed in this index are among the nine Block C members in this 1942 yearbook photo; back row, left to right: Coach Bill Manford, Robert Greene, James Switzer, Charles Clark, Roy Enderlin, and Blaine Huston; front row, l to r: Nick Bardes, Glenn Stockton, Lee Decker, and Bob Johnston.

Index

* Died   ** Missing   *** Prisoner

Chapter 1

January 1-7

The War: The four-month battle of Monte Cassino, south of Rome, begins. The Russian Army enters Poland.

𝔚eekly 𝔊alistogan of January 7, 1944

page 1

Mabel Jewell, director of the county Citizens' Service Corps, announced plans to meet with block leaders in Calistoga for the Food Fights for Freedom campaign. The agency also is collecting used clothing and is gearing up for the Fourth War Loan Drive.

Frank Piner is local chairman of the fund drive – the sale of Series E Savings Bonds. The bonds are issued in maturity values of $25, $50, $100, $500, and $1,000. They cost 75 percent of the maturity value ($18.75 for a $25 bond, for example) and reach the full value in 10 years. California's goal in this drive is $844,000.

The Citizen's Service Corps also oversees the campaign to salvage fat. Residents are paid four cents and two "red points" for each pound of fat returned to mea t dealers. The Office of Price Administration supports this by supplying red points to fat renderers, who buy the household fats from the meat dealers.

New food etiquette rules are suggested by the Food Distribution Administration and the Department of Agriculture. Decline food that is not wanted. Eat ALL you have taken. Tilt the soup bowl and squeeze the grapefruit to get all the food available. Eat lettuce, cress, and parsley garnishes. Pick up chicken and chop bones to get all the meat. Dunk bread in gravy and vegetable juices. Serve average portions to guests. Avoid overloading children's plates. Simplify meals – eliminate needless variety.

Napa County Post-War Planning Board has listed creation of Robert Louis Stevenson State Park on Mount St. Helena among the first projects for development. The board said the park should include the historic toll house, remains of the old Silverado Mine, and the existing monument to Stevenson. The noted author and his bride spent part of their honeymoon at a cabin on the mine site in 1880. The toll house site is owned by Paul Piner of Calistoga.

Note: There are many articles in this book about the park project. Stevenson (1850-94) was a famous Scottish novelist, poet, and travel writer. In 1883, he spent a two-month honeymoon in the Calistoga area – most of it based in a three-story bunkhouse in an abandoned mining camp on the side of Mount St. Helena. He wrote about it in "The Silverado Squatters." The park was established in 1949. It has expanded to 6,042 acres and has trail links to the top of Mount St. Helena and the high rocks. The honeymoon cabin no longer exists. The Silverado Museum in St. Helena is dedicated to Stevenson.

The calendar of rationing dates includes: sugar: stamp 29 in ration book four is valid through January 17; meat, butter, cheese, edible fats and oils, canned milk, and canned fish: stamps R and S are valid through January 29; shoes: stamp 18 in ration book one is valid indefinitely; fruits and vegetables: green stamps D, E, and F in ration book four are valid through January 20 and stamps G, H, and J are valid through February 20; gasoline: No. 9 coupons in A book are valid through January 21. Tires must be inspected as follows: A book holders by March 30; B and C book holders by February 29.

Note: This sort of calendar ran on the front page of every issue.

Katherine Luebeck, a former Calistogan who has served as a Baptist missionary in China for more than 20 years, describes in a letter the hard life there for her and her pre-teen son Jackie. They are at a mission at Meihsien in southeastern China – "the only un-disturbed of all our mission stations." At a previous posting, their home was looted by a youth gang, and there was constant fear of aerial bombing or invasions by "the Japs." Katherine teaches piano and organ, singing, nursing, and religion. Jackie has learned three Chinese languages, plays the piano, and reads a lot.

Note: Mrs. Luebeck and her son returned to Calistoga in 1950. Jackie – known here as John – graduated from Calistoga High School in 1953.

Mina Pfister, 74, a resident of Franz Valley for over 40 years, died at St. Helena Sanitarium after a long illness. Mina was a native of Switzerland. She is survived by four daughters, Mrs.

Frank (Lena) Turner of Knights Valley, Mrs. Walter (Edie) Graham of Franz Valley, Mrs. Gilbert (Minnie) Hunt of Napa, and Mrs. Lowell (Frieda) Gleason of San Francisco, and four grandchildren.

Note: three of Mina's kin still lived in the area in 2012: daughter Minnie Hunt and grandson Frank Turner in Calistoga and granddaughter Betty Turner Becker in Santa Rosa.

Frank Piner, manager of Calistoga branch of Bank of America, is in his 21st year of banking. Piner graduated from Calistoga High School in 1921. He became a clerk and bookkeeper at Calistoga National Bank in 1924. Bank of America bought the business in 1936.

Frank Piner

Piner also is mayor and chairman of the Calistoga War Finance Committee.

District leaders for the Fourth War Bond Drive include: Ida Frediani (Tucker district); Mrs. Walter Tomasini (Knights Valley); and Peter Molinari and Mrs. Winifred Washburn (Calistoga). Ralph P. Winston of the *Weekly Calistogan* will handle public relations.

Mrs. C.C. Simic has been named chairman of women's activities of the War Finance Committee of Calistoga. She plans to organize a Cradle Roll of Honor, which would encourage people to buy war savings bonds for babies.

Boy Scout Troop 18 is collecting empty glass coffee containers for recycling in the war effort. Market owner Al Evans will store the containers and deliver them to companies that recycle them. Troop 18 will get the proceeds.

Servicemen have written heartfelt thanks for Christmas gift boxes they received from the city. "I hope that all of you realize how much support it gives us to know that our home town is behind us at every corner," said Wesley Tucker, a Navy radioman second class in the Underwater Detection Group at San Francisco. Others who wrote: Army private Howard Songey, who was overseas with a Los Angeles APO (Army Post Office) address; Army staff sergeant John A. Ghisolfo, Military Police, Hammond General Hospital,

Modesto; Army private first class Roy Bentley, Alamo Field Air Base, San Antonio, Texas; sailor Bill Wareham, USS Philadelphia, c/o Fleet Postmaster, New York, NY; Army private Jim Switzer, Buckley Field, Denver, CO; Army air cadet Bill Tubbs, Majors Field, Greenville, Texas; Army private first class Eddie Ottonello, Truax Field, Madison, WI.

In his thanks, Wareham said: "Everything it contained, I can use." He went on about his reception on a recent home leave: "It sure was grand to see the home town again. I would also like to thank all the folks who invited me to dinner. Now that I'm back on board, I'd like to get into some more action."

Switzer said: "It really helps a fellow's morale to know that the people at home are thinking about him at the holiday season."

Tubbs said: "I think Calistoga is doing something to be very proud of in sending something to each boy in the service." He added: "I'd certainly like to see some weather from home put in an appearance here. It has been below freezing, with hail and wind to boot. It has not been good for flying, which means we will be flying every day until we get our required time in here." He is training to be a pilot.

Ottonello said: "All the articles were very much appreciated. Quite a number of fellows in my barracks were surprised when I told them the gift was sent by the city. They all want to adopt Calistoga as their home town." He is training to be a control tower operator.

Shortwave radio listeners picked up a broadcast from Japan Wednesday night that carried a message from four Napa men who are prisoners. The speaker identified himself as Lieutenant Albert Finnie, whose parents live along the Silverado Trail. He added that three other Napans – Captain Pearson, Jack Henry, and Marshall – sent regards to their families and friends. Static prevented getting more of the names.

Jack Adams has been dismissed as director of Log Cabin Ranch for Boys. He had been charged with incompetence, insubordination, and inefficiency. Chief Probation Officer R. R. Miller took the action. Adams said he would appeal.

Napa County Clerk Ralph A. Dollarhide said his office collected $10,838 in fees in 1943. That was a slight increase from 1942. He said 257 marriage licenses were issued in 1943, an increase of 31.

Calistoga Rifle Club reported its two most recent competitions. December 23 leaders were Nance, 181; Archuleta, 179; Martin, 169; Hibbs, 180; Leete, 160; and Cohen, 132. December 30 leaders were Nance and Saviez, tied at 186; Hibbs, 180; Archuleta, 177; Ames, 156; Piner, 151; and Morris, 150.

Note: First names were not given in the article. Everyone knew them.

Calistogan Orvall G. Witt is among 294 young men in the pre-flight training school at the Army Air Force's San Antonio Aviation Cadet Center. They are learning the fundamentals needed for actual flight training. Orvall is the son of Mr. and Mrs. W. H. Witt.

page 2

F.E. Williams, chairman of the Calistoga War Price and Rationing Board, wants to clarify misunderstandings about eviction procedures under Office of Price Administration (OPA) rent regulations. Landlords must follow local laws or ordinances governing the eviction of tenants. OPA eviction certificates are "merely permissive." The landlord still has to get an eviction order from a local court.

Williams also announced that the OPA has approved rate increases for truck contract carriers in California. These bring the maximum rates allowed under OPA regulations up to the minimums provided by the California Railroad Commission. The order, signed by Leo F. Gentner, OPA regional administrator, provides rate boosts of 6 percent for trucking general commodities and 3 percent for agricultural commodities, retroactive to January 5, 1943. He said the order would not result in any general increase over rates now charged because virtually all truckers covered by the boosts had been charging the rates set by the railroad commission pending final action on the rate conflict.

Williams also reminded retailers that OPA plans to issue plastic tokens that storekeepers can give as change to shoppers who buy less of a rationed food than a food coupon covers. Applications for tokens must be on file with ration banks as soon as possible to insure retailers an adequate supply when the plan goes into effect February 27.

Napa County's civilian population is 42,000 – about 47 percent higher than the 1940 census count of 28,503, the California Taxpayers' Association estimated.

The association estimated California's population at 8,014,000 – about 16 percent higher than the 1940 census figure of 6,907,287. Solano and Contra Costa county populations have more than doubled since the census, while 21 counties have lost ground.

"Communities with large war industries have drained manpower and population from many California counties," the association said. "Post-war planning should recognize the return to their old homes of many of the people who have gone to war industry areas to work. After victory, the population of many inflated war centers can be expected to drop back to normal. Local governments planning for the future should provide for such a trend of population."

The Folies Bergere at Winterland, San Francisco, has added Saturday midnight shows and Sunday matinees to its daily 8 p.m. performances. The show has a cast of 120, including 80 beautiful girls.

The federal government has charged Bisceglia Brothers, owners of wineries in St. Helena and Fresno county, with failure to pay $43,236 in taxes between November 1937 and January 1939. The complaint in U.S. District Court in San Francisco seeks a 5 percent penalty in addition to payment of the taxes.

Washington columnist James Preston says that when the war is over, the U.S. will have about $17 billion worth of superfluous materials, machinery, and property. Several congressional committees are considering the problem. Many are concerned that the government will force itself into competition with private businesses. "The worry becomes greater as our armed forces drive steadily on toward victory," Preston says.

page 3

From the agricultural extension office's "Vineyard, Orchard and Farm" column:

The Office of Price Administration (OPA) district office has published a farmer's price list on all commodities. Ceiling prices are given, if available. Otherwise, pricing methods are outlined and examples are presented to clarify the method of computing ceiling prices. Farmers may apply for the list at our office in the Napa Post Office building.

Also available there, "How to Make Your Electric Refrigerator Last Longer," a free wartime pamphlet.

Much good wool is idle in home closets. If folks at home cannot wear a serviceman's discarded suits as they are, then it is patriotic and wise to make some of them over into clothes needed now. The U.S. Department of Agriculture's flier "Make-overs From Men's Suits" explains how to go about it. It is available from our office.

From the "Farmers Corner" column by Ralph H. Taylor, executive secretary of the Agricultural Council of California:

Organized labor – railroad men, coal miners, steel workers and more – are seeking sharp wage increases and using the strike threat to enforce their demands. This is in defiance of the Little Steel formula and the directives of the federal government.

Labor leaders argue that inflation has reduced the buying power of labor's paychecks. This disregards the fact that all Americans are in the same boat – and the majority will have to sacrifice more and do with less if some groups win special consideration and benefits. If the President's "hold the line" program is broken by the widespread granting of pay increases, real inflation will come in like a hurricane.

Wages of factory labor increased 99 percent from 1914 to 1939. Farm prices increased only 50 percent. By August 1943, factory wages had increased 297 percent, farm prices only 93 percent. Only 21 percent of family income is used for food – the lowest percent in 30 years.

Safeway's display ad includes price/food stamp details for "rationed merchandise": 11-ounce package of Del Monte seedless raisins – 10 cents and 3 points; can of Gardenside tomato sauce, 5 cents, 5 points; No. 2 can of Country Home golden creamed corn, 14 cents, 13 points; pound of Parkay margarine, 25 cents, 6 points; three cans of Cherub canned milk, 27 cents, 1 point; No. 2 can of Del Monte asparagus, 33 cents, 18 points.

California has been allocated 177 track-type tractors for the first quarter of 1944 – an increase of 51 over the fall quarter – for assignment to individual applicants, on recommendation of county and state committees. Track-tractors are as important in the war effort as bombers and machine guns.

All vegetables canned at home should be boiled for 15 minutes before being used, or even tasted, according to Prof. Karl F. Meyer, director of Hooper Foundation, University of California. He said special care should be taken to follow directions in the UC bulletins for canning the following fruits, which have been known to contain botulism: figs, apricots, pears, apples, apple sauce, apple butter, and tomatoes.

page 4

The editorial page lists C.A. Carroll as editor and proprietor. Subscription rates are $2 per year, $1.25 for six months, 65 cents for three months. The office is at 353 Lincoln Ave. The telephone number is 33.

Note: In 2012, a one-year subscription costs $25; a single copy, 50 cents. The newspaper is located near the historic railroad depot; phone: 942-4035.

Editorials: 1944 is a year of hope, particularly hope for peace.

The Office of Price Administration needs to simplify its regulations. It is estimated that grocers must comply with 7,800 pages of OPA rules. These regulations add to problems caused by food shortages and the lack of adequate help. If the "Washington Wonders" who write the OPA rules were required to work in a grocery store for a couple of weeks, sorting stamps, filling out endless reports, memorizing points and prices, keeping track of inventory, to say nothing of waiting on customers, we are certain there would be a sharp drop in the number and verbosity of regulations.

Congress left a pile of unfinished business when it took a three-week holiday break — taxes, subsidies, young soldiers' voting rights, and mustering out pay.

Woodrow Wilson has been dead 20 years, but his spirit is felt at every international council table where men gather in the interest of lasting world peace. His crusade for a world organization to prevent future wars failed in the aftermath of World War I. He predicted in 1919 that there would be another world war within another generation if the nations of the world did not join together to avoid it. We don't know how successful the League of Nations might have been. We only know it could not have been more unsuccessful than our attempt to avoid war by staying out of the league. We know now that we must strive to get along with other countries in some sort of international association.

What became of the "no strike" pledge that unions gave the President at the start of this war, when Congress was threatening to ban strikes. Now, sailors are being forced to finish building their own ships because union workers walked out on the job, rail workers are threatening strike, and supervisory employees walked out at Ford's biggest bomber plant. Do labor leaders think the war is over? If labor continues to flaunt its pledge, and strikes continue to spread, the people of this nation will have no alternative but to demand that strikes be prohibited by law, with drastic penalties for any violation.

Elementary School News: The school is entitled to fly the "Treasury flag" because 90 percent of the children and teachers are buying war stamps and bonds. The total of stamp sales to date is $2,582. This week's purchases, by grades: first, $18.10; second, $33.90; third, $11.60; fourth, $26.90; fifth, $16; sixth, $12.65; seventh, $8.40; and eighth, $31.75. Lester Cavagnaro and Frances Tedeschi exchanged their stamp books for war bonds.

First graders are making snow men for a border in their room. Mr. Morehouse, the seventh grade teacher, has been sick; Mrs. Conrad Weil Jr. is substituting for him. There was no school Monday because the furnace was out of order.

Note: Students bought 5- or 10-cent war stamps and pasted them into a booklet until they filled it with the $18.75 needed to convert to a war bond. The bond would be worth $25 in 10 years.

Southern Pacific railroad set a traffic record in 1943, for the fourth year in a row. SP will need more manpower and equipment to handle the increasing load, President A.T. Mercier said. More than 14,000 former SP employees are in the armed forces. The company has hired some 4,000 women to do work formerly performed exclusively by men. It has imported about 7,000 Mexican track workers, all efforts to recruit this labor in the U.S. having failed. Mercier cited changes made to handle the unprecedented wartime traffic: heavier loading of freight cars, quick unloading at terminals, better upkeep of rolling stock, and installations of centralized traffic control.

Note: SP had daily freight service to/from Calistoga in 1944.

N.D. Clark, chairman of the Napa County War Board, said fears that farmers might not be able to get sufficient fuel supplies are unfounded. So long as fuel is available for civilian use, farmers

23

will have first call for it, up to the minimum amounts necessary to perform their farming operations. This rule is in Petroleum Distribution Order No. 14.

Farmers have had a preferred position since wartime gasoline rationing began. Some of them have abused this privilege by allowing visitors, employees, etc., to get gasoline for their automobiles from bulk fuel tanks. If such abuses continue, public reaction will be detrimental to farmers and agricultural production in general.

Librarian Elizabeth Wright listed 40 new books available at the Calistoga Library: 12 best sellers, 13 light fiction, 15 non-fiction.

Note: The library was in the same building as now, but shared it with Civic Club.

page 5

American Legion Post 231 hosted an open house at its Lincoln Avenue headquarters New Year's Eve. Twenty-three dozen doughnuts were consumed, and ten pounds of coffee brewed. Plus a large batch of Russian cookies donated by Mrs. V. Dobr.

Community Church greeted the new year with an open house at the Methodist social hall, Cedar and Spring steets. Songs by Janet Caywood, a reading by Mrs. Clifford Bunting, and community singing opened the program. Mrs. Tom Elder directed games. Refreshments were served by Mrs. John Mingus. Rev. A.E. Lucas conducted a devotional service at midnight.

Friendly Circle met in the Methodist social hall Tuesday evening, with Gretchen Ballard, Grace Butler, and Hazel Brown as co-hostesses. Hazel was installed as leader for the coming year.

Calendar of Coming Social and Club Events:
Friday, January 7 – City Council.
Monday, January 10 – Native Daughters, Boy Scouts.
Tuesday, January 11 – The Gleaners, Community Church Service Club and Missionary Society, British War Relief Surgical Unit, War Bond Committee.
Wednesday, January 12 – Rebekahs, Eastern Star.
Thursday, January 13 – Rotary Club, Garden Club, Rifle Club.

Friday, January 14 – Tucker Home Department.

Saturday, January 15 – Silverado Grange.

Monday, January 17 – Community Church Men's Club, Boy Scouts.

Tuesday, January 18 – Eastern Star, Tucker Farm Center, Friendly Circle, Theta Rho, British War Relief Surgical Unit.

Wednesday, January 19 – Odd Fellows, Napa County Farm Bureau directors.

Thursday, January 20 – Bennett Farm Center, Rotary Club, Sunnyside Club, Bennett 4-H Club, Rifle Club.

Friday, January 21 – Civic Club public card party.

High School News, by Allan Forbes: Since its Christmas concert, the high school band has been issued new music. This includes "Atlantic," "March of the Steel Men," "Pavanne," and "Tropical."

The Student Council has set precedent by adopting a budget for the spring semester.

The senior play will be presented on January 22, instead of the originally scheduled date, January 14. The class is erecting scenery and collecting various props.

The A and B basketball teams are practicing strenuously for the league season, which begins later this month.

The sophomore class is far ahead of others in the purchase of war bonds and stamps. It leads in both the percentage of students participating and in the amount purchased.

Note: Allan Forbes was a 1944 graduate of CHS. He is retired as a professor and vice president of California State University - Chico.

Civic Club admitted three new members at its meeting Wednesday. It will host a benefit card party for the library January 21.

Shoe dealers will be allowed to sell certain women's shoes at $3 or less a pair without requiring a ration stamp from January 17-29. This is limited to novelty shoes that women have been reluctant to spend a precious shoe stamp for. A stamp must be collected if the shoes cost more than $3.

People who sell their car must surrender any unused gasoline coupons that were issued for the vehicle to the local War Price and Ration Board as part of the sale procedure. Before the buyer can obtain gasoline coupons, he must present a copy of the sales receipt. This will prevent invalidated stamps from slipping into black market channels.

Gladys Berry returned to her home in Hollywood Tuesday after spending several days in Calistoga with her parents, Mr. and Mrs. Lambert Funke. It was her first visit in four years. Gladys' husband is a Hollywood movie director.

Berkeley radio station KRE is being used to broadcast defense and Red Cross reports again this year. Defense issues are presented Tuesday at 9 p.m. The Red Cross report is Wednesday at 8:45 p.m.

Church Services:
Catholic Church, 901 Washington Street, Rev. William P. Walsh, pastor. Masses Sunday, 8 and 10 a.m.; Monday-Friday, 8 a.m.; Saturday (in Middletown), 9:15 a.m.

Christian Science Society, Berry and Cedar streets. Sunday school, 9:45 a.m.; church services, 11 a.m. Reading room is open every Thursday, 2:30-4 p.m.

St. Luke's Episcopal Mission, Third and Washington streets, Rev. C.A. Homan, vicar. The first Sunday after Epiphany, Holy Communion and sermon, 9:15 a.m.

Community Church, Cedar and Spring streets, Rev. A.E. Lucas, minister. Morning service at 11 a.m.; evening service, 7:15 p.m., with continuing discussion of "After the War, What?" The church is planning a six-week extension of its School of World Fellowship program.

Full Gospel Tabernacle, Washington and First streets, Mrs. Cecilia Nixon and Miss M. Hynning, ministers. Sunday School, 10 a.m.; morning worship, 11 a.m.; evangelistic and inspirational service, 7:45 p.m. Thursday: junior church for boys and girls, 3:30 p.m.; Bible study, 7:45 p.m.

Note: Activities of the Seventh-day Adventist Church at 318 Berry Street were never listed, nor its events mentioned in articles.

Celia H. Kimball, a former resident of rural Calistoga, died at St. Helena Sanitarium December 30. She was 74. Mrs. Kimball was born in Sanger, Fresno County. She moved to Calistoga in 1881. In recent years, she had lived in Hayward. She is survived by one son, one daughter, four grandchildren, and one great grandchild.

Calistoga Garden Club will hold its regular meeting Thursday at 2 p.m. in the room adjacent to the post office.

Franz Valley News: Mrs. E. Michalk and son Bobby spent two days in St. Helena with her sister, Mrs. Peter Ghiringhelli. Mr. and Mrs. R.S. Kettlewell celebrated New Years at home with family, including Mrs. Charles Baptie and daughter, Mary Edith; Mr. and Mrs. Joe Kettlewell and Richard of Knights Valley; and Mildred Kettlewell of Crockett. Mr. and Mrs. J.S. Black spent the New Year's holiday in Gridley with the William Black family. Margaret Black joined them from McClellan Field, Sacramento. The Blacks hosted Laura Sylvester and Jimmy Humphrey Sunday and Mr. and Mrs. William Mattox of Mount St. Helena Monday. The Ivan Boyadjieff family of Oakland seems to have moved into their newly acquired home in the valley; their car was in evidence and lights were on in the house. Mrs. Walter Graham has had word from her husband, ill with pneumonia in New York. Mrs. Robert Sylvester stayed with Mrs. Floyd Goodpasture Monday and Tuesday.

Knights Valley News: The W.W. Kettlewells have been busy. They had 12 guests for Christmas. On New Year's Day, they hosted Private First Class Frank Patton and Sergeant Norman Mihalkevic, both of Camp Beale, near Marysville. Wednesday they had a surprise visit from two cousins of Mrs. Kettlewell – Mrs. Jerry Grove of North Little Rock, Arkansas, and Mrs. Gus Ernst of Santa Rosa. Barbara Kettlewell is home from San Rafael, where she works in the telephone office, recuperating from a severe cold. Irene Harrison returned to the Beck ranch Wednesday after spending the holidays in Fort Bragg with her parents. Mrs. G. Hamilton and children spent Monday shopping in Santa Rosa.

Porter Creek News: Lewis and Ernest Mitchell are visiting at the L.S. Mitchell home. Ernest is in the Navy, stationed at Mare Island. Mr. and Mrs. Robert May are hosting his mother, Elsie May of Bakersfield, for a couple of weeks. Mr. and Mrs. Wes Adams hosted Edith Fechter and family for New Year's Day dinner and then Mr. and Mrs. Ed Kaelin Sunday evening. Mr. and Mrs. Raymond Fechter spent an enjoyable New Year's Eve at Rancho Juan Inez, then hosted son Everett, a merchant mariner, over the weekend. Corporal Bill Sharp has written his sister, Mrs. E.H. Martin, that he has reached his assignment destination in the Pacific.

Bennett District News: Ray Bentley, director of Bennett Farm Center, has appointed a large committee, headed by H.L. Bounsall, to develop its program for work in the community, the Farm Bureau, and Farm Center affairs. The first project will be the War Bond drive, January 10 to February 18. "Farmers have whole-heartedly met every request for increased productions in this time of emergency, and we are confident this new request to invest some of their earnings with their government will be met with equal enthusiasm," Bentley said.

Cerita deBit, a lieutenant in the Army Nursing Corps, and Dr. Leana Gerber of San Francisco were New Year's guests of the Herbert Washburns. While Mrs. Washburn's car is being repaired, the Citizens' Service Corps business is being transacted at her home on the Healdsburg Highway. Phone: 13-Y-21.

Michael Nagy and family of Oakland and Mrs. Ben Cordy spent the Christmas holiday with the H.M. Nagys. Mr. Cordy, confined in Calistoga Hospital for some time, is showing improvement. Mr. and Mrs. A. Brucker spent the holidays with relatives in Oakland. Ditto Mr. and Mrs. Robert Walpole. Captain and Mrs. Fiske were dinner guests of the A.L. Hawkes Monday.

Mrs. Ernest Bentley and daughter, Peggy, are visiting relatives in San Francisco this week. Mr. and Mrs. George Radelfinger and son spent the holidays in Madera with Mrs. Radelfinger's parents. The Radelfingers hosted Mr. and Mrs. Robert Watson of San Francisco early this week. Mr. and Mrs. Lester Mathews spent New Year's with friends in Berkeley. Grace Lincoln is a great grandmother again. The father is grandson Elbert Lincoln of Madera.

Tucker District News: Pearl Fricke hosted Albert and Pauline Klotz and Mrs. Anker Miller of St. Helena for New Year's Eve and dinner the next day. County Supervisor Charles Tamagni returned home from Calistoga Hospital Monday, much improved. Mr. and Mrs. C. L. Tucker finally succeeded in getting a telephone. Katie Morosoli went to San Rafael Thursday, and on to San Jose to spend the weekend with Mr. and Mrs. J. Quinn. Nona Wolleson was visited by Mr. and Mrs. Lauren Brook of Middletown. Mrs. F.A. Wright returned home from St. Helena Sanitarium Thursday and is on the way to complete recovery. About 40 people from Calistoga spent New Year's Eve at the Tucker Farm Center, dining and then dancing the old year out and the new year in. Mrs. J.E. Scott has about recovered from the flu. Dorothy Hagins was over from Sacramento Sunday for a visit with her parents, Mr. and Mrs. J.E. Scott. Their daughter, Beverly, returned home with her. Mr. and Mrs. Richard Lommel spent the past week at Lommel ranch, but have returned home to Walnut Creek. Mr. and Mrs. Walter Tamagni spent the weekend in San Francisco visiting with Mrs. Tamagni's brother, Edward Burnham, who was on furlough from military service.

The newspaper also had detailed reports from correspondents in Lake County and St. Helena. Judge Irwin in Middletown fined two men $200 each and had their rifles confiscated after convicting them of having illegal deer meat – a doe and a buck – in their car. They were arrested as they hunted for more. Another item: every resident of the Veterans Home in Yountville received a Christmas present – 50 cents and a bag of cookies – from a St. Helena women's group, which conducted bingo games to raise funds. And 20 members of the St. Helena unit of the California State Guard took part in the colorful half-time ceremony at the annual Shrine East-West football game in Kezar Stadium, San Francisco, on New Year's Day.

page 7

Ritz Theater Attractions:

January 7-8, a double bill. "Priorities on Parade," a musical comedy about women working in an airplane factory, stars Betty Rhodes, Vera Vague, Ann Miller, and Jerry Colona. "The Leather Burners," a cowboy action flick, stars Bill Boyd as Hopalong Cassidy.

January 9-11, "Reap the Wild Wind," a pirate adventure drama, stars Ray Milland, Paulette Goddard, and John Wayne.

Note: The Ritz always had a newsreel (a forerunner of TV news), which kept us posted on the war, sports, and other events.

page 8

Marine private Dariel Camp wrote from "somewhere in the South Pacific":

"I sure do miss Calistoga and the many friends I have there. I suppose most of the fellows are in services overseas and elsewhere. I haven't run into anyone from home over here yet, but I did meet a cousin of mine that I had never seen before. We meet aboard ship coming here. I don't know where he is now, but I hope to see him again soon."

If you need evening slippers, your dealer can sell you what he has without a ration stamp. Women's slippers with gold or silver uppers have been ration-free, but now brocade, crepe, moiré, faile, and metallic mesh or fabric are exempt too. Dressy afternoon shoes are still rationed.

Calistoga 1944

Army private first class Leslie L. Palmer sent thanks for the Christmas box he received from Calistoga at his base in Iceland. He said he is from San Mateo, but he was born in Calistoga (March 23, 1920) and has an aunt (Eleanor Palmer) and an uncle (Charlie Tucker) living here. "I have been stationed in Iceland for the past 16 months. I can truthfully say that I don't like it here, but I don't want to go back until I know that I can stay there.

"I know you people are doing your part at home, for if you were not, how could we have what we have? We have all we want to eat, three picture shows a week, and other things to make our stay here a more enjoyable one.

"Most people think it is very cold here and that we have a lot of snow. Well, today it is warmer outside than I have seen it at times in Calistoga at the same time of year, and there is no snow, except on the hills. It is true we have very little light, for it is overcast most all of the time this time of year, and the sun seldom shines through."

Lincoln Avenue, looking west.

Chapter 2

January 29-February 4
The War: American forces invade the Marshall Islands
in the Pacific, taking over the major Japanese naval base
at Kwajalein.

𝔚eekly Calistogan of February 4, 1944

page 1

Private Monroe J. (Monte) Shreve has been reported missing
by the Army. Last reports from Monte indicate he was somewhere
in the South Pacific. It is not thought that he was engaged in the
present assault on the Marshall Islands, as casualty reports gener-
ally follow several weeks behind the battles.

Monte, who lived at Camp St. Andrew on Mount St. Helena,
entered Calistoga High School in 1937 and graduated in 1941. He
was active in athletics and distinguished himself on the basketball
team as a forward and on the baseball team as a shortstop and second
baseman. He also played on Calistoga's baseball town team.

Monte enjoyed a reputation of being a good student, both in
class and out. He is perhaps best remembered as a boy who had to
make his own way in life and was doing a very creditable job of it.
Following graduation, Monte signed up with Hawaiian Contractors
and was assigned to a job at Pearl Harbor. He was working there at
the time of the Japanese sneak attack of December 7, 1941. During
the spring of 1942, he enlisted with the infantry. He took part in
many of the battles in the South Pacific.

He is survived by a sister, Evelyn Shreve of Sebastopol. He is
the second St. Andrew boy reported missing in the Pacific. The first
was Frank Burns.

*Note: Monte is among 18,096 World War II veterans missing in
action in the Pacific theater who are honored at the National War
Memorial in Honolulu. His plaque says he died November 21, 1943,
with no other details. Burns is honored in a similar memorial at
the American Cemetery in Manila. It says Burns, a seaman second
class, died on December 1, 1943.*

At least four boys with Calistoga links are known to be in the heavy action taking place on the Marshall Islands in the South Pacific.

Bud Hanly, an aircraft gunner and son of Mr. and Mrs. Charles Hanly, and Robert Winston, aerographer's mate first class and son of Ralph P. Winston, are on the same ship. From the tone of the news dispatches, it may be assumed that the ship is in the action.

Staff Sergeant Loring Tomasini, son of Mr. and Mrs. Walter Tomasini of Knights Valley, is with the 7th Army Division, which has been mentioned repeatedly in communiqués.

Jim Campbell, grandson of Mrs. Ella Campbell and son of Mr. and Mrs. Charles E. Campbell of Oakland, is with a Marine Corps battalion known to be in the action.

Calistoga again demonstrated its willingness and ability to absorb its share of the financial burden of the war, raising $220,000, almost 30 percent more than its required total, in the current Fourth War Loan Drive. As far as can be determined, Calistoga is one of the first towns of the state to meet its quota.

The largest single purchase was made Tuesday by Bob Mondavi of C. Mondavi and Sons, operators of Sunny St. Helena Wine Company and owners of the winery situated on the old Krug ranch near St. Helena. He purchased $20,000 worth of bonds at Bank of America, Calistoga branch, and credited them to the Calistoga quota.

Mondavi said his company feels it is definitely connected with Calistoga, in that Chapin F. Tubbs handles the Mondavi crushing for the upper end of the valley at his Montelena winery. "During the past season, Mr. Tubbs handled the grapes from some 53 different vineyards in an around Calistoga," Mondavi said. "Close to 40 other crops from the upper valley came to our St. Helena plants. We have a definite interest in the Calistoga district and will continue to purchase wine grapes here for crushing at the Tubbs winery and distribution under our labels."

Note: Robert Mondavi created his own world-famous winery near Oakville in the 1960s. His community spirit and generosity continued to his death in 2008.

The last three *Weekly Calistogans* have carried letters from Staff Sergeant Jason Barthel, a gunner on a Flying Fortress bomber, describing harrowing scrapes with death after his plane was shot down near the southern Italian city of Potenza.

The letters are long. Space permits only a summary.

Barthel's B-17 was shot down by German fighter planes. His leg was badly broken in bailing out of the plane. He and five crewmates were captured and spent two weeks under guard in an Italian civilian hospital. They escaped after the hospital was hit by four bombs – apparently from Allied aircraft targeting a nearby railroad bridge. Many patients were killed or injured.

Barthel spent close to two weeks being shifted from hiding place to hiding place by sympathetic Italians. The last place was an abandoned railroad tunnel, which harbored an estimated 3,000 people, about one-fifth of them Italian army deserters. The area was under constant bombing – a different perspective for Barthel. "Every bomb shook me. I'll never get over that. Even now, a plane overhead sets me shaking."

And later, describing the British RAF's nighttime bombing: "Night bombing is worse than daytime bombing. Flares light up the countryside for miles around, and then that eerie sound of the (British) 'screamer bombs', and the ground shakes, and your stomach flip-flops, and your heart pounds – while you wait for the next one."

Another near miss: a "nest" of German snipers attacked the Canadian medical team that had rescued him behind their lines. "The Canadians got the snipers. Some day I'll tell you what they did to the one they got alive. They never take a sniper prisoner. They buried seven."

Barthel was in a hospital in Georgia when his letters were printed. His wife, the former Jacqueline Cole of Calistoga, had left their home in Richmond for Atlanta that week to be with him.

Note: Barthel's letters are in the January 21, January 28, and February 4 issues of the Weekly Calistogan. *They are on microfiche at the Calistoga Public Library.*

Calistoga families who have sons in the Marine Corps can send messages to their boys through the short-wave program "Tell It To The Marines." It broadcasts from San Francisco over KMV (10840 kilocycles) at 1:05 a.m. Monday through Saturday.

Relatives, sweethearts, and other friends may send messages of up to 100 words. The limit applies to the text, the address not being counted.

To send a message, it is necessary to give the full name, rank, and address of the Marine as well as the name and address of the sender. Mail the messages to Public Relations Officer, US Marine Corps, 1 Montgomery Street, San Francisco.

The *Weekly Calistogan* this week initiated a service that it trusts will be of interest to residents of the area. On the wall of our office is a map of the world with all pertinent war information shown upon it. Actions of both the Army and the Navy are clearly indicated, as well as any outstanding events of civil life in all countries.

The service, known as "World News of the Week," will have a new map on the wall every Monday. The map of this week carries all war news of importance January 21–27. It also carries explanatory text.

Readers of this paper with sons in the Navy may be interested in seeing just where Kwajalein, Ailing-Lapalap, Wotje, and Maloilap are located, for there has been recent Navy and Marine action there, and there will be plenty more.

The Italian campaign battle action also may be found on the map.

Voters must be registered by March 2 to exercise their franchise at the city election on April 11. New residents and those who have moved from one precinct to another since the last state and county election must re-register to assure their right to vote.

Three of the five city council seats are up for election. They are those held by E.J. Stevens, J.B. Ghisolfo, and W.H. Butler. The hold-over members are Frank Piner and Ray Oxford. The terms of City Clerk George C. Locey and Treasurer Edmund Molinari also expire in April. They are candidates to succeed themselves.

Aspirants for the various offices must file their petitions for nomination and declaration of candidacy between February 11 and March 11.

The *Weekly Calistogan* is in receipt of the following letter from Bill Tubbs:

"As scheduled, my two months at Major's Field are over, and I am now stationed at Foster Field for my final training phase for pilot. If I graduate from here, I'll be commissioned either as a flight officer or as a second lieutenant and get my wings.

"Graduation day will be around March 10, which is one day after my 21st birthday. I'll then either be assigned to a tactical unit for combat duty as a fighter pilot, or be stuck as an instructor around here. The final training here will be in P-40s if I'm lucky enough to get combat duty. The future instructors do not get either P-40 transition or the gunnery training, which we all look forward to. An instructor's job is a tedious, monotonous, but important, job. I've got my fingers crossed for the 40s.

"I see water again, and the fishing is good here on the Gulf. Please change my Calistogan's address to A-c W.R. Tubbs, 44C Av Cad. Detachment, Foster Field, Texas."

Note: Tubbs eventually flew 53 missions in P-47 Thunderbolt fighter planes in the European Theater. He was recalled to active duty for the Korean War, where he flew 105 missions. Among his honors were a Distinguished Flying Cross with five Oak Leaf Clusters – recognizing six acts of extraordinary heroism. He flew 21 different kinds of aircraft during a 25-year Air Force career. He died in 2007 at the age of 84. He was a 1940 graduate of Calistoga High School.

The first Baby Bond purchased in Calistoga, in a drive running concurrently with the Fourth War Loan Drive, was bought by Captain and Mrs. Charles N. Fiske. It is for their grandson, Thomas Albert Fiske, son of Mr. and Mrs. Stephen Fiske of Berkeley. Purchase of the bond makes the child "an investor in this country's great fight for human liberty and a contribution in a world struggle to make life free and forever peaceful for all men."

The problem: less than two years ago, there was no limit whatsoever on the amount of gasoline a person could buy, other than the money in his pocketbook. Today, the average citizen is counting each quart of gasoline. He must figure very closely the amount of gasoline every little trip will take, and this determines both the number of trips he takes and the distances and places he goes.

The restriction of individual gasoline usage is not a denial of liberty. It is caused by the absolute necessity of sharing a limited amount of gasoline. It is just one of the consequences of war.

When we converted from peace to war, unlimited peacetime gasoline consumption ran into the absolutely essential and steadily increasing demands of our war machine. Obviously, the gasoline needed for war combat and shipping could not be sacrificed. As those needs increased, it became clear that a point would be reached where some uses of gasoline would have to be cut. The sacrifices had to be made by civilians.

The enemy planned on our inability to accomplish the vast and complex task of fueling our part of the war. But the task is being accomplished.

Calistoga 1944

Peter Molinari will describe Indian life in the Napa Valley at next week's meeting of Boy Scout Troop 18. Molinari will exhibit his collection of Indian artifacts, among the finest privately owned collections in the state, and will explain their origin and uses.

Troop 18 is badly in need of an assistant Scoutmaster since the departure of Larry Biancalana for his new job in Sausalito.

Earl Evans – in charge of the troop's coffee jar recycling program – announced that sales of the jars have netted $25.

Last Saturday's tin can pickup was far behind what Calistoga should be able to do toward the defense measure of saving tin for conversion into tools of war. It is a very simple thing to empty a can, bend both ends in, mash the can almost flat, and put it away against the day when there will be another collection. If the start is made now, housewives will find that they have a very respectable pile when the next pickup day comes. The cans are collected and taken to Napa. From there, they are shipped to a reduction plant, where the tin will be removed and converted to blocks for use in the war effort.

Primary elections for state and federal offices – including President – are being consolidated this year and will be held May 16. Would-be delegates to the party national conventions must notify the Secretary of State of their candidacy by February 9.

More thanks from Calistoga service boys who received Christmas packages from the community. Here are some of their comments and, in most cases, their addresses.

Private First Class Angelo Demattei, 1st Rept. Co., 576th AW Btn., Drew Field, Florida: "I want to thank all those who made possible the many Christmas packages that were sent from Calistoga. The whole home town was very much in my thoughts this month. For me, it was the first Christmas I've ever spent away from Calistoga and my family, and believe me when I say I hope it is the last one. The gloom over this field during the Christmas week was so thick you could have cut it with a knife. Everyone seemed to have the same thought in mind all week, and I don't have to tell you what it was. A very, very happy New Year to all the people of Calistoga."

Perry Barber, MM 1/c, 78th NCB, Hdq. Co., c/o Fleet Postmaster, San Francisco. Perry, a Seabee, has been in the South Pacific war zone for the past year. He sent his thanks through a letter to his mother, Mrs. Berwin Barber. He recently encountered Calistogan Blaine Huston on a trip between the islands. Perry says the temperature feels like 135 degrees, although the nights are cooler. He has recently been on a surveying party through the jungles, where every inch of way had to be cut, and the sun rarely reached the ground.

Peter Tedeschi, MM 1/c, USS Hoggatt Bay, CVE-75, Div. M, c/o Fleet Postmaster, San Francisco. "The Christmas present was greatly appreciated. I know how it makes you feel to receive a gift now."

Mr. and Mrs. W.G. McFall Sr. said "Our three boys have asked us to write for them. William Jr., who is somewhere in Italy, wishes to thank the people of Calistoga for their lovely Christmas package, which he received in time for Christmas. It made him feel he was not alone. John, who is in New Guinea, and Gerald, who is in our Navy, were surely pleased with their packages. They expect to thank all concerned in the future themselves."

Charles Westbay, who spent a recent furlough in Calistoga, also thanks all for his Christmas package. Following training at the Merchant Marine school on Catalina Island, Charles is now at sea as an oiler.

Others:

Aviation Cadet Henry Carlenzoli, Class 12-A-1 8B, NAS, Norman, Okla.

Private Albert M. Rose, Co. L, 8th Mt. Inf., 3rd Btn., Camp Carson, Colorado. (Albert recently returned from several months of active service in the vicinity of Alaska. So far as we know, he is Calistoga's only ski-trooper.)

Leo James Suffia, BM 1/c, USCG, Pier 43½, San Francisco Coast Guard cutter Golden Gate.

Note: Back in 1939, Angelo Demattei played the trombone, Perry Barber the baritone, and Peter Tedeschi the saxophone when Calistoga High School won the national small school band championship at the World's Fair on Treasure Island, San Francisco Bay.

Tedeschi returned to Calistoga after military service and a brief career as an infielder for five teams in the Chicago Cubs baseball organization. He was a key figure in development of Calistoga's Little League baseball program. Its stadium is named in his honor. He worked for the post office for 30 years before retirement in the 1980s. He died January 30, 2008.

Calistoga 1944

Aiming to provide recreation for the younger Calistoga group, Mr. and Mrs. "Chick" Hawkins have started Saturday night dances at Redwood Lodge Annex. The first dance, held last week, proved very successful. If the good attendance continues, the Hawkins will make it a regular feature.

The next dance is scheduled for February 12, with the music to start at 8:30 p.m.

Parents are welcome to attend, but if they do not wish to accompany the younger dancers, assurance is given that the dances are well chaperoned.

The March of Dimes drive has been extended to Monday, February 7, chairman Edith Cavagnaro has announced. Your dimes will help win the fight against infantile paralysis. Put them in the wishing wells that are in almost every place of business in Calistoga.

Elementary School News: War stamp and bond sales to date are $3,635.50. This week's sales are: first grade, $28.50, with Billy Weil and Joan Kelley completing purchase of bonds; second grade, $19.40; third grade, $17.90; fourth grade, $28.75, with Gertrude Weil receiving a bond; fifth grade, $14.60; sixth grade, $12.75; seventh grade, $24.85; and eighth grade, $29.00, with Grace Hague getting a bond.

The seventh grade boys are giving the girls of the class a Valentine party.

Calistoga's American Legion Post 231 will hold a card party at the Odd Fellows' Hall at 8 p.m. a week from tonight. A door prize and many other prizes to be distributed among winners.

Members and friends of the Community Church are looking forward to Sunday night, when Mrs. George O. Scarfe Sr. of Calistoga, who spent many years in the Philippine Islands, will talk on the peoples of the islands and their customs. She will display a number of mementos of her stay in the islands. The meeting will be held in the Methodist Church building on Cedar Street, starting at 7:15 p.m.

Chapter 3

February 6 - March 4

The War: Rabaul, Japan's headquarters in the South Pacific, is completely isolated. Russia continues to bomb Helsinki, even as it conducts peace talks with Finland.

Other: Oscar awards (1943 films) – movie: "Casablanca"; actor: Paul Lukas, "Watch on the Rhine"; supporting actor, Charles Coburn, "The More the Merrier"; actress, Jennifer Jones, "The Song of Bernadette"; supporting actress, Katina Paxinou, "For Whom the Bell Tolls"; director: Michael Curtiz, "Casablanca."

𝔚eekly 𝔠alistogan of March 3, 1944

page 1

Two servicemen with Calistoga ties, Lloyd Decker and Bob Winston, have written letters about their experiences – Lloyd in Europe and Bob in the Pacific – and their optimistic feelings about the war.

Staff Sergeant Decker wrote to his parents, the Les Deckers of Calistoga, from England on February 5.

"Today I received the *Weekly Calistogan* you sent, and I was sure glad to read about everyone and their carryings on.

"Mother, please go down to the newspaper office and put an article in it thanking the people of Calistoga for their very welcome Christmas package. Everything it contained was grand and the most usable things a fellow overseas could ask for. If Mr. and Mrs. Carroll want to know what I'm doing or have done, tell them everything I have told you – of my being at the Italy and Sicily invasions. Bill Wareham probably told you a lot about it when he was home.

"The only thing I don't like about England is the way things are rationed. When we were in Africa, there were all sorts of things to buy, but they were mostly junk. I did not have much desire to throw my money away. But over here, where the things are quite similar to those at home, nothing is for sale unless a person has that darned ticket.

Calistoga 1944

"I heard from Aubie (his wife) today, and she says our little girl is growing like a weed. She also says it looks as though the baby is going to have red hair. Can you imagine that? The thing I want more than anything is to get home and be able to care for them myself. Gee, it's been so long since I have seen Aubie and all of you that I'm afraid I won't recognize you. It seems like a life-time has passed since I left.

"It won't be long now, though, until things over here will end. The Jerries can't hold out forever. I'm not much on predicting, but I think, as many others do, that it will be over here by fall."

Note: Lloyd Decker was a 1939 graduate of Calistoga High School. He was an Army Signal Corps telegrapher. He served on ships that supported invasions of Sicily and Salerno in Italy, then Normandy, France, on D-Day later in 1944. In 1945, Lloyd was transferred to the Pacific, where he helped support invasions of Okinawa and Iwo Jima and was on one of the ships escorting General Mac-Arthur in his acceptance of Japan's formal surrender on September 2. Lloyd worked at Ray Oxford's Shell station in Calistoga on his return home, then launched a 38-year career with Bank of America in the Central Valley. He and Auburn live in Yuba City and recently celebrated their 68th anniversary.

Bob Winston, son of *Weekly Calistogan* reporter Ralph Winston and a meteorologist on a Navy ship in the Pacific, expressed hope he'll be home on leave soon. His ship has escaped major damage in recent actions, and he is optimistic about the tide of the war.

"Everything is looking very good, and the tidings of our victories leave me in an extremely optimistic frame of mind. Wouldn't it be great to have the whole thing over by this time next year? We have reached the point where it is possible for us to strike again and again and again, making each blow hurt, and hurt badly.

"I have hopes of seeing you in the near future – am planning on it as much as a man can plan on anything while in the Navy.

"I find so much pleasure in the use of the cigarette lighter you gave me, although I am now reduced to the necessity of using aviation gas in it for fuel. Every time I light a cigarette, a miniature smoke screen envelops me.

"I managed to break my glasses for about the seventh time in the past few months. It is rather difficult to get along without them, but I manage. It is impossible to read very much without producing considerable eye strain, which pains me no end.

"I hope to see you shortly after you receive this letter. Don't neglect writing, however. This leave idea might be a pipedream."

Local semi-finals of the annual Native Sons of the Golden West public speaking contest are being held at Calistoga High School this week.

The goal of the statewide competition is to give students a greater knowledge and understanding of the history of early California.

Senior Allan Forbes, the local winner the past three years, is a contender again. His topic is "John Nobili, Founder of Santa Clara College." Sophomore Audrey Kelley, juniors Virginia Caras and Verna Nicchia, and senior Mermie Tubbs all will talk about General Mariano Guadalupe Vallejo.

The other contenders, by class year, are:

Sophomores – Jim Ingalls, "John Muir"; Shirley Longmire, "The Mormon Trail": Nancy Weil, "The Kelsey Massacre"; and Norman Whatford, "John Weber."

Juniors – Aldo Boland, "Nuestra Senora de la Soledad"; Colleen Kelley, "John Bidwell, Prince of Pioneers"; Andy Richey, "Shasta – Old Town Rich in Memories"; and Patricia Shoemaker, "James Phelan, Scion and Son of California."

Note: Results are in the March 24 Weekly Calistogan.

Napa War Relief is conducting a drive in Calistoga for the collection of cast-off clothing, household furniture, china, glassware, pictures, and any other article suitable for sale in the Salvage Shop at Pearl and Calistoga streets in Napa.

All money raised by these sales is used for war charities. Last year, $10,800 was raised. Most of it was distributed among American Red Cross, the National War Chest Fund, British Relief, Polish Relief, Fighting French Relief, and Russian Relief. Napa War Relief also sends recreational supplies to Navy ships and Army posts.

Mrs. Gordon Hunt, the chairman in Calistoga, said donated articles should be left at the civil defense office. They will be taken to Napa when a truckload has been collected. Two loads have been sent so far this year. Donated clothing should be in reasonably clean and salable condition.

Waste paper is a vital "weapon of war." Blood plasma holders, bomb bands, shell containers, aircraft signals, ammunition chests, parachute flares, overseas containers, and other military needs are made of waste paper.

Open newspapers and tie into packages not more than 12 inches high. Tie magazines into bundles not more than eight inches high. Flatten out boxes and put with wrapping paper and other irregular pieces in bundles not more than 12 inches high.

Tie all bundles both ways and tie securely with string, rags, or wire. Remember, Boy Scouts will have to lift the bundles.

Calistoga schoolmates Sergeant Ward Taylor and Lieutenant Jackson Clary have found each other in England, Taylor says in a letter to his wife.

"Jackson came to see me yesterday. He insisted on my going back to spend the night with him. We talked over old times for hours, and then told each other our experiences since we left home.

"Jackson told me all about being shot down over Germany, and how he got back to England. He is now waiting around for his wife to get her discharge from the service so he can bring her back to the states with him. He will have a 30-day leave, and he says they plan to spend most of it in Calistoga. I imagine you will be seeing something of them. It will be easier for you to ask Jackson about his experiences than for me to try to write it.

"I met Mrs. Clary, and I don't blame Jackson for falling for her. They are coming down here next weekend, and I am to spend my day off with them. I told them they must have Mother's chicken dinner while they are there."

Note: Jackson and Taylor were members of the Calistoga High classes of 1937 and 1940. See the March 31 Weekly Calistogan *for details of Jackson's heroic escape after his plane was shot down.*

The Calistoga Fair Association will elect four new directors at its annual membership meeting at City Hall at 8 p.m. March 13. The terms of George Locey, A.L. Hawke, W.D. Tucker, and George Cropp expire. Chapin Tubbs, president of the association, said the general public is invited to attend the meeting.

Calistoga raised $246,616 – almost 45 percent over its goal – in the recently completed Fourth War Loan drive. The government had stressed the sale of Series E bonds. Those sales totaled $104,400 – 84 percent over the goal, Calistoga War Finance Committee Chairman Frank Piner proudly announced.

There are about 5,000 fewer persons registered to vote in Napa County than in 1942, County Clerk Ralph A. Dollarhide said. He urged people to register now rather than wait until the April 6 deadline approaches.

All persons who did not vote in the 1942 elections, or who have moved since then, must re-register to be eligible to vote in the primary election on May 16. Newcomers must be residents of the state for one year, of the county for 90 days, and of the precinct for 40 days.

Dollarhide also noted that the deadline for registration for the November national election is September 28.

City Clerk George Locey is the registration clerk for Calistoga.

Calistoga's Red Cross branch has a $2,800 goal in its upcoming month-long drive, chairman Mrs. Mitto Blodgett told a kick-off luncheon Friday. Supplies in the form of buttons, window cards, and pledge slips were issued to those present.

Mrs. Blodgett read an excerpt from a letter from Otis (Oat) Cook, a Calistoga boy now in the South Pacific.

"The American Red Cross has a very lovely reception hall for allied servicemen of all branches. I have spent many happy hours there reading, listening to the radio, playing pool or table tennis, eating doughnuts, and drinking coffee or cooling juices.

"There is a great pleasure in meeting soldiers from other countries there."

Mrs. Blodgett said the recreation hall that Cook wrote about is just one of hundreds the Red Cross has established close to the fighting fronts. "There is not a theatre of war that does not have many of the Red Cross facilities for troop entertainment and aid."

She said that 87 percent of the money given to the Red Cross goes directly to benefit our servicemen.

Another Red Cross activity that bears directly on the welfare of our men in battle is the Blood Donor service. The tons of blood plasma that have been shipped to all theaters have been made available through the efforts of the Red Cross. Mobile units to collect bloods will visit St. Helena on March 30, and Mrs. Blodgett urged those interested in donating their blood to get in touch with her for transportation.

Note: Otis Cook was a 1940 graduate of Calistoga High. Neither his branch of service nor his rank was given in the article.

Municipal Judge J.B. Winkelman sentenced two men to jail and fined another heavily during the past week. He found Karl

Rothermund guilty of threatening with a deadly weapon and sentenced him to six months in county jail – with four months suspended. Roland L. Gardner was fined $20 for public drunkenness, with the alternative of spending ten days in jail. He took the jail sentence. Fred Hensen, up on a charge of drunken driving, was fined $200, which he promptly paid.

Calistoga Rotarians enjoyed a surprise celebration of the 20th year of the club's existence at its regular meeting yesterday.

Seated at the head table were six of the 18 original members – Roy D. McCarthy, the president, and Walter H. Johnston, Ed E. Light, John B. Ghisolfo, Owen Kenny, and C.A. Carroll. Also present were members of the Napa Rotary Club in 1924, who helped organize the Calistoga club. McCarthy, now in education work in San Francisco, described the founding and early years of the club.

Historic Hotel Calistoga
(Courtesy Sharpsteen Museum, Calistoga)

Calistoga boasted for some years being the "smallest town in the world with a Rotary Club."

The first official meeting was held at the Hotel Calistoga on February 22, 1924. Officers were McCarthy, president; Wilber R. Snow, secretary; and E.L. Armstrong, treasurer; and C.A. Carroll, Dr. W.L. Blodgett, and E.J. Dove, executive committee.

Our country faces one of the most acute food shortages in its history. Everyone must do his or her part. The Victory Garden program for this season is more extensive than last year's. Everyone is asked to participate in the fullest possible manner.

The Agricultural Department has printed a booklet of suggestions. This will soon be in our possession, and we will, through this column, give you the benefits of its contents.

page 3

Congress has given housewives an effective weapon against overcharges, according to F.E. Williams, chairman of the Calistoga War Price and Rationing Board.

Under the Emergency Price Control Act, Mr. Williams explained, shoppers have the right to sue for $50 or three times any overcharge – whichever is greater.

He said Congress realizes that the battle against inflation can only be won by enlisting the co-operation of the consumer in fighting to hold the line against excessive charges.

The Navy is seeking housing outside the congested San Francisco-Oakland urban area for the families of Navy, Marine, Coast Guard servicemen stationed there. A spokesman for the service branches said they would welcome the help of communities within 150 miles of the Bay Area in moving non-essential families out of the congested port cities. Those wishing to help should get in touch with their local chamber of commerce, which can make the necessary arrangements through the State Chamber of Commerce.

The Women's Army Corps is offering special job assignments for the first time at its San Francisco recruiting and induction office. Women may now enlist, select any of 14 different jobs, and, upon completion of basic training, be returned to the San Francisco office. They may live at home and will receive a liberal living allowance in addition to their salary, clothing, and equipment.

The jobs to be filled are: general clerk, chief clerk, motion picture projectionist, stenographer, classification specialist, stock records clerk, chauffeur, light truck driver, file clerk, clerk-typist, message center clerk, supply clerk, auto equipment mechanic, and canvasser for WAC recruiting.

page 4

Editorial: Figures released by the U.S. Census Bureau reveal a significant shift in population from the eastern part of the country to the West Coast.

In the past four years, New York state has lost approximately one million people, while California has gained about the same number.

During the same period, the industrial and financial importance of the West has greatly increased, and our agricultural production has assumed an even more vital role in the feeding of the nation.

Yet, in spite of this, the West is still a political orphan. There are no westerners in the President's cabinet or among the top administrators in Washington.

Why this slighting of the West? How can the problems of this area be understood and acted on intelligently if we have no spokesmen in high government circles?

The fact that the present administration in Washington has ignored the West in its major appointments has been recognized by Republican presidential candidate Wendell Willkie. In his recent tour, he pointed out the need of western representation in any President's cabinet.

Mr. Willkie's interest in the West can hardly be classified as a mere vote-wooing gesture. He has chosen a western man, Ralph Cake of Oregon, as his national campaign manager. This, in itself, puts him in closer touch with things western than those who live and move only among eastern contacts.

The growing importance of the West gives us the right to demand more representation in the executive and judicial branches of our government.

For those who find the change to tokens in the scheme of rationing somewhat confusing, and the fact that a new series of stamps has been validated, with assigned point values varying from the value printed on the face of the stamps, the following explanation by the Office of Price Administration may be a bit enlightening.

Point values of green stamps K, L, and M in War Book 4 and brown stamps Y and Z in War Book 3 will not be affected by the ration token plan that went into effect Sunday.

All red and blue stamps validated on and after Sunday, February 27, will be worth a flat ten points, regardless of the numbers printed on them.

Green stamps K, L, and M in War Book 4 and brown stamps Y and Z in War Book 3 will continue to have the values of the numbers printed on them – 8, 5, 2, and 1. The green stamps for processed foods and the brown stamps for meats and fats are tag-ends of the old system, and they will expire on March 20.

Red stamps validated for meats and fats last Sunday are A8, B8, C8, and D8 in War Book 4. These red and blue stamps will each have a flat 10-point value and will be good until May 20.

Ration tokens will be given as change by dealers on purchases made with these red and blue stamps.

The OPA emphasizes that no tokens will be given to any consumer, except as change when a purchase is made. Shoppers have been urged to use any outstanding green and brown stamps before they use the new red and blue ration coupons.

W.C. Wiggins gave a report on the importation of Mexican laborers at last week's meeting of the Silverado Grange. He said a pool is now open for farmers to designate how much outside help they will need. Farmers must show they have housing facilities, a requirement for obtaining Mexican labor.

Ralph Goodman Leete, resident of Calistoga and driver for the Greyhound bus lines out of here for the past seven years, died in San Francisco early Tuesday morning. Death came after an emergency operation from which he failed to rally. He was 38.

Surviving are his wife, Henrietta; daughter, Beverly; and eight sisters and brothers.

Sugar stamp 40 in Ration Book 4, which is good for five pounds of sugar to be used only for canning, will be valid until February 28, 1945, the Office of Price Administration has announced. The statement was made to counteract inaccurate reports that the stamp will expire this month.

The OPA emphasized that consumers have no right to use Stamp 40 except for the canning purposes. Stamp 30 in Book 4 is valid for five pounds of sugar for general use. It is good indefinitely. Stamp 31, also good for five pounds of sugar, will become valid on April 1.

page 8

James Milton Overdeck of Napa has been sentenced to two years in federal prison for failing to report for induction in the Army. The sentence was imposed by Judge Martin L. Welsh in U.S. District Court at Sacramento.

The Napa County draft board ordered Overdeck into service on October 4, 1943. He told the board he is exempt from military service because he is a full-time minister of the gospel under the Watchtower Bible and Tract Society of New York State.

Members of the Napa board cast a jaundiced eye over the police record that Overdeck had gathered during his stay in the county seat and decided that his cloak of immunity was tattered and torn. He was ordered into the service.

Overdeck is the third alleged Jehovah Witness minister who has failed to comply with Selective Service regulations. They are all under two-year sentences.

High School News: Students have elected class officers for the spring semester. They include: Seniors – Jack Scott, president; Mermie Tubbs, vice president; Betty Tamagni, secretary; and Jane Jackson, class representative. Juniors – Norman Piner, president; Verna Nicchia, vice president; Mary Bardes, secretary; Colleen Kelley, treasurer; and Milton Petersen, class representative. Sophomores – Shirley Longmire, president; Nancy Weil, vice president; Barbara Fechter, secretary; Audrey Kelley, treasurer; and Marie Pocai, class representative. Freshmen – Bruce Piner, president; Mary Parsons, vice president; Betty Patten, secretary; Geniel Tuttle, treasurer; Ann Richey, class representative.

The Wildcat basketball teams had mixed results last Friday in St. Helena The B team played one of its finest games, beating the Saints 24 to 15. Rudy Urbani led Calistoga with eight points. Others who saw a lot of action were Ernie Zumwalt, Mel Ingalls, Paul Hickey, George Mayes, and Ken Westbay. The A team lost 28 to 20. Robert Howard led the Wildcats with seven points. Other players were Norman Piner, Frank Newton, Jack Scott, Stratton Wiggins, Delbert Pearl, Frank Strebel, and Andy Richey.

Note: Team membership was based on an age-height-weight formula. Bs were smaller-younger. In 1945, the Wildcat's B team, including several 1944 team members, won the league championship.

Greater opportunities than ever before are open to 17-year-old youths in the Navy, according to Jack Balin, in charge of the Navy recruiting station at the Sonoma County Courthouse in Santa Rosa.

Balin said radio technician's school prepares young men for highly specialized work in aiding the war effort, and at the same time qualifies them for an important field that promises to be in great demand when the war is over.

Applicants must be in their senior year of high school, have at least one year of high school algebra, and must pass the Eddy test, which is given at the recruiting station.

Full information may be obtained at the Navy recruiting station in Santa Rosa or from L.P. (Babe) Ames, Navy civilian recruiter for Calistoga.

Pieter Schaafsma of Reeder's Creamery had a surprise visit from two Dutch merchant marines – one a long-unseen nephew – early this week. The young men – both engine room officers – have seen action in the Atlantic and Mediterranean over the past five years, including a role in the evacuation of Dunkirk. They have been re-assigned and expect to be in the Pacific for some time.

Chapter 4

March 19-25

The War: Finland rejects Russian peace terms. The Allies conduct heavy bombing of several strategic German cities.

𝕸eekly 𝕮alistogan of March 24, 1944

page 1

The tragedy of war came to Calistoga Tuesday when a telegram from the War Department informed Mrs. Walter P. Van der Kamp that her husband, flight officer and pilot on a 4-motored bomber, is missing in action over Germany.

Lieutenant Van der Kamp is a member of a prominent family in this community. His mother was Freda Petersen before her marriage. Her family lived for many years on a hillside ranch west of Calistoga, and she grew up and schooled here. Van der Kamp's wife and their infant son, Martin, have been making their home in Calistoga since February 11. They came from Texas, where the lieutenant was stationed before being sent overseas on November 26.

Anxious to serve, even before this country entered hostilities, young Van der Kamp enlisted and trained in Canada. After this country's declaration of war, he transferred to the U.S. Army Air Corps and served for more than a year as an instructor in Texas.

He saw action in the Italian campaign before his recent transfer to the Central European theater. As flight officer, he had been piloting the four-motored bomber, Galloping Ghost, No. 777, with a crew of 11.

Note: Walter and seven members of his crew died when their plane was shot down during a raid on the Regensburg industrial center in southwestern Germany on February 22, 1944. He is interred at the Ardennes American Cemetery and Memorial in Belgium. Jean worked as a waitress and photo shop clerk in Calistoga many years. Martin attended Calistoga schools with class of '61. He has a vineyard and healing center on Sonoma Mountain.

Eddie Cook of Calistoga, taken prisoner when the Japs took Wake Island soon after the outbreak of the war, has been heard from again. The latest message, from a prisoner of war camp in China, was received by Eugene "Daffy" Tedeschi of Calistoga. Typed on a postcard dated July 11, 1943, it reads:

"Well, kid, like a bad penny, I show up once in a great while. Give my love to sisters, brother, mother, and wife. I have written every time I've had a chance, but only received Monkey's first six letters. Tell them not to worry, I'm fine.

"Daffy, old boy, I'll bet you're having fun about now. My life here is quite simple, of course. This place isn't too nice; but, after all, this is war and we must expect to give a little. My job here is similar to the one I had at the old Palisades mine, where my dad was boss; so I'm doing as well as can be expected. The food isn't bad, providing you like rice.

"Say hello to your pretty little wife, babies, and to the gang. How is old Sig Light? Sorry to hear about my old friend, Jack Adams. Give Cecelia my deepest symphony."

Eddie is the oldest son of the late Edward J. Cook of Calistoga and Mrs. Lucy Ashton Cook of Napa. He has a brother, Otis, now serving in the South Pacific with the U.S. paratroopers, and three sisters. He was working in civilian employment on Wake Island when he was taken prisoner.

His return address is: Edward L. Cook, Section 4, Barracks No. 3, Shanghai War Prisoners' Camp, Shanghai, China.

Note: Eddie was a 1927 graduate of Calistoga Elementary School, Otis a 1940 graduate of the high school.

With the Army dipping into the farm-deferred pool to augment its ranks, and with anticipated Mexican national labor far below the promised quota, growers in the Napa Valley face a far more serious labor situation than that which harassed them during 1943.

First requisite for securing Mexican nationals is adequate housing. There are few ranches in the valley that have facilities which will pass inspection by state and county authorities.

Anticipating the needs, the University of California Agricultural College at Davis has prepared plans for units of various sizes. The installations are classed as semi-permanent, and costs vary in relation to sizes. Plans are available for 12-man, 6-man, and 2-man bunkhouses, and a 4-man canvas roofed cabin.

Costs run from $2,000 for the largest structure to $150 for the 4-man cabin.

Lumber yards anticipate having a sufficient supply of materials to meet the demand, and growers will be given all assistance possible from the Farm Labor Offices and the state and county agricultural officials. At the present time, the Farm Labor Office at 1036 St. Helena Highway, Napa, has a supply of plans, with complete details for construction and a bill of materials for each type of structure.

In commenting on the coming season, County Farm Adviser H.J. Baade said, "In 1943, some 6,000 volunteer workers were placed through the three Farm Labor Offices in the county. From present indications, the number will have to be much greater this year. Gasoline rationing will increase the need for accommodations, and the necessity for over-night housing of volunteer workers will be greater than last year."

W.C. Wiggins, director of the Napa County Labor Corporation, states that out of four possible sources of labor which gave promise of providing help, only one remains, and that is Mexican national labor. During the latter part of 1943 and the early part of this year, there was much talk of securing Italian prisoners of war, Italian internees, German prisoners of war, and Mexican nationals. The first three possibilities have been crossed off.

Calistogan William R. (Bill) Tubbs received his second lieutenant's commission in Texas March 13 and then paid his first visit home in over a year. He arrived last Wednesday and left on Tuesday of this week to return to his base, Foster Field, Texas. Having trained as a fighter pilot, Bill now will take five weeks of transitional training. He does not know what his orders will be after that.

The Army Air Force Central Flying Training Command's 11 southwestern advanced flying schools combined for its largest graduation ever – "enough bomber and fighter pilots to replace or redouble the entire American air arm over Europe," the official announcement stated. "Among the new pilots were scores of officers from other branches of the service who had been accepted for pilot training and many former enlisted personnel already decorated for air crew operations over enemy territory."

Navy veteran Robert A. Winston, son of Ralph P. Winston of the *Weekly Calistogan*, spent Monday night at the Carroll home on Cedar Street. Young Winston is spending a 21-day leave on the coast following his return from the South Pacific, where his ship was engaged in the attack on the Marshall Islands. Before that, Bob was at Tarawa in the battle of Santa Cruz, and spent several months north of the Solomon Islands, where his ship was part of the task force engaged in wrecking Tojo's "Tokyo Express" when the Japs were trying to get supplies through by sea to their troops in the south.

Walter Butler has been promoted to corporal in the Army Air Force. He is a radio operator and mechanic somewhere in the South Pacific. He reported in a letter to his mother, Aurelia Butler, that he recently met the first Calistogan he'd come across over there – Staff Sergeant Walter S. Hays.

Still several hundred dollars under the quota, Calistoga's Red Cross drive is approaching its end with every chance of failure to meet its obligation to every man and woman of the armed forces.

Reports pour in from the battle fronts, from the rest areas, from the prison camps in Japan and Germany, telling of the 101 things that the Red Cross does for our forces.

A prisoner of war in Germany wrote his father: "The Red Cross took care of us with clothes and necessities. We have regularly received Red Cross prisoner of war food packages. I have received 16 packages so far. Dad, please write a check in my name and send it to the Red Cross. About a hundred dollars, I guess."

The need is so urgent that every citizen must contribute. The local chapter maintains a table in the Bank of America, where donations will be received. The time is short, and Calistoga must go over the top.

With 27 members signed up, the Calistoga Fair Association moves into the 1944 season, the ninth of its existence. There will be no fair this year, or entertainment of any sort, but the association has certain fixed expenses to meet. Insurance is a principal item. Dues may be handed to any director of the group.

A near fatality occurred on Mount St. Helena Sunday when Ernest Almeida of the merchant marine lost control of his motorcycle and crashed into a car driven by Peter Hansen of Middletown. Almeida, en route to Oakland, evidently misjudged the sharpness of a curve. He and his cycle were pinned under the car. He was extricated with help from passing motorists. Brought to Calistoga Hospital for treatment, he was able to continue his journey on another motorcycle later that evening.

Calistoga High School senior Allan Forbes placed second in the American Legion Fourth District oratorical contest at Richardson Springs over the weekend. He spoke on "John Nobili, Founder of Santa Clara University". Teacher William Manford and student Verna Nicchia accompanied Forbes to the competition.

Calistoga American Legion Post No. 231 will hold a special meeting Monday night to discuss final details for the erection of a memorial plaque dedicated to the men and women of Calistoga who are in the armed forces.

In order that all names may be listed, Adjutant James McCall has requested that relatives and friends of service men and women send names to the *Weekly Calistogan*, which will pass them on to the Legion.

Another ton of waste paper was sent out by the Legion this week, bringing the total to seven tons. They are still collecting and will continue to do so as long as there is any waste paper left.

The first of a series of programs being staged to secure funds for the purchase of uniforms for the Calistoga High School band was highly successful, both in gate receipts and the quality of performance.

The program, held last Friday evening at the high school gym, opened with seven numbers by the high school band, directed by Clifford Anderson. It closed with two one-act comedies staged by high school students.

Lending novelty and enjoyment to the concert was a number entirely different than anything heretofore presented by the band – a modern selection, D. Bennett's "Repartee," featuring Alvin Kuster, principal of Calistoga Elementary School, as piano soloist.

The first one-act play, "Fish For Sale," featured a cast composed of Bill Cook, Tim Foote, Stella Hartinger, Betty Pocai, Betty Tamagni, Ellen Decker, and Frank Strebel.

The second comedy, "Undertakin' Bootleggin'," had a cast made up of Allan Forbes, Pat Shoemaker, Norman Piner, Jack Scott, Allan Ballard, and Norman Whatford.

The high school band, winner in pre-war days of seven regional or national championships, continues to maintain its high standard of performance. With new uniforms, which will be purchased at the conclusion of the present emergency, the band will be ready to bring home new honors to the town and school.

page 2

An interesting letter has come from Perry Barber, MM 1/c with the Navy Seabees in the South Pacific. The letter, addressed to his mother, Mrs. Berwin Barber, says:

"By now you should know just what island I am on. There wasn't a thing here when we made our landing, unless you want to call a few dead Japs something. Now, in less than three months, this place looks like a large city. Navy Seabees really get the work done under any conditions.

"We all say that it is too civilized around here, and hope they send us up to build another base soon. All other outfits are a little bit jealous of the Seabees because we move in and really set up a camp that anyone would be proud of.

"When we left the States, our first stop was at a small Pacific isle. Censorship won't let us say much about it. We only stayed there a few days. The natives were of a queer type, and all seemed to have a bit of American money. Just how they acquired it I cannot say, but all we cared was that they had it. Out came our bottles of hair oil and various face lotions. Needless to say, anything that had a highly perfumed smell brought a high price in return. Most of the boys left with their pockets filled with old musty bills that the natives had had tucked away for some time. Yes, we watered the perfume. All they wanted was the smell anyway. If you wanted any souvenirs, a few cigarettes brought you a grass skirt or some beads.

"Their language consisted of a few grunts and some choice words that the Marines had taught them.

"These 'black boys' really put on a great celebration every time there was a wedding. This always called for roasting a pig. The animal was simply killed by beating it to death with clubs and stones. Then it was laid on a hot bed of coals, without being cleaned in any way. After the pig was cooked to the chef's own taste, everyone sat down around the fire and ripped the flesh off with their bare hands. On top of all this came raw fish. Of course, at this time, the natives had to have their dancing and drink. The drink was something to let alone. It was brew from coconuts, bananas, and oranges. It really gave them pep to beat the drums. I'm sure that if you had their formulas back there, no one would worry about the gas rationing. Some of the boys said that if you spilled any on you, it would take the hair off.

"From there we went to New Caledonia, which is a French settlement. In our spare time there, the mates really set up a fine camp, with wood decks under our tents, and the sides screened in. They have to be screened or the mosquitoes would eat you up in no time. For our lumber, we procured materials from the crates that the airplanes were shipped in. For the screen, we traded a few bottles of beer. Beer was used for all transactions.

"The town there was far behind times. It was very dirty at all times. I would not want to eat anything that came from their stores or markets. The people spoke a very low grade of French, and they always acted as if they didn't know what you were talking about, but they knew the value of the American dollar. In fact, they all preferred it to their own money. As I told you before, the deer hunting was good. We had venison at the galley several times. Our battalion did a lot of work there before leaving. I was glad to leave, as I don't like to stay in any place very long.

"I have told you quite a bit about the island we are now on in other letters. It's the same as most of these islands – heavy jungle growth, lots of bugs, flies, and snakes. I still perspire from morning till night in this heat. We still get lots of tropical fruit to eat.

"I haven't used a foxhole for some time now. It really was the only thing a while back."

Ellen Nicchia, a 1942 graduate of Calistoga High School, is among 800 students who enrolled for the spring semester at San Francisco State College. One of the leading teacher-training schools in the nation, it is putting special emphasis on supplying the elementary and junior high schools in this area with competent teachers to replace the thousands called into the military service. Many teachers who had retired as many as 25 years ago are returning to college for refresher courses as a prelude to going back to their old jobs.

From Sergeant Francis E. Turner, who is taking special training at Purdue University, comes a thank-you note for his Christmas package from Calistoga.

"My first reaction was a strong feeling of genuine pride in my home town. I think you folks are part of the swellest home town a soldier could imagine, and I feel like thanking each of you just for living there, and making it such a first-class community to call 'the home town'."

Frank is the son of the late Robert M. Turner of Knights Valley and Mrs. Rita Turner, who now makes her home in Stockton. His address: Sergeant F.E. Turner, Sect. 3, Co. "C", 1545th S.U., West Lafayette, Indiana.

The Women's Army Corps now offers eligible women the unique privilege of selecting their job, station, and branch in the U.S. Army. New stations now open in this district are Camp Hann, Fort Winfield Scott, and Camp Stoneman.

Camp Hann recruits women to fill such jobs as teletype operator, court reporter, butcher, baker, cook, cryptographic technician, artist, administrative inspector, and truck driver.

Fort Winfield Scott also has a long list, including structural draftsman, photographer, reporter, chauffer, ambulance driver, dietician, dental technician, pharmacist, and personnel clerk.

Camp Stoneman offers surgical technician, optician, dental technician, mail clerk, and laboratory technician. There are many other jobs, all affording women the opportunity to serve their country in time of war and to acquire an interesting and valuable training for a post-war career.

To be eligible for the WAC, a woman must be between the ages of 20 and 49, inclusive, with no dependents; must be an American citizen, in good health, and of excellent character.

See your nearest U.S. Army recruiting station without delay, or write to U.S. Army Recruiting Headquarters, 444 Market Street, San Francisco, 11, California.

page 4

The following amounts were spent for war stamps purchases this week by students at the local elementary school: First grade, $18.40; second, $12.60; third, $11.80; fourth, $13.40; fifth, $8.15; sixth, $25.60; seventh, $22.10; and eighth, $10.45. Three students completed purchase of bonds: Joan Kelley, George Hawkins, and Harry Hawkins.

Calistoga 1944

Belated news received this week tells of the marriage of Andrew Aalders of Calistoga and Agnes Kammerer in Carmel in February. They are making their home in San Jose.

Mr. Aalders, the brother of spa owner Dr. H.J. Aalders, came to Calistoga about a year ago from Los Angeles, where he had been associated with a water filter company. Both he and his new wife have adult families from previous marriages. She formerly managed the S & H green stamp store in Carmel.

Note: Dr. Aalders' spa now is Calistoga Spa.

Editorial: The men and women of our armed forces cannot, by the very nature of things, do much about their future. Individually, they have surrendered a one-time free existence to the military, which is as it must be for victory.

In the military service, they live for this present day, this present hour, the immediacy of a moment which may be the last.

It is for us, then, left safely at home, to be thinking of their future (we can do little enough about their present) – for this future belongs to those who prepare for it.

The Truman committee of the Senate, a diligent fact-finding body which is demonstrably unbiased, has once again pointed the way toward the most effective solution of post-war production and employment problems. It finds that "even in wartime, it is the flow of private initiative that makes possible the success of the war program. This flow must be encouraged in the future."

With the objective clearly defined, then, it is the obligation of each of us at home to project this encouragement to the end that there will be an economic environment which is not hostile to business, prompt liquidation of war contracts, and a reasonable tax program which will encourage individual initiative and incentive.

Let it be remembered that just talking about the future will not bring the results desired. Affirmative and continued action by our lawmakers is of vital importance to safeguard the future.

Editorial: After reading scholarly talks on our tax problems, and after listening to arguments for and against different methods of taxation, one fact stands out clearly – everybody and his dog must now pay sacrificial taxes, and government extravagance must be cut as drastically as taxes are increased.

If we fail to do this, we admit that we prefer to pass on to the boys at the front not only the risk of life and limb but also the obligation of an unnecessarily high public debt. We make no sacrifice in buying interest-bearing war bonds, which create debt, and in perpetuating every boondoggling political project, while our fighting men sacrifice their lives and opportunities and families to preserve us safe from hardship at home.

Unless those enjoying war profits and war wages pay heavy taxes now to hold down the national debt and prevent the devaluation of the dollar, and unless government expenses are cut to the bone, there will be no chance of lowering the tax rate after the war so that industry and the people can have the tax relief necessary to encourage the accumulation of earnings and savings which are essential to industrial expansion on a peace-time basis that will provide permanent jobs for all.

No amount of rhetoric can change these facts.

page 5

Eleven candidates from Calistoga and three from St. Helena were initiated into the Rebekah lodges at a joint meeting in Calistoga Wednesday night.

During the business session, Mabel Mingus and Berenice Martin were elected delegates to the Grand Lodge sessions in Sacramento in May.

The Rebekahs appreciated very much the fruit blossoms and spring flower decorations which the Native Daughters had generously left in the hall after their meeting the night before.

page 6

High School News: The Wildcats baseball team won its first game of the season, 13-11, over the Petaluma High Trojans last Saturday. They scored in every inning except the fifth and sixth. The game was punctuated by nine errors and six hits for the Wildcats, nine errors and nine hits for the Trojans. The first league game will be played a week from Friday with Tomales.

The track team competed with St. Helena and Vallejo at the Saints' track last Friday. It is the first year that Calistoga has competed in this sport. Coach Manford says some of the boys have real possibilities. The next meet will be held in St. Helena today.

The sophomores have elected officers: Audrey Kelley, president; Barbara Fechter, vice president; Jim Ingalls, representative; and Nancy Weil, treasurer.

Calistoga 1944

The freshmen are starting a campaign to collect books for servicemen.

Future Farmers of America: Farm Adviser H.J. Baade is coming to demonstrate the art of grafting. Mr. Federspiel has given the boys an ancient Model-T Ford, which they are endeavoring to fix – if they can get the parts.

The Student Council has donated $10 to the Red Cross. Each class also is collecting money for it, with a goal of $25.

Justus Craemer, a leading contenders for U.S. Senator in the May primary, declared this week that "California faces the fight of its life to save its new industries during the post-war period. That fight will be won or lost, not here, but in Washington, where our post-war policies will be fixed," said Craemer, "and I hope it will be my privilege, as a member of the United States Senate, to take up the cudgels for California in that battle. We simply have to win that fight if we are to have work for our people – and if we are to achieve our destiny as a great agricultural and industrial empire."

Craemer is an Orange County publisher and a member of the State Railroad Commission. He literally "paved the way" for the coming of California's new industrial age some years ago as a deputy director of the State Department of Public Works by insisting that California build a highway system capable of handling military and heavy industrial traffic. During recent months, he has again been in the forefront in a fight against discriminatory federal taxes on transportation and communications that put Western agriculture and industry at a disadvantage with their Eastern competitors.

"California, in years past, spent untold millions seeking new industries and new settlers," Craemer said. "Now we have BOTH, who have been brought here almost overnight by our country's desperate wartime need. But what of TOMORROW? Shall we have closed factories, doles, and bread-lines? I cannot believe we shall risk that bitter anticlimax. If we can prevent Washington politicians from throttling our industries when peace comes, we can keep our factories humming. And we can have work and opportunity for all our people. But we can't do it if we are hamstrung by pitifully weak representation in our national capital. Tomorrow's job is waiting, if we are prepared to fight for it – here and in Washington."

From a Wichita, Kansas, newspaper comes the following comment on a former Calistoga boy – Earl Lander, gunner's mate, 2/c, U.S. Navy. Earl, a grandson of Mr. and Mrs. C.O. Fink, made his home here for a time and attended Calistoga High School. The Kansas paper says:

"Gunner's Mate Earl Lander, 18, has been aboard a ship when it was torpedoed last December and, again, when it was rammed by an ammunition boat. He has been in five battles, including the landing at Casablanca, and his boat is credited with sinking a sub. It has also been attacked upon occasion by Nazi speedboats.

"Lander has just taken a patch off one eye. He suffered this wound when his naval tanker was torpedoed in the Mediterranean. Luckily, the torpedo struck so low that the oil wasn't ignited and the ship was brought into port. He was wounded in the legs on another occasion.

"There is one good thing about a tanker. It is divided into compartments, and when a torpedo slams into a compartment, it is simply shut off and the tanker stays afloat.

"Although only 18, Earl will chalk up two years of service. He is familiar with many Mediterranean ports."

Note: Lander graduated from Calistoga Elementary School in 1940.

An attempt to trade Army gasoline for whiskey led to the arrest of a civilian and an Army sergeant in Napa last week. Subsequent investigation of the case points to a possible traffic in government property.

Two Napa policemen, accompanied by military police, were making their rounds in a prowl car when they noticed an army truck parked in front of a garage in the Westwood area on the outskirts of town. Stopping to investigate, the officers were too late to apprehend a soldier, who ran from the rear of the garage. They did, however, stop a sergeant and a civilian and put them under arrest.

Questioning disclosed that the sergeant was attempting to close a deal whereby he would turn over 200 gallons of gasoline in return for whiskey. The civilian, William Whitcomb of Napa, was to furnish this liquor.

Whitcomb was released from county jail Sunday after posting $2,500 bail. He appeared before the United States commissioner of Sacramento Tuesday. Officials of the FBI are making an extensive investigation to find out whether the incident is isolated, or part of a series.

Chapter 5

Weekly Calistogan of March 31, 1944

page 1

Lieutenant Jackson Clary, an Army Air Force pilot who was reported missing during a bombing raid over Germany last September, shared his experiences with friends in Calistoga Wednesday. They knew he had been reported as safe in England, but his visit here was the first opportunity they had to reassure themselves that the young flier is very much alive, unharmed, and preparing to report to Santa Monica for re-assignment.

Clary, a 1937 graduate of Calistoga High School, originally was a member of the Royal Canadian Air Force. He transferred to our Air Force in June of 1943 but continued to fly for the RCAF.

Flying a British Halifax 4-engine bomber, Clary was returning from his 20th mission over Germany when his plane was hit by anti-aircraft fire. In his words, "It was a calm and very black night. We were flying along serenely when we suddenly received a direct hit. Fragments from the shell destroyed all controls and left me helpless in attempting to maneuver the ship."

The flight engineer died instantly, and another crew member had a leg blown off and a hip wound. Four men bailed out. Clary helped the badly wounded man out of the escape door and prepared to take to the air himself. The plane lurched and threw Clary out. His foot caught in a dangling cable, and he was caught up short, hanging head down. By superhuman effort, he managed to get his hands on the side of the escape door and pull himself up until he could release his ankle from the cable's clutch. The plane continued its dizzying spin. As he fell free, Clary debated whether to pull his parachute's rip-cord. The plane was close by, and he feared he might become fouled up again if he released the parachute too soon. He decided to take a chance and pulled the cord. "The plane shot by me, with the wings perpendicular to the earth. It looked like the side of a house."

After what he later calculated was a 15,000-foot drop, Clary made a safe landing in Occupied France. For military reasons, he could not give any details as to just how he reached and crossed the English Channel. Some idea of the risk involved and the care that had to be taken may be derived from the fact that it took him two months to make it.

Clary said that two of the four men who left the plane unwounded broke their legs when they landed. The other two, uninjured, gave aid. All four were captured and are assumed to be prisoners of war. The boy whose leg was blown off was reported to have landed but to have died in a hospital.

Upon his return to his field, Clary was put through the usual questioning by military intelligence and then assigned to headquarters duty until leaving for the United States something over a month ago. He is being accompanied by his wife, the former Barbara Harrison of England. Mrs. Clary was a member of the WAAF and was on the headquarters staff at the field where Clary was stationed.

Clary says that Sergeant Ward Taylor, also of Calistoga, is an aircraft armorer stationed in England and was in good health the last time they met in London. Two other Clary boys are with the Army Air Force. Everett is a staff sergeant at a Texas field. Peter also is a staff sergeant, stationed with the ground forces at Mesa, Arizona. They are the sons of Mr. and Mrs. Thomas Clary of Alameda, formerly of Calistoga.

Note: Jackson and Thomas Jr. graduated from Calistoga High School in 1937, Everett in 1939.

Directors of the Calistoga Chamber of Commerce have recommended that the city join a proposed soil conservation district. They acted March 23 after hearing two representatives of the U.S. Soil Conservation Service describe the purpose of such a district and its benefits to growers.

Through erosion control and soil and water conservation, land values would increase, with resultant benefit to the community as a whole, they said. Increased activity of the Soil Conservation Service (SCS) will also help provide work for servicemen after the war.

Dr. H.H. Bennett, chief of the SCS, estimates that within six months after hostilities cease, it will be possible to provide work for 80,000 ex-servicemen. Once the conservation program is well under way, there will be work for about 200,000 men.

Rotarians hosted a cosmopolitan group of guests yesterday at their weekly luncheon meeting. They included Bob Honan and Bert Caddies, officers of the Royal Australian Air Force; Dr. R.M. Cossentini, professor of Chinese at Pacific Union College; Chester Wong, Chinese student at Pacific Union who is studying for his doctor's degree; and Henry Carlenzoli, a Calistoga boy who is taking naval air training at Norman, Okla.

Carlenzoli described his naval training. He is due back for more training next week. Wong, speaker of the day, discussed the founding of the Chinese Republic, the attempts to convene a congress and adopt a constitution, and the future aims of the Republic. He emphasized China's determination to carve her own destiny and take her place among the free nations of the earth. Dr. Cossentini described the great progress that has taken place in the teaching of languages since the start of the war. America, he said, is at long last realizing the necessity of being able to carry on trade and cultural pursuits with other nations.

The Australians described the resemblances between California and their country, especially in the smaller communities. The audience sat up with surprise when Caddies mentioned that they had left Australia last Friday night and had arrived in San Francisco Saturday evening. It is a rather startling demonstration of the shortening of time-distance between countries.

Note: Carlenzoli was a 1935 graduate of Calistoga High School.

Constable Ed E. Light was cleared this week in a civil suit alleging illegal entry and attempts to seize certain moneys. Judge A.F. Bray dismissed the claims of Howard J. Bruff and Grace E. Bruff on the basis of written briefs.

Note: No details of the case were given.

Navy Lieutenant George Scarfe, son of Mr. and Mrs. George O. Scarfe Sr. of Calistoga, has written thanking the community for its Christmas package. "The gifts are very nice and show thoughtfulness in their selection. I want to thank you very much for remembering me and including me as one of your home-town boys. No other city will claim me, and it is really almost necessary to have a home town to talk about. I am looking forward to meeting you all in the future."

From Mrs. Louise Culver of Palo Alto, whose home was in Calistoga many years ago, comes a note telling of the death of her son, George Culver Jr., in Italy. "The heartbreaking news came last week that George Jr., at the end of his third year in the artillery, was killed at Anzio, Italy, on February 25. He was in the first invasion of Tunisia, in Sicily, and the Italian campaign."

Culver worked at Standard Oil's Richmond refinery before entering the service.

USS *Napa* has been approved by the Navy Department as the name for a transport attack vessel now being built at a West Coast shipyard. Wartime restrictions prevent advance announcement of the shipyard or launching date.

The action is in response to the Redwood Empire Association's program to have names of rivers throughout its nine-county area given to newly constructed Navy vessels.

One of the largest estates in the valley changed hands last week when Mrs. Frieda Vocke McGill sold her 1700-acre property near Oakville to Martin Stelling Jr., widely known capitalist and property owner.

The selling price, $350,000, marks the biggest realty deal in the county for several years. Stelling recently purchased the adjoining "To-Kalon" vineyards from Mrs. Alice Churchill. The two properties give him holdings which reach along the west side of the valley for several miles and stretch well back into the hills.

Stelling's new property is largely planted to vineyard, with orchard and farm lands comprising the balance. The residence is noted for its landscaped gardens, laid out by the late John McLaren, father of Golden Gate Park in San Francisco. It is reported that Stelling will sell part of the southern end of the acreage, including the mansion, and it will be subdivided for country homes.

Note: Stelling eventually held over 5,000 acres but died before they were developed. They included land developed into vineyards/ wineries by Robert Mondavi, Far Niente, and others.

Considerable interest is being expressed about forming an evening class in Spanish at Calistoga High School to provide growers and others with a working knowledge of the language to facilitate the handling of Mexican national labor on farms and ranches.

Charles S. Morris Jr., principal of the high school, said he would lend all assistance possible in the formation of the class. He said only two things are needed – 12 students and a teacher. It is felt there will be no difficulty in securing either.

The class would be devoted strictly to basic Spanish rather than the intricacies of the language. It will help them direct their men intelligently and understand their wants.

For further information, contact Mr. Morris or call the *Weekly Calistogan* office.

page 2

President Roosevelt's action in signing a law restricting the number of government personnel entitled to free use of the Golden Gate Bridge brings to a successful conclusion a long, difficult campaign of great financial importance to counties within the bridge district.

The new measure will become effective April 12. It limits free government traffic to members of the Army and Navy and civilian personnel when traveling on official business only. Violation is punishable by fine, or imprisonment, or both.

"The Lea-Welch Bill brings to an end unwarranted free use of the bridge by many federal agencies, bureaus, and individuals. That was never the intent," declared Nathan F. Coombs, Napa County's director on the bridge district board.

Sugar stamp 40 in War Ration Book IV is to be used only for sugar for home canning, according to F.E. Williams, chairman of the local War Price and Ration Board. "It must not be regarded as a sugar bonus for general use. Persons who use sugar stamp 40 for other purposes may be denied additional sugar later in the season," Williams said.

Sugar stamp 40 was validated February 1, 1944, and will be good through February 28, 1945.

The Calistoga unit of the Office of Price Administration (OPA) is seeking volunteers who have spare time and are genuinely interested in the federal government's efforts to curb black market operations and maintain compliance with price ceilings.

"We need volunteers for our Price Control Committee, which just recently was granted additional authority to deal directly with violators," local OPA chairman F.E. Williams said.

"These committee members, who will visit designated stores at regular intervals, will not be secret investigators in any sense of the word. They will be duly sworn-in agents of the federal government, and they will make known their identities with proper credentials. Further, they will be of valuable assistance to the merchants who are earnestly trying to comply with the complex requirements which war has imposed upon them.

"Their primary job will be to aid the honest merchant in every possible way to comply. They will bring needed information directly to the merchant, and they will assist in relaying his complaints to the local board. At the same time, they will make periodic checks on the merchants who refuse to obey the laws under which others are expected to operate."

Mr. Williams said prospective committee members should either contact him personally or the board's clerk.

page 4

Myrel Moore, who enters the armed forces April 5, was honored at a dinner party Tuesday night at the Fior D'Italia Hotel. Floral and candle decorations on the long table carried out the patriotic theme in red, white, and blue.

Fior D'Italia Hotel -- today, the Calistoga Inn

Guests included Mr. Moore's co-workers at Safeway and other friends of him and his wife, Amelia. They included Mr. and Mrs. K.L. Smith, Mr. and Mrs. Jack McAvoy, Mrs. Alice Vermeil, Carl Pierce, Mrs. Ida Huston, Jesse Manuel, Mrs. LaVerne Clayton, Mrs. Lena Moiso, and Frank Bechelli.

Mr. Moore has lived in Calistoga five years, during which he was in charge of the vegetable department at the Safeway store. He has made many friends who will sincerely regret his leaving.

Mrs. Moore and their son, Myrel Jr., will remain in Calistoga. She will take over Mr. Moore's position in the Safeway store.

Note: Mr. Moore suffered a heart attack during his military training and returned to Calistoga and Safeway. The son became a four-sport star at Calistoga High; a multi-sport player at Santa Rosa Junior College and University of California, Davis; and a linebacker coach for Oakland, Denver, and New England in the National Football League.

Calendar of Coming Events:
Friday, March 31 – Tucker card party.
Saturday, April 1 – Silverado Grange.
Monday, April 3 – Native Sons, Boy Scouts.
Tuesday, April 4 – Masons, Rifle Club, Library Board of
    Trustees, Friendly Circle, British War Relief
    surgical unit.
Wednesday, April 5 – Odd Fellows, Civic Club.
Thursday, April 6 – Volunteer Fire Department, Rotary
    Club, Sunnyside Club.
Friday, April 7 – City Council.
Saturday, April 8 – Community Church pre-Easter food sale.
Monday, April 10 – Native Daughters, Boy Scouts.
Tuesday, April 11 – Women's Association of Community
    Church, Rifle Club, British War Relief surgical unit,
    Tucker Farm Center annual meeting.
Wednesday, April 12 – Rebekahs, Order of Eastern Star,
    Service Club.
Thursday, April 13 – Rotary Club, The Gleaners, Garden Club.
Friday, April 14 – Tucker Home Department.

A resident of long ago returned to Calistoga last week for a brief visit to the scene of his birth. He is George M. Johnson, son of J.J. Johnson, who was once foreman at the R.F. Grigsby mine north of Calistoga. The younger Johnson, now in his 60s, was born in Horn Canyon, sometimes known as Westerson Canyon. This is his first return to Calistoga in many years.

Observing the fifth Wednesday of the month, Odd Fellows and Rebekahs gathered this week for social time together. The pot-luck supper attracted 75 members and their families. That was followed by dancing to music provided by Miss Edith Cavagnaro and Fred

Tedeschi, and cards for those who preferred. Two Australian fliers who happened to be in Calistoga accepted an invitation to attend. They expressed themselves as grateful for a very pleasant evening.

Only ten Calistoga Rifle Club members were present for Tuesday night's meeting. Nance and Hibbs topped the scoring with 185 and 180, respectively, out of the possible 200. Other scores: Hawkins, 153; Cole, 151; Merry, 150; Morris and Pacheteau, 149; Geary, 132; Ames, 130; and Cohen, 126. Considerable comment was heard regarding Ames' score. Consensus of opinion seemed to be that "Babe" is pressing in anticipation of getting in shape for the coming deer season.

page 8
High School Notes: On Tuesday, the CHS racketeers won their first league tennis match from Healdsburg. Our first singles was won by Allan Forbes, 6-4, 3-6, 6-4. Milton Petersen lost the second singles, 6-1, 5-7, 1-6. Allan Ballard took the third singles, 3-6, 6-4, and first doubles went to Norman Piner and Earl Evans, 6-3, 6-1.

This year's annual staff is as follows: Allan Forbes, editor; Verna Nicchia, assistant editor; Delbert Pearl, business manager; Betty Tamagni, assistant business manager; Ellen Decker, publication chief; Earl Evans, assistant publication chief; and Andy Richey, advertising manager.

The CHS baseball team lost a close game to St. Helena, 10-9, a week ago last Thursday. Calistoga staged a last-inning rally that scored three runs

Allan Forbes, top left, and Delbert Pearl, right

before they were retired with the tying run on third.

Calistoga's line-up was: MacDonald, ss; Newton, 3b; Piner, 1b; Strebel, p; Howard, cf; Urbani, rf; Putman, 2b; Westbay, lf; and Saviez, c. All players except Urbani got at least one hit.

During school physical education periods, the boys and girls have started a mixed doubles tennis ladder. The present standings are: 1 – Mermie Tubbs and Norman Piner; 2 – Nancy Weil and Allan Ballard; 3 – Shirley Longmire and Paul Hickey; 4 – Lorene

Salmina and Brian Putman; 5 – Verna Nicchia and Allan Forbes; 6 – Mary Parsons and Laurence Locey; 7 – Colleen Kelley and Earl Evans; 8 – Audrey Kelley and Ken Westbay.

A report has it that a committee was appointed in Washington to erect a monument to President Franklin D. Roosevelt. The location of the monument was problematical. The committee considered placing the new structure near the Washington Monument, but decided against it as they said George Washington was known as a man who never told a lie. They looked near the Lincoln Memorial, but decided that location would not do, as Lincoln was known as "Honest Abe." After much consideration, they chose a spot near the statue of Christopher Columbus. "Columbus did not know where the hell he was going, nor how the hell he was going to get there. After he returned, he did not know where the hell he had been – and it was all on borrowed money," the committee explained.

Chapter 6

𝔚𝔢𝔢𝔨𝔩𝔶 𝔆𝔞𝔩𝔦𝔰𝔱𝔬𝔤𝔞𝔫 of April 14, 1944

page 1

All five incumbents – three city councilmen, the city clerk, and the city treasurer – won re-election in Calistoga's municipal election Tuesday.

Councilmen Dr. E.J. Stevens, Howard Butler, and John B. Ghisolfo got 207, 187, and 169 votes, respectively, to defeat challengers Owen Kenny, 159, and Fred Tedeschi, 155.

City Clerk George Locey polled 254 votes, City Treasurer Edmund Molinari, 257.

Despite inclement weather and a seeming disinterest in the election, close to 60 percent of the city's registered voters cast ballots.

The election board consisted of Mrs. Evalyn Wolleson, inspector; Mrs. Elsie Rockstroh, judge; and Mrs. Adele Light and Mrs. Mazie Lawson, clerks.

A hero of more than 50 combat missions over the European theatre of war chose death last Sunday rather than bail out of his spinning airplane and allow it to crash in the business section of Napa. Hundreds of people watched as the plane crashed into the Napa River. Several jumped into the river in an attempt to attach a line to the plane, but it was Monday morning before the wreckage was recovered.

Lieutenant William W. Murphy, leading a formation of four planes on a training flight, was demonstrating combat maneuvers when his plane suddenly went into a vertical dive and then a spin. It plunged directly toward the Conner Hotel at Third and Main streets in Napa. Lieutenant Murphy stuck with his plane and managed to clear the buildings. He crashed into the river some 500 feet below the Third Street bridge.

Calistoga 1944

Florence Barber of Calistoga was among 60 honored participants in the Fifth Annual California 4-H Club All-Star Conference in Berkeley, April 3-6.

Florence, a junior at Calistoga High School, was Napa County's only representative. She was selected on the basis of her outstanding work in 4-H projects for a number of years. She is the daughter of Mrs. Berwin Barber of Tucker district and is a member of the Tucker 4-H club.

Florence was accorded a special honor when she was selected to speak before the Berkeley Kiwanis Club. She described projects that 4-H Club girls undertake, including those that won her the All-Star honor.

The All-Stars stayed at the Hotel Shattuck. They enjoyed lectures by professors of the University of California. Social activities included a trip to San Francisco for a War Memorial Opera House concert by the baritone John Charles Thomas.

Note: 4-H, then as now, is a youth development organization. The name represents four focus areas: head, heart, hands, and health.

Excerpts from letters written by Mike Nagy, now taking naval training at Purcell, Oklahoma, will be interesting to his friends in Calistoga, where he attended school and resided until he joined the Navy several months ago.

"I'm writing from the USO in Purcell. Earlier today I went to North Base at Norman to see Jerry Senter from Calistoga. We spent almost all day together. He had to fly for three hours while I was there, but he brought out some *Weekly Calistogans* he had, and I read them while he was flying. I'll bet I read almost every word in them. It was sure swell to read about all the guys you know and the different things that are happening around home.

"My school is almost finished, as I have only a couple of weeks left.

"Purcell is a small town, about the size of Calistoga. It's a nice little town, but there isn't much doing. They have two shows and the USO, and that's about all there is for us to do. You don't spend much money here, so I'm trying to save a little, just in case I get a furlough at my next base.

"The weather has been rotten. It started to snow last night, and it hasn't stopped yet. I guess the weather in California is pretty good, everything getting green. Here, nothing is green.

"School is getting along fine, but it's hard. We have to learn codes of all kinds, and my head is so full of dots and dashes that it's ready to break open. We have to learn to shoot machine guns. That's a lot harder than I expected.

"I have been going out for boxing and have done pretty well. The physical training instructor has been getting us into shape. I think he's killing me instead of making me better, but I've lost a little weight (from 175 down to 163), and I feel much better. Every day, he makes me run three miles, work out four 3-minute rounds on the bag, and box three 3-minute rounds. I'm about ready to drop, but then he makes us do calisthenics, and then I am real dead. But I'm getting into shape."

Mike's address is Michael Nagy, S 1/c, N.A.G.S., Purcell, Oklahoma.

After a two-month search from Mount St. Helena to the hills opposite Napa, the Army plane reported missing from the Santa Rosa airport on February 22 was found in the hills near Lokoya Lodge late Wednesday afternoon. The body of the pilot, Lieutenant D.V. Clough, was in the cockpit.

A note has been received from Mrs. Lurline Cook of Richmond, who sends the *Weekly Calistogan* to two brothers serving with the Army in the Pacific theatre. They all attended Calistoga schools in the 1930s.

The older brother, Harry Clark, is seeing action in the New Guinea area. His address is Staff Sergeant B.H. Clark 39838525, Co. C, 592nd Engineer Regiment, APO 503, c/o Postmaster, San Francisco, Calif. The younger brother, Charles, is "somewhere in the Pacific." His address is Private Charles F. Clark, 39131908, Co. A, 57th Engineering Battalion, APO 716, c/o Postmaster, San Francisco, Calif.

What started as a peaceful Easter Sunday sun-bath ended up with a burning house when William Mory fell asleep with a pipe in his mouth and woke up with a blanket on fire and the house alongside of him in full blaze. The flames had such a headway before the fire engine arrived that it was impossible to save the building.

Mory had been "squatting" in the house on the old Hiltel place, now owned by William Otte. Chief of Police Ed E. Light took him to the county infirmary Sunday evening.

Growers and interested citizens of the Calistoga area are being offered the opportunity to attend classes in Spanish that will, in a comparatively short time, teach them enough to converse with Mexican nationals who may be assigned to the upper valley as farm laborers.

The classes will be devoted to a strictly streamlined course for colloquial Spanish. It has been designed to give the pupil a sufficient command of the language to enable him to give orders, understand the wants of his employee, and exchange the usual social amenities.

E.M. Murray of St. Helena will be the teacher. He comes with an excellent reputation. The first class will meet in the Calistoga High School next Monday, April 17, at 8 p.m. The public is welcome to attend.

page 4

There are 14,727 registered voters in Napa County, according to County Clerk Ralph A. Dollarhide. That includes 7,996 Democrats, 6,475 Republicans, 32 Townsendites, four Prohibitionists, four Socialists, one Progressive, and 215 declined to state.

Note: The Weekly Calistogan *listed Republicans first and described the Democrats' margin as "slight." In 2012, Napa County had 67,589 registered voters. By party, these included 31,440 Democrat, 18,813 Republican, 1,967 American Independent, 774 Green, 387 Libertarian, 204 Peace and Freedom, 323 other, and 13,683 declined to state.*

Private Eddie Taylor is spending a two-week furlough in Calistoga with his wife and mother. Eddie is serving with the Army at Indian Springs, Nevada. This is his first return home in a year.

Lieutenant Scott Nagel is stationed at the Naval Air Station at Pensacola, Florida. Before entering the Navy, he was in charge of this district for Standard Oil.

Chapter 7

𝔚eekly 𝔠alistogan of May 12, 1944

page 8

High School News: The Wildcats attended the sub-league track meet for the first time ever, competing against bigger schools like host Santa Rosa, Petaluma, Sonoma, and Healdsburg. Jack Scott placed fifth in the varsity 100-yard and 220-yard sprints. Jack McIntyre placed fifth in the varsity half mile. The Cats did better in the B and C divisions for younger/smaller boys. Ernie Zumwalt placed third in the B 440-yard run. He teamed with Allan Ballard, Paul Hickey, and Jim Ingalls for fifth place in the relay. The C team won its division. Brian Putman took second in the low hurdles and third in the shot put. Bob MacDonald tied for second in the high jump. Bruce Piner took third in the 50-yard and 100-yard sprints. Those three and Gus Kelperis teamed to win the relay.

The Wildcats baseball team played one of its best games of the year, beating Sonoma, 3 to 2, here last Friday. They had beaten a Napa High team, 8 to 4, that Wednesday. They ran their winning streak to three when they swamped Middletown, 15 to 4, Monday. Pitching duties were shared by Frank Strebel, Frank Newton, and Rudy Urbani, while Frank Saviez did the catching.

The boys' tennis team suffered its first league defeat, 2 to 1, to Analy last Saturday. They had beaten Sonoma, 5-1, last Wednesday. The team is comprised of Milton Petersen, Allan Forbes, Earl Evans, and Allan Ballard.

This week, the senior class topped all others by having a 100 percent participation in the purchase of War Stamps. Their purchases totaled $5.40. The juniors had 30 percent ($3.60), the sophomores 35 percent ($4.80), and the freshmen 33 percent ($7.95).

Chapter 8

May 14-20

The War: Allied forces finally win the battle of Monte Cassino in Italy. Allied troops capture the important air base at Myitkyina, Burma. Japanese resistance ends in the `Admiralty Islands north of New Guinea.

Weekly Calistogan of May 19, 1944

page 1

With the entrance of Ralph Wareham into the Navy Monday, Calistoga has a five-star service family – the Josiah Willard Warehams, who have made their home in and near town for several years.

Ralph has been accepted by the Navy despite having had polio when he was 11. It is not known where he was sent for training. He had been working as a machinist's helper at Mare Island.

His four brothers who serve are Vernon, in naval training in San Diego; Waldo, with the Army at Camp Grant, Illinois; William, in the Navy on the Atlantic side; and Robert, with the Army at Fort Knox, Kentucky. Robert and Ralph are married. Robert's wife and their two children live in Bakersfield. Ralph's wife and their infant son live in Santa Rosa.

Unless found unfit because of an operation undergone a short time ago, another brother, Harry, may enter the service before long. The Wareham boys have a sister in Calistoga, Mrs. Susan Ames.

Note: Ralph Wareham trained at, and then taught at, the Navy radio school in San Diego. He returned to Mare Island after the war and retired in 1977 as mechanical group planning supervisor. He was founder-drillmaster of The Campions, a Santa Rosa youth precision drill team that won three national championships. Vernon served as a pharmacist aboard a destroyer in the Pacific during the war. He worked as a cabinetmaker after the war, but died in an explosion in 1982. Waldo was a civilian employee at Pearl Harbor when the Japanese attacked. He served as a medic in the Pacific theater during the war, and became a dentist and professor of dentistry

76

after the war. Bill served as a gunner's mate on the USS Philadelphia, *a light cruiser that hunted submarines in the Atlantic, then supported landings in North Africa, Sicily, the Italian mainland, and France. He retired from the Navy in 1960 and worked in construction. Robert drove trucks in support of Army troops during fighting in six European counties. After the war, he drove displaced persons in Europe to centers where arrangements were made for their return home. Back in the U.S., he drove car carriers until retirement in 1981.*

A total of 543 Calistoga voters cast their ballots Tuesday in the consolidated primary election and, in general, followed the state trend in voting for United States Senator and the amendment to allow the state to tax federal property.

State-wide returns give Democratic incumbent Sheridan Downey and Republican Lieutenant-Governor Fred Houser the nominations for the U.S. senate race in the November elections. Downey garnered the largest number of local votes too, with a total of 125 (45 Republican and 80 Democratic). Houser came in second with 89 votes (63 Republican, 26 Democratic).

Incumbent Congressman Leroy Johnson, running on both tickets, tallied 375 votes (236 Republican, 139 Democratic).

The amendment to allow the state to tax federal property found 351 supporting the measure, 144 opposed to the move. This measure carried the state by a substantial margin.

Mrs. Mitto Blodgett of Calistoga won a place on the Republican County Central Committee.

Major Newton D. Hagins of Calistoga has been awarded the Legion of Merit honor for service as the engineering officer of an Army Air Force fighter group in North Africa from June 4, 1942, to August 4, 1943.

Major Hagins, while not widely known here, is the son-in-law of Mr. and Mrs. J.E. Scott of the Tucker District and considers Calistoga his most permanent home address.

The Legion of Merit citation said that Hagins, then a captain, arrived with his group to discover the planes to be used were British Spitfire fighters, entirely new to them. But he supervised training of his mechanics with such efficiency that the group began operational flying eight days later. They worked in exposed front-line airdromes during the Tunisian campaign, lacking many essential tools and supplies, but, nevertheless, maintained an unusually high rate of 89 percent of aircraft in commission.

Major Hagins has seen action in Italy since the African victories. Prior to his service overseas, he was stationed in the Panama Canal Zone and at Chanute Field, Illinois.

Mrs. Hagins – Dorothy Scott before her marriage – lives in Sacramento.

Note: Dorothy was a 1927 graduate of Calistoga High School.

Representatives of the State Agricultural Extension Service met with growers last week to discuss the problems of the coming harvest season. Housing for workers and their families occupied the greater part of the meeting.

Discussion brought out the fact that the simplest solution will be for growers to house workers on their individual ranches. The idea of a central camp was dismissed because compliance with various state laws would require too large a managing staff.

The California Farm Production Council stands ready to rent housing equipment to growers at very reasonable rates.

A partial list of equipment available, and the rents, include: 12x14-foot tents, with platforms, $4 per month; cots, each 35 cents per month; mattresses, each 35 cents per month; cooking equipment, 20 cents per month, per person. The minimum rental is for a 15-day period. Ranges, ice boxes, and other miscellaneous items are also listed.

Growers interested in renting any of the above-mentioned items may get full information from the Calistoga Farm Labor Office after it opens on August 1. Before that, a letter to the California Farm Production Council in Napa, to the attention of Mr. Eisley, will bring full information.

A note from Mike Nagy states that the Navy has moved him from Oklahoma to Florida for flight training. The letter reads, in part:

"Well, here I am in Florida, a long way from home. Boy, flying is really the thing. We formed a squadron and are having our final training.

"I had a nice little trip down here. We had nine-hour lay-overs in both Memphis and Atlanta. I like Atlanta a lot better than Memphis. In Memphis, they treat servicemen like dogs. In fact, all the South isn't too friendly to servicemen. Florida isn't too bad. I have a little tan. I still stick to California.

"I am in a TBF squadron. We fly half a day and go to ground school the other half. I have a good pilot and a good radio man. TBFs are only three-man jobs, but they are big planes for only one motor.

"I receive *The Calistogan*. Will you please give them this new address: Michael H. Nagy, S 1/c, Aircrewman Squad, 26-B, NAS, Fort Lauderdale, Florida."

An additional 12 million pounds of dried prunes from the 1943 crop are being released by the War Food Administration through regular trade channels for civilian consumption. This brings the total of dried prunes made available for civilian use to 248 million pounds out of a total 1943 pack of about 432 million pounds. Of this total, California packed 92.5 percent, Oregon 7 percent, and Washington the remainder.

Packers were required by War Food Order 16 to set aside the entire 1943 pack of dried prunes, raisins, apples, apricots, peaches, pears, and currants for government war use. However, WFO 16 provides for release of such quantities of these dried fruits for civilian consumption as are not needed for direct war purposes.

Seabee Donald Williams, enjoying a 30-day furlough, came up from Berkeley with his wife and child and spent the weekend with his parents, Mr. and Mrs. A.R. Williams of the Porter Creek district.

Donald has spent the past two years in the Aleutians. He plans on soaking up some California sunshine, and hopes to spend a large part of his furlough in the Calistoga area.

Note: Donald was a 1938 graduate of Calistoga High School.

Starting next Monday, Napa County War Relief will conduct a one-week drive to collect warm clothing to be shipped to devastated areas of Russia. Heavy coats, sweaters, mittens, and other articles suitable for wear in cold climates are desired.

It is requested that clothing donated be as clean as possible, as shipments will start immediately after the close of the drive.

With hundreds of towns in Russia practically obliterated, and inhabitants facing the terrible task of rehabilitation, with little or nothing for use as a beginning, the Russian War Relief drive should bring a generous response.

Mrs. Gordon Hunt, chairman of the drive in Calistoga, advises that donations may be left at the office of the Citizens' Service

Corps, next to the post office, on Mondays, Tuesdays, Wednesdays, and Fridays between 2 and 4:30 p.m.

Commencing July 1, there will be a small increase in the subscription rate of the *Weekly Calistogan*, necessitated by increased costs of production. The new rate will be $2.50 for one year – up from $2.

The increase, less than one cent a week, is necessitated by the increased costs of materials and labor, largely the latter. In 1895, when the present publisher purchased the paper, he paid a printer $1.25 a day. Now he pays approximately that same sum per hour.

A large percentage of the weekly newspapers of the country have long charged $2.50 for a year's subscription. Many have been increased to $3. In many cases, their size has been cut, too. *The Calistogan* does not want to decrease size nor quality, so it has chosen the other alternative – a slight increase in subscription rate.

Anyone who wants to start or renew a subscription for one year at the $2.00 rate may do so between now and July 1. However, no subscription will be taken at the old rate for more than one year.

Note: The 2012 rate is 50 cents an issue, $25 per year.

As in years gone by, Calistoga will observe Decoration Day on May 30, with a parade and appropriate ceremonies at the cemetery.

Details will be finalized by the Calistoga Cemetery Association next Wednesday, May 24. C.L. Petersen, head of the association, urges all local organizations – civic, farm, religious, and fraternal – to send representatives to the meeting and to make plans to participate in the parade wearing the regalia of their order.

The schools will take part, and the high school band will be among the marching units.

As is the custom, the parade will form in the open space adjacent to the Southern Pacific depot and will start moving at 10 a.m. It will proceed to the cemetery, where graveside ceremonies will be held. The sequence of marching units, a complete line of march, and other details of the graveside rites will be announced in next week's issue of *The Calistogan.*

Note: Memorial Day is the modern name for this holiday, honoring men and women who died while in military service. The holiday dates back to the 1860s, just after the Civil War.

Boy Scouts of the North Bay, including Calistoga, are assured of a permanent summer camp in the high Sierra following the purchase by the Silverado Area of rights to facilities on 17.5 acres on the upper Echo Lake, 50 miles north of Placerville.

The camp has over 1,500 feet of sandy beach along the lake shore, three large lodges, three shower houses, a hospital, administration buildings, doctor's quarters, an electric power plant, boiler plant, boat house, corrals and stables, and several smaller buildings.

Recreational equipment includes three outboard motor boats; a cabin cruiser; an open launch; a speed boat powered with a Lycoming motor; 18 canoes, including four war canoes capable of carrying 12 boys apiece; 16 rowboats; 12 paddleboards; two water bicycles; and several aquaplanes.

The camp has been operated for many years by Sierra Camps, Inc. as an exclusive summer retreat for the children of the wealthy. It represents an investment of some $75,000. Silverado Area secured it for $25,000. The price includes buildings and equipment only. The land is under a long-term lease from the federal government.

Funds for the initial payment came from individuals and firms within the Silverado Area. It is anticipated that the remainder will be raised in the same manner.

Three camping seasons are planned for the coming summer: July 5-19, July 19-August 2, and August 2-16. At the present time, 110 Scouts are registered for the three sessions. A full program is planned for each of them.

Note: I was one of the lucky kids who enjoyed that camp. I had two weeks there in 1946 and worked all three sessions as the pot-washer in 1947.

The Calistoga Chamber of Commerce has agreed to act as a sponsoring body for the proposed Robert Louis Stevenson Memorial Park on Mount St. Helena.

In a meeting May 11, chamber directors acted after being briefed by Ralph P. Winston of the *Weekly Calistogan* on what would be necessary in the way of finances and publicity to bring the park into being.

V.M. (Bob) Moir, manager of the North Coast Council of the State Chamber of Commerce, said he would aid in bringing state officials to Calistoga to survey the area suggested for inclusion in the park.

Calistoga 1944

Weather permitting, the Calistoga Elementary School band will give a concert downtown tomorrow night, under the direction of Clifford Anderson, music director for Calistoga schools. The band will play at the corner of Lincoln Avenue and Washington Street, beginning at 8 p.m.

The program includes: "Star Spangled Banner"; "Honor Band March" by Weber; "Yesternight Serenade" by Eisenberg; "Promotion March" by Chenette; "Blue Moon Waltz" by Ribble; "Forward March" by Chenette; "Village Chapel" by Ribble; "Playground Waltz" by Chenette; and "Vanguard March" by Hollingsworth.

A collection will be taken toward the close of the concert, with the proceeds going to the band uniform fund.

page 2

The *Calistogan* wants to share a letter paying tribute to the late Mrs. Lillian Bell Miller, who was president of the Calistoga School Board when the writer, Miss Ellen Franklin of Napa, was a high school student here.

"Few of us ever offer to the world so much good in our short lifetimes.

"I recall the incident when she averted a strike by the students in Calistoga High School. The pupils realized the injustice and penuriousness of the citizens in failing to vote bonds for adequate school equipment, in a rich community. We signed a petition to walk out and attend our rival school, St. Helena.

"Lillian Miller was president of the school board. Upon receiving our declaration, she had the principal, Miss Florence Marvin, assemble the students, whereupon she explained the laws governing our schools – how each district receives a certain sum of money from the attendance of each child in the district; that we could not attend St. Helena High, even if we were willing to degrade ourselves to such an extent; and that we would but succeed in cutting off our educational source, inadequate as it seemed.

"Then she suggested we force the trustees to hold another election by circulating a new petition, signed by two-thirds of the voters in the school district. This we did. Visit CHS and know that Mrs. Miller was a politician par excellence. I learned my greatest lessons on citizenship and co-operation right then and there."

Note: Ellen Franklin was a 1920 graduate of Calistoga High School.

Farmers Corner column by Ralph H. Taylor, Executive Secretary, Agricultural Council of California: The U.S. Treasury Department, in its drive to stimulate the buying of war bonds by farmers, has delved into what farmers are doing with their money — now that agricultural earnings are above normal — and has reached the conclusion that too great a share of the cash surplus is on deposit in rural banks, where it constitutes a potential inflationary menace.

Quite naturally and logically, the Treasury Department urges the purchase of more war bonds to dissipate this danger — advice which is certainly sound, both from the standpoint of the country's welfare and from the standpoint of the individual farmer, who needs to put something away for the inevitable rainy day.

However, it is this writer's opinion that farmers should also be putting more of their extra cash into the retirement of their debts, so they will be better conditioned to weather the economic storms which are certain to come during the post-war period. Many farmers could increase both their bond purchases and their payments on their debts and still have more left for running expenses than they have had for many years.

Treasury estimates gross farm income in the United States from sales of crops and livestock in 1943 at $19.1 billion — 23 percent more than in 1942, and 2.3 times as great as in 1940. To the marketing income can be added an estimated $600 million that farmers received in government payments in 1943, making a total cash farm income of $19.7 billion.

Cash farm expenses for 1943 were estimated to be $9.7 billion, and cash expenditures for family living and personal expenses at $8.7 billion, leaving a balance of $1.3 billion. Add to this, Treasury says, $3.5 billion in cash received by farmers from non-farm sources and there remains $4.8 billion in the hands of farmers as cash available from 1943 for savings and payment of incomes taxes.

This is the time for farmers to put it away — in war bonds and in debt retirement payments. There may not be another such time in our lifetimes. Don't fritter it away.

The question of when hamburger is ration point-free and whether chuck requires ration stamps has been a source of much confusion, according to the Office of Price Administration.

Hamburger is point-free when it is made only from the point-free meats. That is, when it is made of any of the following beef cuts: necks, flanks, heel of round, briskets, plates, miscellaneous beef trimmings and fat, or when ground from any portion of Grade D dressed carcasses.

If any steak or roast cuts, which still require ration points, are ground for hamburger or used for stew meat, points must be collected in accordance with the ration value of the cut used. Chuck meat still requires ration points because it is classified as a roast instead of stew meat, the OPA explained.

Chapter 9

May 21-27

The War: Allies increase bombing in France. U.S. troops break out of their beachhead at Anzio and link up with other forces headed to Rome. U.S. troops land at Biak, Dutch New Guinea, but it will take three months to oust the Japanese.

Weekly Calistogan of May 26, 1944

page 1

Two Knights Valley teenagers rescued the pilot of a Navy Hellcat fighter plane that spun out of control and crashed on the Beck ranch Sunday.

The pilot bailed out during the airplane's 40,000-foot plunge. Geniel Tuttle and Bill Cook, watching the parachute as it drifted, jumped in a car and headed into the hills near the Yellow Jacket Ranch. They clambered up a steep hillside searching for the pilot, later identified as Lieutenant Anderson. They found him tangled up in brush, hanging head down and unconscious.

Bill Cook

They cut him free from his parachute harness and carried him to a nearby stream, where they bathed his face and arms. Coming to, Lt. Anderson's chief concern was whether or not he would be grounded. It was the second time he had parachuted from a falling plane. His injuries seemed limited to scratches and bruises.

Knights Valley residents found the plane wreckage on the Beck ranch after a lengthy search. A Navy crew from the Bay Area took away all the scrap metal.

Note: Bill graduated from Calistoga High School a few weeks later. He has ranches in California and Montana and business interests in Arizona, where he lives during the winter months. Geniel graduated in 1947. She married another Knights Valley boy, Ray Hausknecht. She died in 1999.

Calvin J. (Jack) Rannells, a teacher and coach at St. Helena High School the past 11 years, was named principal of Calistoga High School by the unified district school board Wednesday night. He will take over the duties July 1.

Rannells is a graduate of Chico State Teacher's College, with a master's degree from Oregon State College and advanced studies at University of California, Berkeley. At St. Helena, he taught shop, mechanical drawing, history, and mathematics, and he coached the football, basketball, track, and tennis teams.

Calvin J. (Jack) Rannells

The school board considered about 20 applicants to fill the vacancy created by the resignation of Charles S. Morris Jr., principal for the past three years.

Note: This article oddly omitted the fact that Rannells – my dad – was hired as superintendent of the school district as well as the high school principal. Also unstated, but probably not a matter of record, was his commitment to start a football program. Calistoga High fielded a football team in 1945, won its first championship in 1946, was undefeated in 1948, had only one touchdown scored on it in 1949. My dad's teams had a 36-17-3 record and included two players who later became National Football League coaches – Myrel Moore and Dick Vermeil. My dad's track teams also won many honors.

He resigned from the school district in February 1952. He worked for the State Department of Education and then Tehama County, helping rural schools form more effective unified districts. He died of cancer in December 1954.

My mother, Marguerite, taught at Calistoga Elementary School and then in Pope Valley and the Carneros and Salvador schools on the outskirts of Napa. She and her second husband, Primo Baldi, moved to Chateau Calistoga in 1986 after being flooded out of their home in St. Helena. She died in 2000.

Columbus Banta, a resident of Calistoga since 1891, died at St. Helena Sanitarium Saturday. He was born in Nicholas, Sutter County, in 1876. He farmed here for some years and then became a building contractor – associated for the past 25 years with Harry W. Coulter. His first wife, Bertha, died four years ago. He is survived by his second wife, Alice; three sisters, Evelyn Wolleson and Octavia Brown of Calistoga and Erma Scott of Oakland; and a number of nieces and nephews, including Thelma Wright of Oakland and Calistoga. The service was conducted at Simic Funeral Home in Calistoga. Pallbearers were W.W. Kortum, Emil Rockstroh, Frank Tamagni, Frank Turner, Charles Tamagni, and L.E. Light. Interment was at Calistoga Cemetery.

An honor roll is being compiled of Napa County men and women in the military service. Enrollments will be taken June 2 from 2:30 to 4:30 p.m. in the Citizen Service Corps rooms next to the post office. Only relatives can sign up people for the honor roll.

Newcomer Charles Corwin White took top honors with a score of 181 at the Calistoga Rifle Club meeting May 16. Vincent Archuleta hit a record low of 16.

The Fifth War Loan Drive will be conducted from June 12 to July 8, with a nationwide goal of $16 billion. That is $2 billion more than the fourth drive.

"With D-Day and invasion scheduled for the not too distant future, and with the war in the Pacific moving ahead on all fronts, citizens of the United States are to be asked again to lend their money to their government in order that there may be no slackening of the war effort and that our fighting men may be amply supplied with the machines and equipment of war," the announcement said.

Frank Piner continues as chairman of the Calistoga War Finance Committee. No local quotas have been announced. "Calistoga met its $170,000 quota in the fourth drive last January and February, and there is little doubt but that the community will meet the increased demand with the same spirit, and the same speed, that has put Calistoga over the top before," Piner said.

Edith Fechter defeated Al Evans 159 to 22 in an election for a seat on the Calistoga School Board last Friday. Mrs. Fechter succeeds her brother-in-law, Raymond E. Fechter, who retired.

Napa County has not met its quota in supplying blood for the blood bank and in making surgical dressings. Surgical dressings are made in the Citizen Service Corps office every Tuesday afternoon. Volunteers should contact Mrs. Jack Matthews there.

C. L. Petersen has been elected president of the Calistoga Cemetery Association. Other new officers are Ray Oxford, vice president; Katie Butler, secretary-treasurer; Dr. E. J. Stevens, Alvin Kuster, and F.W. Martin, executive committee.

The Calistoga branch of American Red Cross Home Service offers four programs to help current and former servicemen and their families, chairwoman Mrs. Curtis Wright said. They include aiding communications between servicemen and their families; co-operating with military authorities in questions about emergency furloughs or discharges for servicemen; helping disabled ex-servicemen and their dependents, and dependents of deceased servicemen, present claims for compensation and other government benefits; and helping get financial aid and other assistance for servicemen's families' special needs.

There also is Home Service for civilians, Mrs. Wright noted. This includes help for those seeking information about persons in foreign countries, or who wish to send messages of a personal nature to relatives and friends in enemy-occupied territory.

Calistoga's Home Service workers recognize the need for safeguarding military information and the confidentiality of personal matters, she said. Calistoga's Home Service workers include Mrs. C.E. Ingalls, Main Street, phone 84-M; Mrs. Carl Jursch, Lincoln Avenue, phone 84-W; and Mrs. Wright, Maplewood Ranch, phone 15-Y-4.

Ensign Harrison Bidwell of Knights Valley has completed an internship at the Marine Hospital in San Francisco and expects to return to sea duty. He has seen considerable duty with the Maritime Service (merchant marine). On one trip, his ship was hit and he spent a few weeks on an island in the Atlantic, but he escaped injury.

page 2

Corporal Walter Butler makes interesting comments on the South Pacific areas he has seen since going overseas with the Army, in a letter to his mother, Mrs. Aurelia Butler of Calistoga.

"I guess I can take time out to tell you a little about New Guinea and all of its wonders. I wonder why the Japs want it. I sure don't. The country is scenic in a gruesome way, and looks much better from a few thousand feet up than from an Army engineers' highway. I've seen a lot of it from both points and, undoubtedly, will see more of it before I'm through with this little game we're playing over here.

"My first reactions were much better than I expected. There is definitely the American touch all over the place, and to me it was not nearly as bad as the press led one to believe. It's hot, but livable, if you know how to do it. Siestas and things like that are a great help in this climate.

"Before coming to New Guinea, I had the good fortune of seeing the majority of Australia's cities and countryside – a regular GI sightseeing tour, as we call it. Australia is quite a place and has possibilities of being the land of opportunity after the war. The American touch is starting to predominate in most of the country already."

Napa's first effort to provide amusement for the younger generation, and to cut down on the tendency toward juvenile delinquency, took place last Friday night when over 300 teenagers gathered at the Napa Pavilion for the opening of a canteen sponsored by the city, civic groups, and individuals.

Prominent Napans gave brief talks and outlined the plans for entertainments every Friday night from 6:30 to 10:30 p.m.

page 8

Excerpts follow from two recent letters received from Mike Nagy, now undergoing training in Florida as a Navy air crewman.

"I just finished a hop over the ocean. Boy, you can't imagine how tired you get when you fly. Today, we had two flights of about one-and-a-half hours each, and I am almost out on my feet.

"On the first hop, we didn't do a thing but fly and look for enemy subs. On the second, we had a bombing run, and after that we shot at an oil slick in the water. My radio man got sick while we were up, but after a while he was OK. We were supposed to drop eight bombs, but something happened, as usual, and we only dropped four.

"You asked if I am a gunner, or if I repair the guns. Well, when you are an aircrewman, you are a gunner and everything else that goes with a plane. I will get my rate sometime this month or next.

Calistoga 1944

"Florida is a nice state, but it's a lot like a jungle. There are no mountains or hills – all swamps. The weather is a lot like California. The fruit they raise here isn't as good as what they grow in California, and the soil is no good at all. It seems to be all sand.

"When I graduate, I get my wings. They are air crewman's wings. Have you ever seen them? Not too many guys have them. If I wash out, I won't get the wings and will have my rate taken away. We are supposed to graduate about the first of July. Then I think I'll go to Virginia to get a carrier."

Elementary School News: Tuesday was war stamp day, and the grades bought stamps as follow: first grade, $12.65; second grade, $10.33; third grade, $20.65; fourth grade, $11.35; fifth grade, $6.75; seventh grade, $20; and eighth grade, $9.80. Bonds were bought by Gene Allen, Elvin Mariani, and Margaret Gavin.

The fourth grade received a letter from Caroline Drake, who transferred from the class several months ago.

High School News: Thursday was traditional Senior Sneak Day. Seniors reported for roll call at the first period class, and then left. They took the 9:30 Greyhound bus to St. Helena and, from there, hiked out to White Sulphur Springs. The class enjoyed

Calistoga High School of 1944. The building has been replaced.
(Photo courtesy of Sharpsteen Museum, Calistoga.)

swimming, tennis, and fishing. At noon, they indulged in a wiener roast with all the trimmings. At 5:30, the class caught a bus back to Calistoga, got a bite to eat, and went to the movies.

They were chaperoned by Mrs. E.M. Tamagni and teacher Claude A. Bryner.

On May 30, the band will march to the cemetery and play a few selections for Memorial Day. The American Legion and the Calistoga Cemetery Association, under the direction of Dr. E.J. Stevens and C.L. Petersen, respectively, are making the arrangements. The Legion honor guard will head the parade. Upon arrival at the cemetery, the firing squad will give a salute. Author Charles Corwin White will give the address of the day.

Summer plans: Betty Tamagni will be working at Lommel's Creamery while looking forward to September, when she will start nursing school. Mermie Tubbs, Betty Pocai, and Jane Jackson will be busy studying for their entrance exams to college. Mermie and Jane will be preparing for Mills College, Betty for San Jose State. Allan Forbes will be waiting to hear from Uncle Sam. If that doesn't come through, just look for Al at St. Mary's College.

CHS's war bond and stamp sales have totaled $4,955.60 this year.

California Scholarship Federation pins for the first semester were awarded to seniors Mermie Tubbs and Bill Cook; juniors Lucille McFall, Ann Tamagni, Pat Shoemaker, Andy Richey, Colleen Kelley, and Earl Evans; sophomores Norman Whatford, Audrey Kelley, and Kenny Westbay; and freshmen Catherine Evans, Anne Richey, and Lorene Salmina.

Photo caption: A Liberty Ship built at the Permanente Metals Corp. shipyard in Richmond stayed afloat 83 hours after being hit by a Japanese torpedo in the South Pacific. It was struck on the port side while carrying war materials. A photograph shows it making its way to an Australian port with its bow seven feet out of the water and the stern submerged. The photo caption ends: "Yes. Liberty ships – 1,800 all together – are tough."

Chapter 10

June 4-10

The War: U.S., English and French troops capture Rome – the first Axis capital to fall. D-Day begins with the landing of 155,000 Allied troops on the beaches of Normandy. It is the largest amphibious military operation in history. They quickly break through the Germans' "Atlantic Wall" and push inland. Russia attacks Finland, with the intent of defeating it before pushing for Berlin.

𝔚eekly 𝔠alistogan of June 9, 1944

page 1

Calistoga, jubilant over the success of D-Day and in the mood to celebrate the start of the victorious invasion in France, will join in a mass meeting Monday night which will serve the double purpose of paying tribute to our men who are fighting on the European continent and on all other fronts, and to get the Fifth War Loan drive off to a flying start.

With the high school band out in full force, the meeting will get under way at 8 p.m. in front of Hotel Calistoga. The street will be roped off so there will be no interruption from traffic, and there will be room to accommodate what is hoped will be the largest crowd ever to assemble on the streets of Calistoga.

Various civic officials will address the crowd over the public address system, and representatives of the county Fifth War Loan organization will speak upon the importance of the present loan campaign.

The action-front in the South Pacific will be described by a veteran of 62 missions in that theater. Staff Sergeant Walter Hays, 5th Air Force, will tell of his experiences and bring home to his listeners the necessity of supporting the war effort through the purchase of bonds.

To facilitate their purchase, the Treasury Department has announced that bonds, with the exception of Series E, F, and G, may be purchased for 10 percent down, with the balance due within six months. Also, the government has agreed that, in response to hundreds of requests, all bonds bought up to, and including, June 12 will be dated June 6 (D-Day).

Little Larry Patton, first grader at the Calistoga Elementary School, can grow up as the first local child to be saved by the use of the new wonder-working drug, penicillin.

Stricken with meningicoccic meningitis, Larry was rushed to the St. Helena Sanitarium and immediately put in an isolation cottage due to the highly contagious and communicable nature of the disease.

Doctors gave the boy penicillin and, at the present reading, he is well on the road to recovery. Penicillin has been used elsewhere in the county in previous cases, but Larry is the first patient from this area to benefit from the drug.

The Calistoga Unified District School Board filled three remaining vacancies on the elementary school faculty Wednesday night, completing the corps of teachers who will conduct the school next year.

Appointed were Mrs. Conrad Weil, Miss Margaret Grauss, and Mrs. Helen Dixon. The latter has been teaching in St. Helena during the past year. Her husband is with the armed forces in the Aleutian Islands. Miss Grauss, the daughter of Mr. and Mrs. F.L. Grauss of Calistoga and well known here, has been teaching in Napa in recent years. Mrs. Weil, also well known in Calistoga, has lived in this community for a number of years. She is a Stanford graduate and is returning to the teaching profession during the current shortage of teachers. Her husband is a lawyer and engineer.

Leaving the faculty are William Morehouse, Mrs. Irma Changus, Mrs. Gladys Hernandez, and Mrs. Delpha Snow. The board received with particular regret the resignation of Mrs. Snow, who has been a member of the faculty for many years, and whose services have been valued. Mrs. Snow has not made known her plans for next year.

Principal Alvin Kuster has not yet made the teachers' grade assignments.

Farmers of Knights Valley are up in arms following loss of stock through the actions of hunters who, either deliberately or accidentally, wound and kill cows and horses.

Calistoga 1944

Latest grower to suffer a loss is William Beck, who last week found one of his purebred Jersey cows shot in the shoulder. The animal was due to drop a calf next week. Bert Noble, Hooper Jackson, George Cropp, and Lew Cook also have suffered from the stupid carelessness of hunters.

In practically every case, the embryonic nimrods have hunted on private property without showing the courtesy of securing permission from the owner.

Ranchers of the valley have banded together to protect themselves, and it promises to go hard for anyone found hunting without permission from the owner of the property. The law provides stringent penalties for such offenses.

The Albright Realty Company reports the sale of four properties this week, one within the city limits, two on Mount St. Helena, and one in Lake County.

In Calistoga, Mr. and Mrs. H. Topalian of San Francisco purchased the Charles Nance holdings on Wapoo Avenue. The three houses are occupied by the Joe Olaeta, Tom Garrett, and J. Brown families. The new owners will not move to Calistoga for some time, and present tenants will remain.

On Mount St. Helena, the old Guile place, owned by Paul Piner, was sold to Mr. and Mrs. Earl Atherton of San Francisco. The Athertons plan on using the place as a summer home until after the war, when they will make their permanent home here.

The 15-acre ranch adjoining the Guile place, now occupied by Tom Martz, was bought by Mr. and Mrs. L.F. Wiloth of St. Helena. They, too, plan on having the property as a summer home for the present. Martz will remain as caretaker.

Ida's Place, well-known roadside restaurant on the Lake County Road, has been sold by Mr. and Mrs. Vic Holmsteadt of Middletown to W.H. Verbiscio of Richmond. The new owner will re-open the sandwich and refreshment shop in the near future.

Robert W. Johnston, son of Mr. and Mrs. W.H. Johnston of Calistoga, is enrolled as an aviation cadet in the Army Air Force pre-flight school at Maxwell Field, Alabama. He is receiving nine weeks of intensive military, physical, and academic training.

Cadet Johnston graduated from Calistoga High School in 1942 and attended the University of California, Berkeley, 1942-43.

His address is now: A-T Robert W. Johnston 19186833 Sec. P, Sq. H., Flt III, Class 45-B, Maxwell Field, Alabama.

Note: Johnston received his commission in April 1945. After the war, he returned to UC Berkeley and then worked in management of construction and public works projects. He is retired in Foresthill, California.

Robert Johnston

Calistoga Post No. 231, American Legion, reports that it has raised enough money to erect a memorial plaque honoring current servicemen. It will be located adjacent to the telephone office near the Lincoln Avenue bridge.

Commander Dennis Ward and Adjutant James McCall again ask that the parents and friends of Calistoga men and women who are in the service leave their names at *The Calistogan* office in order that there may be a complete listing.

Names have been coming in slowly. They have not begun to approach the expected total, which is something over 200.

Note: The memorial was built, but it was removed many years ago.

Dr. H.M. Pond, a highly esteemed resident here for many years, died in an Alameda hospital Monday evening after a long illness. He was 88.

Dr. Pond was born in Downieville, Sierra County, in 1856. He graduated from University of California in 1876 and from that institution's college of medicine in 1880.

He practiced medicine in St. Helena and then Alameda. He moved to Calistoga in retirement in 1917 and built his lovely home on the northwest outskirts of town.

Dr. Pond served for a number of years as director of the Napa County Apricot and Prune Growers' Association. He was a member of the Elks, Native Sons, and Odd Fellows.

Note: Dr. Pond's home stands at the front of Rancho de Calistoga mobile home park, a 1970s development.

Calistoga, through its indifference toward aid from state and county agricultural officials, stands a very good chance of not having a labor office here for the coming season.

Calistoga 1944

Recently, four representatives from the Berkeley office of the University of California Extension Service and two officials from the county agricultural office came to Calistoga to meet with growers and outline to them just what the season promises in the way of labor, and the requirements that will have to be met by the individual grower. Only three growers attended.

During the past week, Berkeley has advised that there are many, many families that have signed up for their vacation periods or longer and are willing to come to the country and help harvest crops. But it is absolutely necessary that farmers provide housing.

In order to help those farmers who do not have adequate housing, the California Farm Production Council has made available a considerable amount of equipment that may be rented at an extremely low figure. Equipment includes tents, cots, mattresses, blankets, stoves, eating utensils, cooking utensils, ice boxes, and miscellaneous items. Rentals are for a minimum of 15 days. If the grower so desires, the money paid for rental may be applied toward purchase of the equipment.

Full details, price lists, and information as to delivery dates may be secured by contacting the Napa County Farm Adviser's office in the Napa post office building.

Representatives of the farm adviser's office said that Calistoga's delay in naming a manager for the labor office may result in having the needs of the community served only by a field representative. Such a situation would mean that Calistoga would be left holding the well-known sack, as far as securing sufficient labor is concerned.

Chapter 11

June 11-17

The War: Germany attacks England with destructive, un-manned V1 flying bombs.

In the Pacific, U.S. troops invade Saipan in the Mariana Islands.

𝔚eeklp Calistogan of June 16, 1944

page 1

Seventeen seniors will graduate from Calistoga High School tonight in ceremonies in the school's gym/auditorium.

The graduates are: Robert E. Bjorklund, Lew Wilkins Cook, Ellen Luella Decker, Gilbert E. Foote, Allan Edward Forbes, Jack F. Geary, Stella K. Hartinger, Jane Elizabeth Jackson, Alberta Lorraine Lawson, Jack V. McIntyre, Delbert L. Pearl, Betty Lorraine Pocai, John M. Scott, Frank M. Strebel, Betty L. Tamagni, Merritt Reid Tubbs, and Charles William Westbay. Westbay is serving in the Merchant Marine and will not be present, but he earned his diploma before leaving school.

Class president Jack Scott will give the welcome address. Student body president Allan Forbes will describe "The Benefits of a High School Education." Mermie Tubbs will speak about "Nations Brought Closer by Air Travel." The band, under the direction of Clifford Anderson, will play Sibelius' "Finlandia" and Lewellyn's "My Regards," the latter featuring a tenor saxophone solo by Betty Tamagni. Principal Charles S. Morris will review highlights of the year and present special awards. School board member Frank Pocai will present the diplomas.

Sunday night, the robed seniors attended a baccalaureate service. Rev. A.E. Lucas of Calistoga Community Church delivered the sermon "Opportunity in Service." Rev. William P. Walsh of Calistoga Catholic Church gave the invocation. Then a mixed chorus, directed by Clifford Anderson, sang "The Lord's Prayer" and "Hear My Prayer, O God." Mrs. Joe Olaeta was the accompanist. Rev. Lucas closed the event with the benediction.

Calistoga 1944

Calistoga High School's 1944 graduates included: left to right, front row – Betty Pocai, Betty Tamagni, and Stella Hartinger; middle row – Jane Jackson, Ellen Decker, Mermie Tubbs, and Delbert Pearl; top row – Jack McIntyre, Gilbert Foote, Jack Scott, Allan Forbes, and Bill Cook. Five others graduated but weren't present on photo day.

Thirty eighth graders graduated from Calistoga Elementary School last night. They are: Vladimir Baeff, Patricia Boland, Glenn Conner, Helen Derrick, Bill Driver, Betty Elder, Earlene Elder, Jack Fechter, Virginia Fisher, Wayne Gardner, Dorothy Garrison, Margaret Gavin, Ed Greer, Grace Hague, Harry Hawkins, Richard Headley, Robert Johnson, Jeannine Lathrop, William Lindsey, Stanley Locey, Norma Manley, Norman Mariani, Jack Martin, Wayland Metcalf, Elfriede Meyer, Donald Nixon, Howard Ruff, Dale Sherrill, John Tamagni, and Richard Thorsen.

The graduation included numbers by the band, under the direction of Clifford Anderson; songs by the chorus, under William Morehouse; and the address to the graduating class by Rev. Burton Alvis of Middletown.

Note: Girls made their own graduation dresses. The little corsages on the girls' dresses were pansies grown at the school. The eighth

Calistoga Elementary School graduates in 1944 included: left to right, front row – Richard Headley, Norman Mariani, Dorothy Garrison, Helen Derrick, Betty Elder, and Wayland Metcalf; second row – Glenn Conner, Stan Locey, Midge Gavin, Pat Boland, Jeannine Lathrop, Grace Hague, and Howard Ruff; third row – Norma Manley, Dale Sherrill, Elfriede Meyer, Miss Ford, Beanie Fisher, Earlene Elder, Bob Johnson, and Red Gardner; and back row – Bill Lindsey, Vladimir Baeff, Skip Tamagni, Jack Martin, Bill Driver, Harry Hawkins, Dick Thorsen, Ed Greer, and Jack Fechter.

grade teacher, Julia Ford, began working with them as seventh graders. She taught them to make dish towels and learn embroidery. In the eighth grade, the focus was on the graduation dress.

Renovation work has begun for creation of Hospitality House for visiting servicemen. Mr. and Mrs. John Stelzner, owners of the building on the north side of Lincoln Avenue, east of the bridge, are having its foundation repaired and the outside painted. Furniture and other equipment will be added to make the place a comfortable headquarters for servicemen who chance to pay Calistoga a visit. Funds for the interior remodeling are being raised by a local group headed by Mrs. John Mingus. A card party last Friday night raised $93.50 for the project. Others on the steering committee are Ben Schuman, vice president, and Bernice Wiggins, secretary-treasurer.

Joe Olaeta, a teacher at Calistoga Elementary School, has been appointed manager of the new Calistoga Farm Labor office. It will open August 1 in the building occupied by Charles B. Corkett Insurance Company at 1220 Washington Street, immediately behind the Bank of America. Corkett will act as secretary, and, thus, there will always be someone in the office to take care of the needs of growers.

Calistoga 1944

Mr. Olaeta's appointment sets at rest rumors that Calistoga might not have a labor office this year.

Army Air Force Staff Sergeant Walter S. Hays, home on leave, purchased the first bond in Calistoga's Fifth War Loan drive. He made his move at the drive's kickoff rally Monday night in front of the Hotel Calistoga. Hays attended high school here. He has chalked up 412 combat hours as a tail gunner on bombers in the New Guinea area, and is credited with shooting down at least five Jap planes.

Calistoga's quota for this drive is $200,000.

Calistoga Elementary School students have set an example by purchasing $2,243 in war bonds and stamps during the Fifth War Loan drive. It is a figure that should spur adults to greater efforts. The school children have bought $7,974 in bonds and stamps so far this year.

Police Chief Ed Light arrested two tourists – a man and a woman – yesterday for separate incidents of stealing newspapers from in front of business establishments along Lincoln Avenue. Judge J. B. Winkelman fined each of them $5.

Army Air Force Lieutenant Melvin Ceder held the rapt attention of 45 Calistoga Rotarians and guests as he described his experiences with the Flying Tigers – an American volunteer group that helped the Chinese fight the Japanese early in the war. Much of the lieutenant's talk cannot be published. Suffice to say that every person who attended left with a clear and vivid picture of the nature of the Jap, particularly when the Jap has the upper hand.

Lieutenant Ceder is a San Francisco boy and former student at the University of California, Berkeley. He holds 22 medals, including three Purple Hearts for wounds in action.

Now assigned to recruiting service, he was accompanied by Corporal Knutzen of the Women's Army Corps. They are touring Northern California during the current drive for WAC enlistments.

Note: The Flying Tigers' fighter planes, painted with a shark face, are among the most recognizable combat aircraft of World War II. They were flown by former military pilots, recruited under Presidential sanction and commanded by retired Army Air Force Brigadier

General Claire Lee Chennault. They had notable success during the lowest period of the war for U.S. and Allied Forces, giving hope to Americans that they would eventually succeed against the Japanese.

The historic Palisades Mine site and mining rights have been sold to V.C. Harrison, realtor Alice Fisher announced this week. The former silver mine is near the road to Middletown, at the eastern base of Mount St. Helena.

Palisades began operations some 65 years ago and was a profitable producer of silver for many years. The founder, Robert F. Grigsby, always claimed the mine could be worked at a profit indefinitely. However, its ownership has changed many times, and no owner seemed able to show a profit. The last owners, upon giving up, dismantled the mill and stripped the workings of all equipment.

Oat Hill Mine, among the Calistoga area's oldest producers of quicksilver, ceased its operations yesterday. In steady production since the early days of this war, it was forced to join with other quicksilver mines in closing down due to the falling price of the metal. Recent legislation designed to protect cinnabar smelters has failed to peg the price high enough to warrant continuing operations.

Note: The mine was located along the dirt road between Calistoga and Pope Valley, now a popular mountain biking trail.

Handkerchiefs and wash cloths are needed for returned servicemen in hospitals, according to Mrs. John Mingus, chairman of the local Camp and Hospital Committee of the Red Cross. If you have anything along this line, please see Mrs. Mingus. Also needed are old sheets and bath towels, as these can be used to make handkerchiefs and wash cloths.

page 4

Cupid and Uncle Sam conspired to provide a very happy furlough for Eugene Frediani of Calistoga, who has been stationed at the Galveston Air Field, Texas, in recent months.

Arriving home on a 15-day furlough, Eugene was married on June 10 to Miss Jeanne Mortensen of Berkeley. The ceremony took the form of a nuptial mass in St. Columbus Church, Oakland. Alfred Frediani, brother of the bridegroom, served as best man.

Calistoga 1944

Following the ceremony, there was a reception at the bride's home in Berkeley. On June 14, the newlyweds were honored with a dinner at the home of the bridegroom's mother, Mrs. Ida Frediani of Calistoga. The couple will be leaving shortly for Texas.

Eugene graduated from Calistoga High School in 1937, worked for a time here and at Basalt in Napa, and then entered the service.

Note: Gene and Jeanne returned to Calistoga after the war. He was a rancher. They had four kids, including two CHS grads: Judy, '64, and Mary Sue, '71. Gene died in 1978. Jeanne celebrated her 91st birthday on May 14, 2012.

Mrs. A.R. Jewell of Napa, state vice chairman of the Parent-Teacher Association, discussed juvenile delinquency Tuesday at a meeting of the Women's Association of the Community Church.

Mrs. Jewell gave as some of the causes of delinquency the following: truancy from school, unstable pattern of home life, working parents, frequent absence of older brothers and sisters, improper housing, lack of privacy, improper food, glamour of uniforms, loneliness of those not in uniform, and other factors. She went on to show what has been, and can be, done in Napa county, and praised the efforts of local girls and women in helping set up the "Hospitality House" for visiting servicemen. Wholesome recreation for youth, according to Mrs. Jewell, is one of the best preventives of juvenile delinquency.

Local News Briefs: Mrs. Ada Lavering left Sunday for Rio Vista, where she will visit for a time with her daughter and family, before continuing to Oregon for an indefinite stay with her mother. It was with regret that Calistoga saw Mrs. Lavering leave. She owned and operated a local beauty parlor for a time and later opened and ran the Calistoga Florist shop.

Mrs. Vincent Archuleta was hostess on Tuesday and Wednesday of this week to her sisters, Miss Pat Dowrick and Mrs. Erin Srock. Mrs. Archuleta and her daughter, Maureen, returned to the Bay Area with Miss Dowrick and Mrs. Srock. They will remain there while Mrs. Archuleta attends a 10-day course at the Institute of International Relations at Mills College.

Calistoga Elementary School students enjoyed a party at the Ritz Theater Wednesday afternoon. They saw the popular picture,

The Ritz Theater on Lincoln Avenue, looking east
(Courtesy of Sharpsteen Museum, Calistoga)

"Johnny Come Lately," starring James Cagney and Grace George. The party took the place of the school picnic, not held this year because of transportation difficulties.

Mrs. Mitto Blodgett will leave Calistoga next Wednesday, bound for the Republican National Convention in Chicago.

Chapter 12

June 18-24

The War: U.S. Navy pilots sink three Japanese aircraft carriers and other ships in the Battle of the Philippine Sea. British troops take Perugia, Italy. Allies take the offensive in Burma. Russian forces destroy the German Army Group Center in Belarus – considered Germany's greatest defeat in the war.

𝔚eekly 𝔠alistogan of June 23, 1944

page 1

Milton Petersen and Andy Richy of the class of 1945 at Calistoga High School are in Sacramento attending the annual, week-long session of Boys' State. The program acquaints a select group of boys with the functioning of a democratic government. They set up city, county, and state governments and stage elections and court scenes.

Boys' State is sponsored by the American Legion. Participants are selected by their school's faculty members on the basis of scholarship, citizenship, and interest in government.

Milton is the son of Mr. and Mrs. C.L. Petersen. Andy is the son of Mr. and Mrs. T. A. Richy.

Five awards were announced at last Friday's Calistoga High School graduation. Class Activity Cup: won by the class of 1947 (freshmen) and received by class president Bruce Piner. Class Scholarship Cup: class of 1944, received by class president Jack Scott. Top Scholar Cup: senior Lew (Bill) Cook. Bausch-Lomb Medal for outstanding promise in scientific study: Cook, again. Citizenship Cup: senior and student body president Allan Forbes.

Note: Chapter 11 has graduates' names and other graduation details.

Harry Wagnon of Calistoga was being held in Sonoma County Jail on multiple charges after an auto accident that injured three bystanders – one critically – Wednesday night. His bail was set at $5,000.

Wagnon faces charges of driving while intoxicated, causing personal injuries, driving on the wrong side of the road, and driving without a license. Police said his car hit three men who were standing by their cars talking. One had fractures of both legs, back and arm injuries, and severe shock. The others suffered minor injuries.

Four Boy Scouts were awarded rank badges at Troop 18's court of honor at the high school Monday night. Kenneth Smith received his Tenderfoot badge. Pete Marciano, Wayne Merry, and Phillip Snow received badges for the next higher rank, Second Class. Scoutmaster Bill Connolly and Scout Commissioner John Opman made the presentations.

Four members of Troop 18 will attend the recently purchased Boy Scout summer camp at Echo Lake in the Sierras this summer. L.P. (Babe) Ames is sponsoring Bob Johnson for a two-week stay at the camp. Bob was chosen as the Scout outstanding in leadership, interest, and accomplishments in Scout work. Lew Cook of Knights Valley is sponsoring Wayne Merry and Phillip Snow. Earl Evans, senior patrol leader, will attend the camp. He plans to stay a full month. Connolly advises that all Scouts who plan to attend summer camp must have physical examinations first.

Connolly announced that 10 Army surplus sleeping bags donated to Troop 18 by his brother, Steve Connolly, have arrived from the South Pacific. They are being dry-cleaned and soon will be ready for use by the troop.

Note: Bob Johnson and Pete Marciano eventually became Eagle Scouts, the highest rank. In 1958, Wayne Merry was on the two-man team that was the first to climb the face of El Capitan in Yosemite National Park. He later worked as a ranger at Denali National Park in Alaska and in wilderness rescue in Canada.

This community was grieved and saddened by the untimely death last Saturday of Mrs. Armand Tedeschi, a young woman whose many fine qualities had endeared her to a wide circle of friends. She had had a series of operations over the past year and a half.

Born in Calistoga on August 10, 1909, Anna Barberis Tedeschi spent her life here, graduating from the local elementary and high schools. In September 1928, she became the bride of Armand. She is survived by four children: Frances, 14; Rosalie, 12; Edward, 8;

and Richard, 4. Other close relatives are her parents, Mr. and Mrs. D. Barberis of Calistoga; sisters Mary Saviez, Lena Carlenzoli, Milena Barberis, and Edythe Triglia, all of Calistoga; and brother, Corporal Frank Barberis, now serving with the Army at Camp Knight, Oakland.

Rosary was held at the Simic Funeral Home in Calistoga Monday night. The funeral was held Tuesday morning from Our Lady of Perpetual Help Catholic Church. Pallbearers were John Nolasco, Charles Nolasco, Edmund Molinari, Mario Cavagnaro, Frank Pocai, and Fred Monfre. Interment took place at St. Helena Catholic Cemetery.

Native Daughters of the Golden West's Grand Parlor has unanimously endorsed the proposed Robert Louis Stevenson Memorial Park on Mount St. Helena. Individual delegates to the Parlor's meeting in San Jose promised the whole-hearted support of their various parlors.

Native Sons of the Golden West previously had voted its support, including financial aid. Newspapers throughout the state are taking an active interest and bringing the park to the attention of their readers. Harriet Hinsdale, widely-known Southern California writer, is handling publicity and organization in the southern part of the state.

A central committee is being formed. An active mail campaign will be initiated, publicity will be increased, and state officials will be brought into the picture. While the park is definitely a Napa County project, and particularly a project that concerns Calistoga, there has been a most gratifying interest shown throughout the state. No one locally will be unduly burdened with the necessity of raising funds, as donations will be coming in from all of California.

Charles S. Morris Jr., who recently resigned as principal at Calistoga High School, has been selected principal of Williams High School in Colusa County. During his three years in Calistoga, Morris made many friends, who wish him every success in his new job.

Adjutant James McCall of Calistoga Post 231 of the American Legion has issued a call to all honorably discharged veterans of the present war to get in touch with him at the earliest possible moment to file any claims they may have against the government arising from disability incurred in the line of duty.

"The request is directed particularly to those men who have been discharged for reasons of physical disability," McCall said. "They must file claims within a year of the date of discharge. The local post has the necessary forms, and officers of the post are ready to assist any and all veterans who may apply."

Former Calistogan Burch Bachtold was commissioned a second lieutenant June 5 at exercises for Army aviation cadets in meteorology at the 3709th Army Air Force Base Unit, University of California, Los Angeles. His parents, Mr. and Mrs. Caspar Bachtold, now live in San Francisco.

Jack Rannells, Calistoga's new high school principal, has purchased the Isabel Tamagni home at 921 Main Street, according to Fisher Realty Company.

Note: Is this page one news? Street names/numbers have changed since 1944. The address now is 1514 Foothill Boulevard. It's the red house. It was white in 1944, the only home my parents ever owned. They paid $4,000 for the 9,000-square-foot lot with a two-bedroom main house and a two-room cabin in back. Parts of the house date back to the 1880s. The only toilet/bathtub was on an open back porch at the rear of the house – one step up from the original outhouse. There was no garage. We did get a chicken house and 20 laying hens in the deal, plus lots of space for a victory garden. Landscaping included a goldfish pond, a palm tree, two redwoods, black walnut trees, a rose garden, a fig tree, a quince tree, and an acacia that gave my dad hay fever every spring. Laundry was done in a washer-with-wringer on the back porch. It was hung to dry on lines next to the cabin where my brother David and I lived.

page 8

Army Private Lloyd Camp, son of Mr. and Mrs. W.A. Camp of Calistoga, writes from "somewhere in England":

"Received the *Weekly Calistogan* and sure was glad to get it. I see where Lt. Jackson Clary has arrived safely back home. I sure would like to have seen the places he has been, and I probably will before long. I only hope that I don't have the luck that he had – bad luck, I mean. He sure went through some experiences that I hope never to encounter. I don't mean that I am afraid, or anything, but I just don't think that I would have as good luck as he did in getting away. Give him my regards and tell him that I think Lady Luck was hugging him real tight. I sure was sorry to hear that he was lost in action; but now that he is back, everything is OK, I hope.

"Well, I see where the draft is getting the rest of the boys that are left behind. I only hope that they leave enough labor behind to take care of the ranches. I will try to contact the boys by their APO numbers I received.

"I hope that the deal about the labor office goes through. I think that Mr. Wiggins will pull through all right. He usually does when he starts out to do something."

Lloyd's address is: Pvt. Lloyd V. Camp, 39127164, Co. B 526 A-1-Bn., U.S. Army, APO 134, c/o Postmaster, New York, NY.

Note: The March 31 issue of the Weekly Calistogan *gives details of Lt. Clary's escape after German gunfire destroyed his plane over France.*

Mare Island Naval Shipyard in Vallejo plans to appoint 400 apprentices in 14 mechanical trades in July. During a 27-month program, participants will receive training in their trade and a high school diploma, if they don't already have one. Males ages 16 through 21 who have IV-F draft classification are eligible.

The apprenticeships will be for sheetmetal worker, machinist, electrician, shipfitter, blacksmith, boilermaker, coppersmith, pipefitter, molder, patternmaker, sailmaker, painter, shipwright, and rigger.

Apprentices have been trained at Mare Island since 1869. The apprentice school system was founded in 1912. It is recognized all through the world as an outstanding training program.

To qualify, youths must pass a mechanical aptitude test. This exam will be given between 9 and 11 a.m. and 1 to 3 p.m. daily, except Sunday, in the Labor Board office at Wilson and Tennessee streets, Vallejo.

Mare Island operates a bus service to-from Calistoga for the exclusive use of its employees. This enables 16-year-old apprentices to enjoy the comforts and advantages of a normal home life while, at the same time, making vital contributions to the nation's war effort. Appointments to the program will be made in compliance with War Manpower Commission policies.

Chapter 13

June 25-July 1
The War: Finnish and Russian troops clash at Tali-Ihantala -- the largest battle ever fought in the Nordic countries.

𝔚eekly 𝔠alistogan of June 30, 1944

page 1

Special agents of the Federal Bureau of Investigation ended a nationwide search in Calistoga Tuesday with the arrest of Virginia Gladys Biunno, who came here some two weeks ago and secured employment as cashier at a local bingo parlor.

The woman is alleged to have fraudulently collected government dependents' allotments from at least three servicemen. She was indicted by a federal grand jury in Pensacola, Florida, on May 5. She came across the continent to Oakland and lived there until she came to Calistoga with the help of a former local businessman. Agents of the FBI had followed her trail and finally localized the hunt in this area.

She will be returned to Florida to face trial in the federal district court.

Army Air Force Corporal David Newton makes some interesting comments on his experiences at the Flying Fortress School in Seattle, Washington, in a letter to his parents, Mr. and Mrs. George Newton of Calistoga.

He is taking training on the B-29 superfortresses that were credited with making the war's second raid against the Jap homeland.

"I finished the electrical phase of my training last week and came out with a 4.2, highest in the class. The phase I'm in now is easier, but has more to remember. Saturday I will be half through, with 35 days of schooling left. In a way, I'll be glad to finish. I have seen enough of Seattle and want to see some other country."

David added a PS – "Our B-29s finally did something in Japan. Hope they leave some for me."

Note: David was a flight engineer on 13 B-29 raids on Japan in 1945, and won a Distinguished Flying Cross for heroism on one of them. Flak from Japanese guns knocked out one of his plane's engines. David stripped off his flight gear, crawled into the plane's bomb bay and – at an altitude of 16,000 feet – found the problem, spliced some cables, and got the engine running again. David remained in what became the Air Force after the war but died during a peritonitis attack in 1958. He was a 1936 graduate of Calistoga High School. His widow, Rosella Proaps Newton, a 1938 CHS graduate, lives in Napa.

Calistoga's Hospitality House for servicemen will soon be a reality. The foundation has been finished and volunteer carpenters and painters are now at work on the interior. Last Sunday, a hot lunch was served to the workers, a pile of lumber serving as a table. Later, the workers and their wives enjoyed a waffle supper at the home of Mr. and Mrs. W.C. Wiggins.

Theta Rho girls, under the supervision of Mrs. Ward Taylor, will work this week on the draperies and curtains.

A dance at the Masonic Auditorium on Monday, July 3, and a card party at the Odd Fellows' Hall on Tuesday, July 4, will raise more funds for renovation and maintenance of the house. Anyone who wishes to help by donating merchandise or cakes for prizes, please contact Mrs. Tom Elder.

Following many months of starts and stops, legal consultations, and court appearances, the suit instituted against the City of Calistoga by the Valley Construction Company was settled in favor of the city on June 23.

Builders of Calistoga's municipal dam, Valley Construction, sued the city for $15,026 allegedly due for extra work caused by the change in plans to move the spillway from the western end of the dam to the eastern end.

The case was heard in the courtroom of Judge Harold Jacoby of Contra Costa County Superior Court. City Attorney Lowell Palmer presented the city's defense, assisted by Nathan F. Coombs and Conrad Weil Jr.

Tomorrow, July 1, marks the 49th anniversary of the day that the present owner of the *Weekly Calistogan*, Charles A. Carroll, took over the then *Independent Calistogian* and entered the newspaper game as a full-fledged owner, editor, and proprietor.

Receiving his early experience on the *Mendocino Beacon* in Mendocino City, Mr. Carroll later worked on both of the Ukiah papers and then the *San Francisco Chronicle.*

Wishing to own his own paper, Mr. Carroll watched for an opportunity to buy a country weekly. Early in June of 1895, he heard that the *Independent Calistogian* was on the market.

Journeying to Calistoga by train, he spent several days of negotiations with the owner, I.N. Bennett. On July 1, 1895, the papers were signed, and Mr. Carroll took over the plant. He has remained the owner since then. Some 14 years after assuming ownership, Mr. Carroll changed the name of the paper to *Weekly Calistogian.* About 18 years ago, he changed it to its present name.

The 49th anniversary of his purchase of the paper finds Mr. Carroll the dean of newspapermen of Napa County. All of those who were active owners and publishers at the time he entered the field have passed on.

Mr. Carroll has seen the growth of the mechanical end of newspaper publishing, and he has gone through the days of hand-set type, Washington hand presses for printing the paper, gasoline-driven presses, and on up to the days of the linotype, electric-driven presses, and mechanical folders.

Note: By 1944, Mr. Carroll's daughter, Lois, and her husband, Ralph (Scoop) Winston, did most of the work in producing the paper. Carroll died in 1946.

Costume jewelry is widely used by our troops throughout the South Pacific and is valuable to them through the fact that the bright pieces are accepted by natives where money is scorned. It is more in demand now than at any time since the boys discovered its value.

Napa County War Relief Inc. is conducting a drive for any and all kinds of costume jewelry. The local chairman, Mrs. Gordon Hunt, asks that anyone who has pieces to spare please leave them at the office of the Citizens' Service Corps next to the Bank Club on Lincoln Avenue in Calistoga. Office hours are from 3 to 4 p.m. on Monday, Wednesday, and Friday and from 2 to 4 p.m. on Tuesday.

Fond memories of the annual shoe sale clearance will be brought back to Mrs. America on July 10, when certain odd lot shoes will be ration-free at reduced prices.

For three weeks, beginning that day, the Office of Price Administration will permit dealers to dispose of the normal accumulation of broken sizes and other odds and ends. Each dealer will be limited to a certain percentage of his stocks of these shoes.

The dealer also will be required to reduce the price of shoes sold ration-free to 25 percent less than the charge as of June 1, 1944. The release of odd lots of shoes applies to men's and women's shoes and boys' shoes of sizes one to six.

Mrs. Joseph J. Fereday, a resident of Calistoga since 1915, passed away at her home last Saturday after an illness that started 15 years ago. She had spent a great deal of the past two years in the local hospital.

Jean Fereday was the daughter of Joseph Jordan, who came to California during the 1840s gold rush. She was born at Sutter Creek, Amador County. The family moved to Idaho, but she and her husband came back to California in 1908. Mr. Fereday is a building contractor. Mrs. Fereday was a home-loving women, whose only outside affiliation in recent times was with the Calistoga Community Church.

She had three daughters; ten grandchildren, including five grandsons now serving their country; and four great grandchildren.

The funeral service was held Monday from the Simic Funeral Home in Calistoga. The service was preached by an old-time friend, Rev. J. Sherman Potter of San Leandro, who served the Presbyterian pastorate in Calistoga some 25 years ago. Pallbearers were Frank Muller, J.A. Taylor, Joseph Franz, George H. Short, and J.B. Winkelman, all of Calistoga, and George Wood of Vallejo. Interment took place in the St. Helena Cemetery.

Robert Greene's most recent letter to his parents, Mr. and Mrs. H.A. Greene, reports that he has been made a corporal and is "somewhere" in France. He described the type of dugout in which he has spent a great deal of time of late and his joy at a chance meeting in France with his particular buddy of training days in the States, Don Gregory.

Note: Robert was a 1942 graduate of Calistoga High School.

Page 8

Maximum hourly and piecework wage rates for picking apricots for the fresh market, canning, and drying were announced this week by the national War Food Administration. The rates for Napa County and 13 other central California counties are 80 cents an hour or $13 a ton. They are lower – 75 cents or $12 – in the southern San Joaquin Valley counties and higher – 85 cents or $13 a ton in parts of Alameda and Santa Clara counties.

Roland F. Ballou, executive officer of the California WFA Wage Board, emphasized that the rates are maximums. He said violations of the wage ceilings make both workers and employers liable to severe penalties, ranging up to one year of imprisonment, a $1,000 fine, or both. An employer may also be disallowed deduction for income tax purposes of all wages paid in violation of the ceiling order.

Chapter 14

July 9-15

The War: Saipan is taken — 30,000 Japanese troops died in its defense.

Politics: FDR announces he will seek an unprecedented fourth term.

𝔚eekly 𝔆alistogan of July 14, 1944

page 1

Calistoga did it again!

At the close of business on July 8, the last day of the Fifth War Loan drive, Chairman Frank Piner reported that the total amount subscribed was $262,520. In exceeding the quota by $62,519, Calistoga chalked up an over-subscription of 31 percent – an enviable record.

With E bond sales stressed by the Treasury Department, Calistoga was given a quota of $62,350. The end of the drive found a total of $106,431 in E purchases – an excess of 71 percent.

Calistoga sales lagged at the drive's halfway mark, but several sizable allocations came in from corporations and local wineries to push the drive over the top. Calistoga and St. Helena were among the first towns in the state to make their quotas.

"The fact that the quota was exceeded by 31 percent can be directly attributed to the untiring efforts of those who solicited from door to door and from ranch to ranch," Mr. Piner said.

Those who have read of the heroic work of American nurses serving with the invasion forces in France will be interested to know that a Calistoga girl is there on the fighting front. She is Lieutenant Emily Musante, daughter of Mr. and Mrs. Giuseppe Musante of this city.

Emily was the first Calistoga girl to receive a commission with the U.S. fighting forces. Enlisting in December of 1941, she trained first at Stockton, Calif., and later in the East. She has been overseas for many months and now is "somewhere" in France.

She was a 1931 graduate of Calistoga High School. She took her nurse training at the University of California Hospital in San Francisco. Then she nursed in Queen's Hospital in Honolulu and in County Hospital in Shanghai, China. She was in Shanghai when it was bombed by the Japs, and did emergency duty there before returning to this country. Emily has three sisters – Mrs. Theresa Mainini, Miss Catherine Musante, and Mrs. Marcella Losco – all well known here.

Note: Emily's father founded Calistoga's mineral water bottling company in 1924 and owned it until 1970. He is the lively fellow depicted in the metal sculpture near the now defunct bottling plant on the Silverado Trail. More on Emily in Chapter 22.

Calistoga's proposal for a recreational dam on the Napa River received the attention of the State last week when D.S. Cleavinger, associate hydraulic engineer, Division of Water Resources, came to town to look over the site and advise as to the practicability of building such a structure.

Cleavinger later made an informal report at the Rotary Club meeting. He said the project is feasible but fraught with many difficulties.

Calistoga would be faced with a very considerable amount of grief before the construction could start, and a great deal of responsibility if the dam were built. It has been stated that an eight-foot dam would give four or five feet of water in the river near Pioneer Park. That does not provide sufficient depth for diving and would mean a constant source of danger to those who might think they could dive in.

Boating also has been discussed; but with so little water backed up, there would scarcely be room enough for boats and swimming too, according to those who have really given the matter mature thought.

Note: The dam was proposed where the crossing has been built between Sharpsteen Museum and Pioneer Park.

During the past two War Loan drives, there has been a drive-within-the-drive for "War Bonds for Wartime Babies." Up until now, only babies up to one year old could be honored with these bonds.

Tuesday, it was announced that the War Baby Bonds can be purchased in the names of children up to six years old. They will receive a special certificate from the United States Treasury. Designed by Walt Disney, it is bordered with characters like the Seven Dwarfs, Pinocchio, Bambi, Mickey Mouse, Donald Duck, and Pluto.

Mrs. Elizabeth Simic, the Calistoga War Finance Committee member in charge of soliciting the War Baby Bonds, welcomed the change. She said the bonds are a way to give children a nest-egg to be used when college days roll around.

More complete information may be secured from Mrs. Simic or by inquiry at the Bank of America, Calistoga branch.

Walnut growers of Lake and Napa counties will attend an important meeting next Tuesday afternoon at Konocti Bay, on the shores of Clear Lake.

Sponsored by the California Walnut Growers Assocation and the University of California Extension Service, the meeting will feature talks on marketing, cultural, and equipment problems facing the grower for the coming year.

Included on the list of those attending are Walter Christie, field manager for the California Walnut Growers Association; A.E. Gilbert, manager of the association's Calistoga processing plant; and Gene Serr, extension specialist in deciduous fruits and nuts.

Note: The walnut plant was a fixture in Calistoga from 1939 to 2000.

Members of the Men's Club of the Community Church, their ladies, and guests will hear an outstanding speaker Monday evening during their monthly meeting and pot-luck supper in the Methodist Church social hall.

The guest speaker will be Calistoga newcomer Charles Corwin White, a former New York business executive, world traveler, and well-known analyst of current affairs. Mr. White has chosen for the theme of his address, "A Reasonable Ambition."

Following his graduation from Yale University, Mr. White entered the business world. At the age of 26, he became president of the Manger Hotel chain in New York City. Later, he cruised for a year on his yacht, and then toured Finland, Lapland, Labrador, and other distant places.

He once pedaled his way on a bicycle from New York to Los Angeles, making inquiries of hundreds of people as he conducted a personal survey concerning the possible entry of the United

States into the war. Following the attack on Pearl Harbor, he spent months with the American Red Cross in the Pacific Coast area as field director and first aid instructor.

Mr. White is now engaged in research in history, economics, and allied fields, specializing in the study of the United States today and tomorrow in relation to the rest of the world. He and Mrs. White have been making their home in Calistoga for several months.

Anyone who wishes to attend next Monday's event is invited to do so. Members of the Men's Club will provide bread and butter, coffee, and dessert. Those who attend are asked to furnish other dishes for the supper, which is set to start at 7:30 p.m.

County Assessor S.J. Webber announced last week that with the completion of the assessment roll for the current year, Napa County showed an increase in property values of $969,970. With an increase in evaluations of public utilities of $82,970, that makes a total increase of assessments of $1,052,140.

He stated that while this did not compare with the increase of $2,876,165 last year, when the gain was centralized in the area of Napa township due to war building and housing, the increase this year is divided among all districts.

According to a report of the State Equalization Board last week, public utilities in the county indicated assessed values of $2,597,260. Property assessments outside cities total $15,386,950; those inside corporate cities total $10,629,840.

Former Calistogan Carl McDonald, has tendered his resignation as Napa County Superintendent of Schools, effective August 1, to accept the position of principal of the Walter Colton School in Monterey.

McDonald came to Calistoga in 1937 as principal of the elementary school. He soon established himself as an outstanding educator and a forward-looking member of the community. He took the county job a year ago. During his six years here, he was active in all civic affairs and entered into war defense work as an instructor in disaster relief and first aid, as applied to civilian agencies.

In March 1943, he was named president of the Napa County Tuberculosis Association. His leadership brought the association to the peak of its usefulness.

Note: McDonald's son, Malcolm, lives in Calistoga. He retired after 25 years as a teacher and administrator in St. Helena schools.

Following are some reports and actions at the City Council meeting on June 30:

Police Judge J.B. Winkelman reported that 16 cases were heard in his court during June. Fines amounting to $75 were levied and collected.

Police Chief Ed E. Light reported that he issued one traffic citation, arrested three persons on warrants, and arrested one person on a charge of drunkenness. Officer Otto Bohn reported issuing six traffic citations and arresting four persons for drunkenness.

The Council approved increasing the salary of Mario Cavagnaro to $35 per month, effective July 1, for care of the city's fire trucks and ambulance. It named D.C. Wall to replace E.D. House, who resigned as general utility man for the various city departments. Wall's salary was fixed at $160 per month.

The council advised Alexander Gering to postpone a building project on his Lake Street property until such time as the present federal restrictions are removed. If he wants to proceed at this time, he must secure priorities from the War Production Board and present a detailed plan of the proposed structure for City Council approval.

page 2

Army Sergeant Harry C. Drake gives a colorful description of his station "somewhere" in New Guinea in a letter to Mr. and Mrs. J.B. Ratto.

"I'm safely salted away over here, where there is a sample of everything that walks, crawls, or flies. We are close to a stream, also the ocean. Just like a summer resort. And just think, we are getting paid for it!

"I understand that Walter Butler is over here somewhere, but trying to find out where is just about impossible. This is a big place, and there are lots of places where a person could be. I intend writing him soon.

"I wanted in the worst way to get up to Calistoga before shipping out, but time sort of caught up with me before I could do all the things I wanted to.

"Thanks a million for the cigarettes. We keep pretty well supplied with them over here, free of charge. The boys who chew have a little trouble, though, as they are overlooked in most cases.

"So far, I haven't been any place to spend any of my hard-earned cash. If a person were to stay over here 75 or 80 years, he could accumulate quite a fortune. I will take mine out in the Napa

Valley. I'd give my next month's pay for a box of second crop grapes right now.

"The food situation here isn't a bit bad. We have fresh eggs regularly, and some fruit – apples to be exact. There are some native fruits in the jungle, such as bananas and coconuts. The bananas are difficult to find, as the natives keep them well cleaned out. They know where the good spots are.

"The other day while I was messing around in the jungle, I ran into a vine that had a gadget on it that looked much like our home-grown cucumbers. I cut it open, and darned if it wasn't – and it tasted the same too.

"I brought along some fishing tackle and have had a little luck in the ocean on some small fish. There aren't any large enough in the streams to fool with.

"The land crabs here take all prizes. When you goose one with a stick, he takes off sideways, never straight ahead. It is very confusing.

"Here is one for Ted Tamagni. The other day, I was taking a dip in the ocean, and in the shallow water I saw a fish that looked to be about a foot long. I made a pass at it with my hands, and all it did was swim up to the water's edge and crawl right out and hide under a rock on dry land.

"Forward a message to those responsible for the nice Christmas package that I received from the City of Calistoga. The articles are all most useful and in constant demand. I hope to receive the *Weekly Calistogan* soon. Jean has them on the way, along with copies of the *Chronicle* Sporting Green.

"Say hello for me to all my friends along Lincoln Avenue."

Sgt. Harry Drake, 39009605, Hq. Btry. 983rd FA Bn, APO 9788, c/o postmaster, San Francisco.

Note: Harry was a 1926 graduate of Calistoga High School. He fought on Leyte in the Philippines later in the war. He returned to Calistoga, where he ran a service station and later worked in a hardware store. His daughter, Carol, was a 1952 graduate of CHS and is the wife of retired NFL coach Dick Vermeil.

Chapter 15

July 16-29

July 16-29

The War: In the Pacific, U.S. Marines invade Guam
Island and Tinian Island, which will become the base for
our atomic bombers a year later. General Hideki Tojo
resigns as chief minister of the Japanese government.
Allied troops break through German defenses in Normandy. Soviet troops liberate the first of many German
concentration camps. Germany scores the first victory for
a jet airplane, damaging a British RAF reconnaissance
aircraft. U.S. forces take Leghorn (Livorno), far up the
Italian "boot."

Other: At exactly 10:17 p.m. on July 17, two immense
explosions, five seconds apart, devastated Port Chicago, a
military weapons loading facility on Suisun Bay in Contra Costa
County. Several ships were blown apart, and 322 military
and civilian workers were killed. People in the upper Napa
Valley saw the flashes in the sky and heard/felt the explosions. Many assumed it was a Japanese bomber attack or
an explosion at Mare Island, where friends or neighbors
worked. Workers at Port Chicago refused to return to
loading jobs and were charged with mutiny.

𝔚eekly 𝔠alistogan of July 28, 1944

page 1

Calistoga's Farm Labor Office at 1220 Washington Street will
open for business Tuesday, August 1, Manager Joe Olaeta
announced.

Olaeta said the success of the office depends on it knowing in
advance just how many workers are needed at the various ranches.
That will help him steer the available workers to places where they
are needed. He expects that this year, as last, volunteer labor from
the Bay Area will be available every weekend. C.B. Corkett will be
office secretary.

There is still an opportunity to sign up for Mexican nationals.
Information can be obtained from the Napa County Farm Labor

Corporation in the Hotel St. Helena building in St. Helena. Growers who have had Mexicans on their places for some time past say that they have proven to be very satisfactory.

The ration value of creamery butter has been increased from 12 to 16 red points a pound to cut down on civilian consumption. The OPA put the change in effect at 12:01 a.m. Eastern War Time, Sunday, July 23.

The change was made after preliminary reports showed civilian consumption of creamery butter is running as much as 20 percent over the July allocation of 100 million pounds. Slowing down civilian consumption will help the armed services obtain their required supplies, the OPA said.

A.L. Hawke of Calistoga was installed as president of the Napa County Farm Bureau for the coming year at a meeting in Salvador Farm Center on July 19. The Farm Bureau and its Home Department have ten centers in the county.

Calistoga area Farm Center officers include: Bennett – Ray C. Bentley, director; C.W. Scott, vice director; R.L. Page, secretary; Mrs. Milton Sherwood, treasurer. Tucker – Charles A. Davis, director; W.D. Tucker, vice director; Mrs. Nona Wolleson, secretary; and Mrs. Katie Morosoli, treasurer.

Calistoga area Home Department officers include: Bennett – Mrs. H.A. Goudy, chairman; Mrs. Grace Lincoln, vice chairman; and Mrs. W.T. Bentley, secretary. Tucker – Mrs. Nona Wolleson, chairman; Mrs. Bernice Cahill, vice chairman; and Mrs. Katie Morosoli, secretary.

Following many weeks of hard work by its sponsors, Calistoga's Hospitality House opens tomorrow night as a respite for members of the armed forces who visit Calistoga.

Hospitality House, near the Lincoln Avenue bridge, started as a project of Theta Rho, but it has claimed the attention of a large number of local people, who volunteered labor, donated furniture, and worked long and hard to make the quarters attractive and comfortable for visiting servicemen.

Much of the credit must be given to Mr. and Mrs. John Stelzner, who donated the house rent free and paid for all major repair and renovation work. Mrs. John Mingus, adviser to Theta Rho, is chairman of the project's board of directors.

Calistoga 1944

The opening ceremonies will start with playing of the Star-Spangled Banner by Norman Piner, first trumpet player of the Calistoga High School band. Next will come the invocation by the Rev. A.E. Lucas. Following that, Del Caywood will sing a solo. The Navy will be represented by Commander Robert England of Mare Island, the Army by an officer from the Santa Rosa air base. Guests of the evening will include Gold Star mothers of Calistoga, local service men and women who are in town on furlough, and visiting members of the armed forces. Following the dedication, the Calistoga Lodge of Rebekahs will host a reception at the Odd Fellows Hall.

With the nationwide paper shortage becoming more acute every day, it is imperative that every citizen save every scrap of paper possible.

Old newspapers, magazines, and pasteboard cartons should be bundled for pick-up by the American Legion, which will take them to the collection center in San Francisco. Call Adjutant James McCall at 149-M to schedule a pickup. Bundles should be large enough to be handled easily.

Bill Adams, Calistoga boy now in the Navy, shoves off tomorrow to rejoin his ship after spending a two-week furlough in town. Bill saw action in the Marshall Islands, in New Guinea, the Hollandia raid, and had a ringside seat during the landings at Saipan.

Nathan F. Coombs, chairman of the county Republican Central Committee, was guest of honor and speaker at yesterday's meeting of the Calistoga Rotary Club. Coombs, who attended the recent Republican national convention in Chicago, described highlights of the convention, its delegates, and the candidates.

When W.C. Wiggins checked out the cabin on the old Corkett ranch on the road to Knights Valley last Friday to see if it was salvageable, he found the body of a man who had been dead for a very long time.

Wiggins notified Chief of Police Ed E. Light. The body was in an advanced stage of decomposition, but a draft card in his pocket identified the man as Alonzo Flagg of Vallejo. Light recalled that he had checked a transient with similar clothing and bed-roll in that area back on January 16.

Flagg was buried at St. Helena Cemetery after efforts to locate relatives failed.

page 4

A free clinic on home canning will be conducted here next Friday under the sponsorship of Calistoga's Civic Club, in cooperation with Pacific Gas and Electric Company and Standard Oil of California. It will stress approved methods of home canning, as well as prevention of food spoilage and food poisoning.

The clinic will be held at 2 p.m. at the Civic Club. It will be led by Bernice Redington, well known home economist and canning expert.

page 5

Technical Sergeant Peter Nolasco, a Calistoga boy who took part in 25 air missions over Europe, deserted the ranks of the single men last Saturday and journeyed to the altar with Miss Claudia Paden of Los Angeles. Pete is stationed at an Army air field at Taft. Claudia will join him there, if they can find housing; otherwise, she will remain in Los Angeles for the time being.

Ellen Nicchia and Robert Orsi took their vows in Reno on July 5. Both attended Calistoga schools. Ellen attended San Francisco State College for two years after graduation from Calistoga High School in 1942. Orsi, playing with Art Rowley's band, is at present at Rio Nido, where he and the new Mrs. Orsi are living. From there, they will go to Santa Cruz for a band engagement, and from there to the state of Washington.

Staff Sergeant John A. Ghisolfo, better known as the Adonis of Lincoln Avenue, finally decided that the life of a bachelor has its disadvantages and took unto himself a bride. Miss Ruth Cummings, a very charming resident of Lynwood in Southern California, journeyed to the altar with Johnny there. He hopes to bring his new bride to Calistoga sometime in August.

Rev. Cecilia Nixon returned to Calistoga Wednesday from a month's vacation in Oregon. She attended the Assembly of God camp meeting and convocation in Brooks and held meetings in the churches of Coquille and Port Orford, which she formerly pastored. The Port Orford church was built under her ministry.

Chapter 16

July 30-August 5

The War: The 63-day Second Warsaw Uprising begins; Russia fails to provide aid expected by the Polish rebels.

Allied troops, under General Stilwell, complete the take-over of Myitkyina in northern Burma. Allied troops liberate Florence, Italy; the retreating Germans destroy bridges, historic buildings.

𝔚𝔢𝔢𝔨𝔩𝔶 𝔆𝔞𝔩𝔦𝔰𝔱𝔬𝔤𝔞𝔫 of August 4, 1944

page 1

Leroy Johnson, congressman from this district, addressed the Rotary Club Thursday on the subject of "War Contract Terminations and Reconversion."

His focus was on the War Contract Termination Act recently passed by Congress. Its goal is to enable the productive capacity now tuned to war to be quickly turned to peacetime production and provide employment and opportunities for the millions of discharged servicemen and war workers who will be looking for jobs.

A basic provision of the law is that contract changes will be settled by negotiation. Contractors and government procurement agencies will sit down and determine the amount due the contractor for the work performed. Provision is made so that the winding up of these contracts will be speedy and fair to both the contractor and the government.

Mr. Johnson noted that thousands of contracts already have had to be terminated because of the changing demands of the various war fronts. When the war ends, it is estimated that contracts totaling $100 billion or more will have to be terminated.

Mr. Johnson said the Army has over 100,000 prime contracts and a million sub-contracts that will be affected. Provision has been made for review of all settlements where the payment exceeds $10,000. The settlements will be final, except in the case of fraud. A contractor can be punished for fraud any time that it is detected.

Mr. Johnson said it is up to war contractors to work with the government in doing this mighty job. In a sense, he said, the private enterprise system is on trial. If they handle this job well, it will give the system that has made America the land of opportunity and wealth an opportunity to continue. If not, it may mean more and more government encroachment in the domain of business.

Army Aviation Cadet Robert W. Johnston, son of Mr. and Mrs. Walter Johnston of Calistoga, was recently awarded an expert's medal for his accurate firing of the .45- caliber automatic pistol at Maxwell Field, Alabama. Bob, a 1942 graduate of Calistoga High School, is in a nine-week course for military, physical, and academic training.

Note: Bob received an officer's commission in April 1945. After the war, he earned an engineering degree from University of California, Berkeley. He worked for 43 years in design, construction, and management of public works projects. He lives in retirement in Foresthill, CA.

Jumping the gun on deer season may prove costly for three hunters who were arrested by Game Warden M.F. Joy Monday night near Aetna Springs. The season didn't open until Tuesday.

Sig Light shows his forked-horned kill to Mayor Edward L. Stevens, left, and Police Chief Ed Light.
(Photo courtesy of Sharpsteen Museum, Calistoga)

Louis Taucher and Ord Allaway, owners of the Tuxedo restaurant in San Francisco, and Earl Hunt, miner from the Toyon mine, were found with a pair of three-point bucks. Judge J.B. Winkelman released them on $100 cash bail apiece. They will face charges before him Tuesday morning.

Meanwhile, here are some reports from legal hunters. Herman Klotz, Jackie Pacheteau, and Harry Cohen each bagged a three-pointer. The Carlenzoli party brought in two bucks, as did the John Nolasco party. George Pease and Carl Pierce bagged the biggest buck of the day near Monticello. It dressed out at around 130 pounds. Kenneth Grimsley, Vince Archuleta, "Gus" Gustavic, and Cyril Saviez each brought one in.

News reached us this week from "somewhere in England" that Lewis Ward Taylor has been promoted to staff sergeant. Taylor is an armament inspector, playing an important role in keeping bombers and fighters in condition. He is a 1940 graduate of Calistoga High School and trained as a mechanic before entering the service.

Ryan Aeronautical Company, considering post-war establishment of an airline serving the North Coast and adjacent inland areas, is studying possible feeder routes.

Eugene R. Scroggie, who will direct operations of the projected airline, is scheduled to visit Calistoga. He will make a detailed survey of potential business that might be diverted to air-borne freight.

Police have reported conditions that "made us ill" during the investigation of a home for crippled and mentally deficient children on the old A.B. Mangus ranch on Santa Rosa Road some three miles from town.

They found a Mrs. Lucy Weeks, with her husband and daughter, operating the "home" and using the old barn as quarters for 20 children, ranging in age from three to twenty years. The barn had been only partially cleaned out, there were no sanitary facilities, no running water, no lights, and the windows were unscreened.

The children ran the gamut from morons to imbeciles. Some were so badly crippled that they were helpless. Others were suffering from serious skin diseases. All were in filthy clothes and had not been bathed for a considerable period of time. There was no evidence of any exacting supervision, and the children were allowed to roam at will.

Following the original investigation by Chief of Police Ed Light and two sheriff's deputies, Assistant District Attorney Lowell Palmer was called into the case.

"I have never seen human beings kept in such filthy surroundings," Palmer told the *Weekly Calistogan*. "Of the 20 I counted, not one was mentally able to care for himself any better than a baby. They were seemingly on their own, and it was obvious that the filthy conditions would become worse."

Palmer said the Weeks family was receiving $45 a month for each child.

Chapter 17

August 6-12

The War: In the Pacific, U.S. troops liberate Guam; the Marianas are all in U.S. hands and will become major air and naval centers.

𝔚eekly ℭalistogan of August 11, 1944

page 1

One of the most devastating forest fires to strike Napa County during the past few years started on the Cravea ranch, in the Bell Canyon area, shortly after noon Sunday.

Fanned by a brisk wind, the flames swept up the canyon, and by night were threatening homes in the vicinity of the St. Helena Sanitarium. Pacific Union College was also in the path of the spreading blaze, but fighters managed to hold the fire at that point.

Forestry officials estimate that several thousand acres were laid waste. Two homes and two barns in Bell Canyon were reported to have been destroyed.

A detachment of soldiers from the Santa Rosa air base has been assigned to patrolling the area until all danger is past.

Technical Sergeant David Sharp of the Porter Creek district has been recommended for the Distinguished Service Medal for exceptionally meritorious service in the European, African, and Middle Eastern theatres of war between November 13, 1942, and May 15, 1944.

In support of the award, his commander, Captain Carl Scull, Army Medical Corps, said:

"Sergeant Sharp has been with 6619th Prisoner of War Administrative Company since it was activated in July 1943. At that time, our work was tremendous and it was impossible to get medical personnel from the replacement depot, but through the efficiency of Sergeant Sharp, and his capacity for maintaining long hours of work, we were able to give medical aid not only to our own attached American soldiers, but to as many as 20,000 prisoners of war. At the same time, we had only four medical personnel out of sixteen allotted.

"In the construction and arrangement of hospital facilities at Prisoner of War Enclosure No. 101, largely from a heterogeneous accumulation of captured German hospital equipment, Sergeant Sharp performed exceptionally meritorious services in assorting, and making useful, equipment that looked beyond any use at all.

"Later, when our medical detachment had its full quota of men, and we were at St. Denis du Sig, and still later at Bizerte, awaiting orders for more active duty, it was only Sergeant Sharp's sturdiness of character, his almost paternal guidance, and his cheerfulness, that kept the morale of our Medical Detachment and officers at a high level. Sergeant Sharp's morale building not only affected our Medical Detachment, it permeated into the unit as a whole.

"At Prisoner of War Enclosure No. 326, Italy, his services have not only been indispensable, but miraculous, in that, at all times, regardless of whether our intake of prisoners was at a minimum or at a maximum, Sergeant Sharp had supplies for us with which we could work.

"For services beyond his call of duty, he never hesitated. At the time of the Anzio beachhead, many refugees were evacuated. Many of them were sick, wounded, pregnant, and dying. Sergeant Sharp promptly set up first aid stations outside our camp, where it was attempted, 24 hours of the day, to give them help until the American and British Red Cross were able to take over."

Note: Sharp was in the Calistoga High School class of 1938. After the war, he worked as an inspector for the Sonoma County Agriculture Department. On retirement, he turned a taxidermy hobby into a full-time occupation. Dave died in 1997.

Thirty-one servicemen signed the register during the first week of Calistoga's Hospitality House, according to Mrs. W.C. Wiggins, chairman of hostesses. All available beds were signed for by nine o'clock Saturday night, and the directors had to send out an emergency call for more cots.

If anyone has an extra cot and mattress or blankets that they can lend for the summer months of housing shortage, please phone Ray Oxford, who will pick them up.

Calistoga 1944

Last Saturday night, a young sailor and his wife and an Army Air Force officer, his wife, and baby asked for help in finding rooms. For these people and for boys who would prefer to pay for a private room, the hostesses of Hospitality House could save many precious leave-hours and much weariness if they could direct them to available rooms. Have you a room you will open to them? If so, phone Hospitality House, 172, or Mrs. Wiggins, 174-W, and your rooms will be listed.

Many of the boys who come to Calistoga are farm boys from the Mid-West. They are intensely interested and curious about California farms. One boy asked a hostess if she knew where he could find a pitch-fork. Another said he'd "love to milk a cow again." If you will take these boys home for a few hours, a home meal, or a weekend, list your name at Hospitality House.

Last Friday, the representatives of 14 women's organizations met at Hospitality House to formulate staffing plans. It was decided that the House would be open Friday afternoon and evening, all day Saturday and Sunday, and that each organization would take a weekend and be responsible for providing hostesses and entertainment for that time. Rebekah Lodge members will have charge this weekend.

The senior hostesses expressed the hope that the younger girls of the town will sign up to work with them. Every girl who wishes to serve must be sponsored by an organization or by a member of the board of directors. She will be assigned, together with a senior hostess, to definite hours, and only girls so sponsored will be permitted in the House at any time. Girls who are sixteen or less must bring the written consent of their parents.

Following are the organizations which will co-operate and have signed for dates: Colfax Rebekah Lodge, Friendly Circle, Calico Club, Civic Club, Civilian Defense, Sunnyside Club, Franz Valley Mothers' Club, The Gleaners, Women's Association of Community Church, British War Relief unit, Tucker Home Department, Catholic Ladies, Native Daughters, and Eastern Star Service Club.

Any girl or woman who wants to help, independent of an organization, may phone Mrs. Wiggins at 174-W.

In another development, articles of incorporation as a non-profit organization were issued last Friday. Dues were set at one dollar per month, with all funds to be devoted to maintaining the center, supplying entertainment, and providing for the welfare of visiting service personnel. Directors of the corporation are: Mabel

Mingus, Ben Schuman, Bernice Wiggins, Dorothy Matthews, Ray Oxford, Howard Butler, and Lois Elder, all of Calistoga.

Mr. and Mrs. W.A. Camp recently received a letter from their son, Pfc. Lloyd Camp, who has been in England for many months. Lloyd's letter, dated July 25, leaves his whereabouts uncertain, but it is thought that he is having a part in the invasion of the European continent.

Lloyd states that he is not in a position to write as often as he used to, but that he is "in the best of health and aims to stay that way."

"Please don't worry about me any more," he says, "as I am safe, and if anything does happen to me, you will be the first to know about it."

Asking his folks to renew his subscription to the *Calistogan*, Lloyd gives the following as his address: Pfc. Lloyd V. Camp, 39127164, Co. B, 526th Armored Infantry Battalion, APO 654, c/o Postmaster, New York, NY.

Housewives! Don't forget that there is a can collection tomorrow, starting at 9 a.m.

Cut the ends out of the cans, if you have not already done so. Flatten them until the sides are between one-quarter and one-half inch apart. Put them in a container on the curb in front of the house.

The tin shortage is attaining serious proportions, and every tin can that is collected and sent in to the reduction plants means just that much more tin for war materials.

The City Council met in regular session last Friday night with Mayor E.J. Stevens, Frank Piner, Ray Oxford, J.B. Ghisolfo, Howard Butler, and City Attorney Lowell Palmer in attendance.

The regular monthly report of City Treasurer Edmund Molinari was read, approved, and ordered filed. Fund balances as of July 31 were as follows: general, $6,936; water, $42.91; library, $599; ambulance, $673.93; special gas tax, $8.12; street improvement, $490.50; in lieu tax, $620.82; A.B.C., $162.16; sewer assessment bond, $1,452.64; and cemetery, $60.83.

Police Chief Ed Light reported the issuing of eight traffic citations, the arrest of one person on warrant, three persons for drunkenness, one person for disturbing the peace, and one person for vagrancy.

Police Officer Bohn reported the issuing of 46 traffic citations, the arrest of three persons for drunkenness and one person for disturbing the peace.

Police Judge Winkelman reported that 58 cases had been cited into his court during July and were disposed of as follows: three suspended sentences, three dismissals, three sentences, 46 fines totaling $154, and nine cases pending disposition.

The Council set the tax rates for the next fiscal year: 92 cents per $100 of assessed valuation for general purposes, 8 cents per $100 for the library.

Mayor Stevens appointed committees as follows: fire – Piner; streets, lights, and sewage – Ghisolfo; police – Butler; water, parks, cemetery – Oxford; finance – Mayor Stevens and councilmen Piner and Oxford.

Due to gas restrictions keeping Bay Area deer hunters confined within "A" card distances of their homes, the counties north of San Francisco Bay are faced with the problem of handling hundreds of hunters who, anxious to get their venison, ignore "No Trespassing" signs posted by land owners and swarm over ranches and range land.

Napa County is particularly infested with such nimrods. They not only enter posted land, but, once there, they defy the owner and refuse to get off. One owner reported that 50 hunters were on his property in absolute violation of the notices.

Monday, three hunters from Mill Valley were arrested by Sheriff Joseph Moore and later given fines of $25 each in the court of Judge David Wright of Napa. They were apprehended while trespassing on posted land. The Calistoga area, including Knights Valley, has been pestered with a horde of amateur hunters.

David Newton has been transferred from Army Air Corps training in Seattle to Denver, Colorado, according to his latest letter to his parents, Mr. and Mrs. George Newton of Calistoga.

"I finished school top man and tied the highest score on that field, which wasn't so bad. I hope I can do the same here. They say this is no push-over. I'll find out, I hope. A lot of the fellows want to wash out. I'll finish anything I start, if they will let me. The course here is 10 weeks, same as B-29, only the last five weeks we fly and get flying pay. We get 50 hours as co-pilot on B-17s and B-24s, and eventually end up in B-29s.

"It sure is hot here – some change from Seattle. I will enjoy this weather. May get rid of some weight, if I work hard enough."

"Oregon looks like the nicest country. It is green, which is more than I can say for Idaho or Wyoming."

Note: See David's earlier letter in Chapter 13.

Paul Rametta, former janitor at the high school and more recently cutting wood on contract, met with serious injuries Wednesday when he, in some unknown manner, fell into the saw as he was cutting wood on a power-driven unit.

Cutting wood on the Charles Davis ranch south of town, Rametta had been working all morning. Shortly after noon, Mr. and Mrs. Davis noticed a change in the sound of the saw, but they paid no particular attention. Some 30 minutes later, Davis went out to where the equipment was set up and found Rametta on the ground, badly cut up and bleeding profusely. He had lost three fingers from his left hand, the inside of his right arm was ripped open from arm-pit to wrist, and there were severe cuts on his face.

The city ambulance rushed Rametta to Calistoga Hospital. After emergency attention there, he was sent to the St. Helena Sanitarium. Reports yesterday stated that he was resting well and would recover.

With the 1944 prune harvest getting under way this week, and deliveries being made to dehydrators, agricultural experts estimate that the county will produce some 11,000 dry tons of prunes, as opposed to 16,800 tons last year.

While the War Food Administration has not yet released prices for this year, it is thought that the basic figure will be at least nine-and-a-half cents a pound -- one cent higher than in 1943.

The quality of the crop is expected to be high. No figures have been given out as to the tonnage that may be

Students Barbara Hughes, Rosalie Tedeschi, Angelene Saviez, and Jean Kelly helped in the prune harvest.

released to the consumer market this year, but it is expected to be higher than at any time during the past three years, due to the fact that a large part of last season's large crop is still in military warehouses.

Harvest and dehydrater help is none too plentiful, but it is thought that the situation will improve as the season advances. More Mexican nationals are expected to arrive within the next few weeks, and considerable local labor has signified a willingness to aid the harvesting. Fifty dehydraters are prepared to take care of the prune crop as it comes in from the orchards.

The recent burglary of the safe at Aalders' Roman Plunge has not been solved, nor a couple of other similar jobs here in town. The proprietors of the plunge reported a loss of $125. Questioning of local suspects failed to break the case.

Public pool at Dr. Aalders' Hot Springs, a popular spot for Calistoga kids as well as tourists in 1944. Now it is known as Calistoga Spa.
(Photo courtesy of Sharpsteen Museum, Calistoga)

Flight Officer Dan Taplin, who has just completed 18 months of pilot training in Arizona and California, arrived home in St. Helena this week on a 15-day leave. He is accompanied by Mrs. Taplin, the former Miss Virginia Switzer of Calistoga, who has been with her husband at his training center. Following stays with both sets of parents, they will go to Victorville, where Mr. Taplin will receive a new assignment.

Note: Virginia was a 1940 graduate of Calistoga High School.

Work continues on the making of articles to be included in the Christmas packages which will be sent to all Calistoga men and women in the armed forces as a holiday remembrance from their home town.

Out of 150 packages sent last year, only one was returned unclaimed. A second package did come back, but, by coincidence, the mother of the boy to whom it was addressed was present when the package came in. She was on her way to San Francisco to see her son, who was passing through the bay city, so she presented the gift to him personally.

After spending two years here with her grandparents, the J.E. Scotts, little Joan Scott is now on her way back to Panama, home of her parents, the Donald Scotts. Joan came to California when the Japs appeared to be a likely menace to the Canal Zone, but with that threat removed, at least to a large degree, her parents decided it would be safe for her to return home. Accompanying Joan to Los Angeles, where she will catch a plane, was her grandfather, J.E. Scott. War-time restrictions do not permit children under 12 to travel alone on trains, but no such restrictions govern plane travel.

Many incidents that occurred during the Port Chicago disaster July 16 proved the value of civilian defense training.

Says the editor of a nearby publication: "I saw Port Chicago's movie house 40 hours after the explosion. It is not a place in which I would have cared to have been on the evening of July 16. The giant fist of the blast had struck one side of the building a blow so mighty that the wall was bent crazily over one whole section of seats.

"Joe Meyers, proprietor of the movie, told me that children had been sitting in those seats when the explosion occurred. They had been told by their teachers how to act in case of bombing. When the wall came in, every one of them scrambled under the seats. And not one child was even scratched.

"There was no panic among the 196 persons who were attending the show at 10:16 on that Monday night. In good order, they filed out within a few moments after the blow had struck. Only two people out of the 196 were hurt, and they were merely scratched.

"Civilian defense training, it was a darn good thing for Port Chicago."

page 8

The engagement of Ellen Decker, eldest daughter of Mr. and Mrs. Lee Decker of Calistoga, and Charles S. Jackson of St. Helena was announced informally last week.

Ellen graduated from Calistoga High School in June and is employed in the office of the local ration board. She has two brothers in the service. Lloyd has seen considerable action on several European invasion fronts. Leland is with the U.S. Marines. She also has a sister, Bernice, of Calistoga.

Jackson is the son of Mr. and Mrs. Charles S. Jackson of St. Helena. He graduated from St. Helena High School this spring and will leave tomorrow for Florida to enter V-6 naval aviation training.

Advertisement by Greyhound bus service:

"Greyhound needs auto mechanics, body and fender men, auto trimmers, electricians – 6-day week, 8-11 hours daily, time-and-a-half over 40 hours. You can earn $350 per month and over. Men with 4-F and 1-A limited draft classifications – discharged military men – men engaged in non-essential industries.

Advertisement: NOTICE: NO HUNTING permitted on property of undersigned. Trespassers will be prosecuted to full extent of the law. Yellow Jacket Ranch, A.J. Dyer, Chick Hafey, Bert Noble, E.D. Woodruff.

Classified advertisement: "FOR SALE: 8.5-acre ranch: 5 acres young bearing grapes, 3 acres prunes and mixed orchard; 4-room house, good barn, chix houses and equipment for 1,000. Price includes everything on place, 800 hens, cow, 2 sows. Located 2 miles north of town on highway. Price $9,500. Albright Real Estate. Phone 233.

Classified advertisement: Want to exchange, with Mare Island employee, rented home in Vallejo for one in Calistoga or St. Helena. Have 3-bedroom home in government project. Leaving Vallejo because of health. D.H. Lewis, 256 Alaska St., Vallejo.

New officers for Calistoga American Legion Post 231 are: Dennis Ward, past commander; Carl Pisor, commander; Larry Duff, vice commander; James McCall, adjutant; Ben Schuman, chaplain; Richard Tucker, sergeant-at-arms.

Volunteer blood donors are reminded that the Red Cross mobile unit will be in St. Helena on August 31. Sixty Calistoga donors are wanted, so those who have not yet put their names on the list are asked to see Mrs. Mitto Blodgett, chairman of the Calistoga branch of the American Red Cross, at once.

Many people of Calistoga are concerned because there is no place here to participate in this vital and dramatic miracle of the war. Mrs. Blodgett explained that after blood is taken from a donor, it must be refrigerated in special containers and delivered to the Army and Navy processing laboratory within 24 hours. The Red Cross, the official collecting agency, has 35 blood donor centers throughout the United States. Mobile collecting units circulate within a safe operating radius of each center.

As long as the existing centers succeed in attaining Army and Navy quotas, the opening of additional centers and processing laboratories cannot be justified from the standpoint of saving manpower and Red Cross War Fund dollars, Mrs. Blodgett said.

Last year, the Red Cross filled its quota of four million pints, drawing from 75,000 donors each week. This year, the Red Cross feels that an increased quota of five million pints can be achieved from the existing setup.

Chapter 18

August 13-19

The War: French Resistance begins uprisings in Paris as Allied troops approach the Seine River.

𝔚eekly 𝔠alistogan of August 18, 1944

page 4

Editorial: We have spent some little time in wondering just why the Commander-in-Chief took that recent trip to Honolulu and the Aleutians.

Surely it could not be politics that dictated the trip, for he has stated that he was "not going to campaign in the usual sense."

It must be pure coincidence that he, after two and a half years of giving the Pacific action the well-known "brush off," calls MacArthur in from the battle fronts, has Nimitz and Halsey stand by, and then takes a United States cruiser and journeys to Honolulu.

We predict that from now until election time, the President is going to use the war as his chief means of getting votes. He is going to trade upon the hard-won victories of our fighting men, the victories won by the strategic planning of our generals and admirals, and the victories won by the blood, sweat, and tears of our sons.

As we read of the Honolulu conference, we wondered just what thoughts were passing through MacArthur's mind. We wondered if he remembered the days on Bataan, and the tragic days on Corregidor. We wondered if he remembered the early days of the campaign in the Solomons and New Guinea, when he fought with so few tools that his victories will go down in history as military miracles.

We wondered if he harked back to his own turmoil of mind when he realized that the Commander-in-Chief had his eyes turned to the East, sending armor, ships, and men to England, while the remnants of a fine army struggled against a superior foe in the Southwest Pacific.

The mid-Atlantic conference was held. Quebec took the spotlight when the Commander-in-Chief journeyed there to sit in council with the men from the East. Cairo came and went. The Teheran conference became history – and still the western front took the crumbs from the feast of arms and carried on.

But now the story changes. Nimitz, Halsey, MacArthur, Spruance, Stillwell, and a host of other commanding officers have wrested victory from apparent defeat, and now, with the election less than three months away, the Commander-in-Chief stoops to use those victories, and those men, to perpetuate himself in office.

The Commander-in-Chief is going to play upon the heartstrings of millions of Americans in an endeavor to convince them that he, and he alone, is responsible for our success in arms, both in the Pacific and European theaters.

It reminds us of a prize fight, where the victor has stood up under heavy punishment and, by dogged perseverance, has won his battle. His arm is raised as a token of victory, and just then his manager hops into the ring and dances around, hands grasped above his head, shouting, "We won! We won!"

Local News Briefs: Charles Westbay, who has recently returned from service in the South Pacific, is spending two weeks in Calistoga with his mother, Mrs. R. Westbay.

Stella Hartinger, daughter of Mr. and Mrs. John Hartinger, left for San Francisco during the early part of this month. She will enter St. Joseph's Hospital for Cadet Nurse Corps training. Stella graduated from Calistoga High School in June. She is the first local girl to join up for this important work.

Calistoga High School had an average daily attendance of 108 during the 1943-44 school year. The total for Napa County was 1,380 students.

Note: In 2012, CHS has 250 students in grades 9-12.

Chapter 19

September 3-9

The War: Allied troops free Brussels, Antwerp, and other key centers in Belgium. The first German V2 rockets explode in London. Gen. Charles DeGaulle forms a provisional government in France. Bulgaria makes peace with Russia, declares war on Germany.

𝖂𝖊𝖊𝖐𝖑𝖞 𝕮𝖆𝖑𝖎𝖘𝖙𝖔𝖌𝖆𝖓 of September 8, 1944

page 1

News was received this week that Corporal Bertram Washabaugh has been reported as missing since August 17 following action in France with an anti-tank division.

Bert, son of Mrs. Robert Sylvester of Franz Valley and brother of Laura Sylvester, joined the Army some time before Pearl Harbor. He was sent overseas in May of this year and landed in France on the third day of the invasion.

A graduate of Franz Valley Grammar School, he later attended Santa Rosa High School and a business college there. He worked for Pacific Gas and Electric Company in the Sacramento and San Joaquin valleys.

Washabaugh is the fifth Calistoga boy reported as dead or missing in action.

In the fall of 1943, Lieutenant Jackson Clary was listed as missing following an air mission over Germany. Clary turned up in England after having landed in occupied territory, where the French underground helped in his escape.

Flight officer Walter P. Van der Kamp died when his plane was hit during a bombing raid in Germany last February (see *Weekly Calistogan*, Chapter 4). His wife recently was notified that he had received two awards and that they will be presented to her at ceremonies at the Santa Rosa air field.

Staff Sergeant James Barthel, whose wife is the former Jackie Cole of Calistoga, was shot down over Italy and listed as missing in action. The story of his landing by parachute, his rescue by Italian soldiers, and the bombing of the hospital where he was recuperating formed an intensely interesting document (see Chapter 2). He eventually was hospitalized in South Africa and then returned to the United States.

Frank Burns, one-time high school student here, has been reported missing since shortly after the start of the war in the Pacific. Hope is held that he is a prisoner of war.

During September of last year, Ensign Dave Senter, son of Mrs. Mabelle Senter, met his death in a plane crash on the East Coast.

Don Camp, one of four Camp brothers in the service, received his medical discharge about a year ago, after having been wounded in action in the South Pacific. He is now home.

Two local boys are known to be prisoners of Japan. Jack Cole, son of Howard Cole, was captured when Corregidor fell. He is in a prison camp in the Philippines. Eddie Cook, son of Lucky Cook, was captured at Wake Island, where he was a civilian employee in construction work. He is in a camp in Shanghai, China.

With more and more wounded being hospitalized at Mare Island and other Bay Area service hospitals, the need for crutches and canes has become acute.

American Legion posts are collecting all crutches and canes that can be spared. The Calistoga post asks that local residents who have the needed equipment bring it to the Legion Hall on Lincoln Avenue. Donations may be left in the barrel in front of the hall.

Every pair of crutches will enable some wounded serviceman to get up and about. Those men who are less seriously wounded and in the process of recovering will welcome a cane to help them get the exercise necessary to their full recovery.

Following months of negotiations with the Federal Communications Commission and other federal agencies, the Napa County Sheriff's Office has received permission to install a two-way radio system to operate between headquarters and all patrol cars.

Long a "dead spot" within the net of law enforcement communications in Northern California, Napa County is, at last, able to modernize the system of communication between the sheriff's office and the prowl cars that are constantly on the move. A teletype machine was installed some time back, and through its functioning, the office has been kept in constant touch with various agencies outside the county. Unfortunately, such bulletins lost the greater part of their value due to the inability of the officers in charge to communicate with outside deputies.

Once the new system is in operation, Napa County officers will be able to keep in touch with the officers of sheriffs in all of the North Bay area. Arrangements will be made with Sonoma and Marin counties whereby Napa County will be able to use the repeater stations on Mount St. Helena and Mount Tamalpais, at no cost to the local organization. Construction will get under way in the next 60 days.

Longtime resident Domenico Barberis died Sunday at Calistoga Hospital after an extended heart ailment. He was one of the best known of the old-time vineyardists of this end of the valley, a long-time member of Bennett Farm Center, and a director of the St. Helena Co-operative Winery.

Mr. Barberis was born in Murialdo, Italy, April 22, 1880. In April of 1901, he came to the United States, and almost immediately to this valley. After a few months of employment in the St. Helena area, he went to Oat Hill, where he worked in the mine for a brief time, and then to Dawson, New Mexico, where he was also engaged in mining.

In 1907, he returned to Calistoga and purchased a ranch which had been owned by J.R. Thairwall. Soon afterward, he sent for his bride-to-be, Gilda Ermene Stella. Their marriage took place in St. Helena in 1908, and together they had lived on the ranch ever since.

He is survived by his wife, Gilda, and five adult children – Mary Saviez, Lena Carlenzoli, Milena Barberis, and Edythe Triglia, all of Calistoga, and Corporal Frank Barberis, who is stationed with the Army at Fort Knight, Oakland; a sister, Mrs. Severina Parodi of St. Helena; a brother, John Barberis of Calistoga; other brothers and sisters in Italy; and nine grandchildren.

The Rosary was recited Monday evening at Simic Funeral Home. Tuesday morning, the funeral service was held at Our Lady of Perpetual Help Church in Calistoga, where a Requiem High Mass was celebrated for the repose of his soul. Father W.P. Walsh officiated. Burial took place in the St. Helena Catholic Cemetery.

Jackie Pacheteau was injured early yesterday morning while riding toward St. Helena on his motorcycle. As he made the turn at St. Gothard Tavern, a large bus swung into the path of the motorcycle before Jackie could swing out of the way. A crash resulted. Examination at the St. Helena Sanitarium, where he was taken after the accident, revealed that Pacheteau was suffering from a broken leg, cuts, and contusions.

Note: After the war, Jack was a prominent race car driver.

Gwendolyn Tuttle, assistant director of the Napa Welfare Board for the past six years, left for Washington, D.C., yesterday for service with the American Red Cross as assistant field director – military service. Miss Tuttle will take a three-week course in Washington and then be assigned to active duty overseas, she hopes. Mrs. Ralph Merry of Calistoga has been appointed to the post vacated by Miss Tuttle.

Judge J.B. Winkelman handled three cases in the local court this week. Henry Moranda pleaded guilty to drunken driving. He was fined $150, which he paid. Paul Carr, arrested on a charge of assault and battery, also pleaded guilty. He was fined $25. Louis Taucher, Ord Allaway, and Earl Hunt, arrested July 31 for violation of game laws, changed their minds regarding a jury trial and pleaded guilty. They were fined $125 each. All paid.

In the service since August 9, Ray Leggitt is now with the Army military police at Fort Custer, Michigan, according to his wife, the former Marian Newton of Calistoga. Mrs. Leggitt is staying here with her parents, Mr. and Mrs. George S. Newton. She plans to go East, however, as soon as she is certain that her husband will be there for a considerable period of time. Before Mr. Leggitt's induction, they made their home in San Jose.

Reporting the sale of the former Elizabeth Wright home on Cedar Street, Mrs. Alice Fisher of Fisher Realty Co. states that the new owners, Mr. and Mrs. George Dixon of San Francisco, plan on making their home here in the near future. The Dixons will remodel and modernize their new property and will probably convert part of the house into apartments.

Fifty-seven Calistoga residents journeyed to St. Helena on August 31 and made their donations to the Red Cross Mobile Blood Bank.

They are: Mrs. Josie Ratto, Mrs. Clarence Thom, Mrs. Donna McGreane, Miss Julia Ford, Mrs. Grace Molinari, Mrs. Earl Nance, Edna Patton, Mrs. Lauren Procter, Mrs. William Manford, Mrs. Al Evans, and Florence Barber.

Mrs. L.P. Ames, Mrs. Mabel Coolidge, Mrs. C.J. McGill, Mrs. Odette Schmitt, Mrs. Buford Clark, Mrs. Minnie Katzman, Mrs. H.C. Staub, Irene Caril, Mrs. H. Hart, Mrs. R.L. Page, Mrs. H.L. Bounsall, Mrs. George Locey, Mrs. Pearl Simms, and Mrs. Leoni.

Mrs. W.T. Bentley, Mrs. O. Ottonello, Mrs. H.W. Johnston, Arthur Label, Fred Lerner, Mrs. C.C. Simic, Allan Forbes, Mrs. Bill Cavagnaro, Mrs. Hembrow, Mrs. Stanley Locey, Mrs. R. Westbay, Fred Tedeschi, Mrs. L.S. Mitchell, Miss Virginia Harmon, Mrs. Edith Fechter, La Verne Clayton, Mrs. Calhoun, Mrs. Stilipec, and Joan Ward.

Mrs. June Snodgrass, Mrs. Jack Kelley, Mrs. A.M. Pearl, George Miller, Mr. and Mrs. Frank Tamagni, Mrs. C.E. Boland, George Newton, Mrs. Thelma Tamagni, Mrs. Kathleen Levy, Mrs. Jack Matthews, Mrs. Frank Pocai, Mrs. Chapin F. Tubbs, Mrs. Glenn Grier, and Mrs. Carl Ball.

Calistoga's annual Christmas project, a gift-box to every local man and woman with the armed forces, is taking shape rapidly, with various organizations and individuals working every day to have the boxes ready for mailing ahead of the deadline for such mail.

Mrs. C.J. McGill and Grace Lincoln are making handkerchiefs to be included with the many other gifts contained by the boxes, says Mrs. Jack Matthews, who is in charge of the packing.

Albert (Mickey) Mercer, in charge of listing names of the servicemen, reports that there are many names still lacking. He states that several families of Calistoga men in the service have left the vicinity, and he urges any friends or relatives of such men to bring in their names and addresses at the earliest possible moment. The committee in charge of the assembling and mailing of the gifts wants every person from Calistoga who is in the service to receive a gift box. Unless the names are turned in, there may be some who will be neglected.

More funds are needed, as there are more boxes going out this year, and each box will carry more items than those that have gone out in previous years. Frank Piner, at Bank of America, will receive all donations.

Napa County residents who wish to cast their ballots in the November general elections must register on or before September 28, according to County Clerk Ralph A. Dollarhide.

Dollarhide urges unregistered citizens to call immediately at the registration office in the courthouse at Napa, or to see a registration clerk in their own communities.

Voters who failed to cast ballots in the 1942 elections must register again, if they did not re-register before or since the May primary this year. Those who have changed residence also must register. Newcomers may register to vote in the November election if they have resided in California at least one year, in Napa County for not less than 90 days, and in the precinct in which they will vote for at least 40 days.

In a statement aimed to clarify the recent grape price figures released by the Office of Price Administration, Dewey Baldocchi, member of the OPA advisory board on juice grapes, advises that the $66-a-ton figure used in press releases does not mean growers will receive only that price. Nor does it mean, he said, that there is any ceiling on wine grapes.

Wineries are already paying $95 a ton in the San Joaquin Valley, and they are free to pay any price they please, as there is no ceiling at the grower level.

The $66 figure, said Baldocchi, is only a minimum which reflects the technicalities of the law governing OPA, which must guarantee parity to farmers.

Baldocchi said growers should receive $125 a ton this year, on the basis of wine ceilings. He said they received $80 per ton last year, when OPA set $30.30 as the legal price.

Public Notice: The J.B. Garrison family wishes to thank all of their white friends who made it possible for them to stay in Calistoga as long as they did, and who have as their motto, "Live and let live."

My family and I would have stayed longer had we not believed in peace.

There are a few white people in the little town of Calistoga who do not like Negroes, and the Garrison family made a problem for them. Some of these Negro haters are in business and educational work, so we are going in order that we may have rest.

We are not able to pay all of our white friends in dollars and cents for what they have done for us. But our Heavenly Father, who owns this whole world, will pay you double for your kindness toward his colored children who have been among you. For it is as He says in his Holy Bible: "Inasmuch as ye have done it unto one of the least of these, my brethren, ye have done it unto Me."

May God give you long life and happiness. And some day, if ever you hear of the Garrison family, you will say to yourself, "I helped them when they were in the city of Calistoga."

To the Negro haters, we wish to say only this: all of your crooked work and what you did to scare the Garrison family failed. The other colored people who were here ran before they found out who was back of it – people who were smiling in their faces, but at the same time making trouble. But I want you to know that everything you have tried has failed, even though you thought of having the health board here write something and say it was from Los Angeles. I want you to know that I wrote to them, too, and received a good reply from them, and from San Francisco too; so I was smarter than you thought.

But we believe in peace, and that is what we want you to have – rest, if our Heavenly Father is willing for you to have rest.

J.B. Garrison

Note: See reactions in Chapter 21 and Chapter 26.

Chapter 20

September 10-16

The War: U.S. troops liberate Luxembourg. The first Allied troops enter Germany near Aachen. U.S. troops reach the Siegfried Line – the western wall of Germany's defense system. U.S. Marines land on Peleliu island east of the Philippines; dug- in Japanese troops will fight for 10 weeks.

𝔚𝔢𝔢𝔨𝔩𝔶 𝔠𝔞𝔩𝔦𝔰𝔱𝔬𝔤𝔞𝔫 of September 15, 1944

page 1

Representatives from Calistoga, Napa, St. Helena, and the Veterans' Home outlined their programs for post-war construction Wednesday at a meeting with a State Senate interim committee in Napa. In turn, they listened to a resumé of just what the state plans to do in assisting municipalities to provide work for returning servicemen and build up a back-log of construction projects designed to protect the state, as a whole, against unemployment and a consequent depression.

City Clerk George Locey gave a detailed account of Calistoga's need for an adequate distribution system to handle the water from the recently constructed municipal reservoir. He said the city is supplied by a six-inch main, which was installed some 50 years ago and is not capable of handling the present-day needs.

County Supervisor Thomas Maxwell presented a six-point program prepared by the Napa Planning Council. It includes the Conn Valley dam project, sewage disposal for the City of Napa and contingent territory, construction of an adequate approach to the new four-lane Napa-Vallejo highway, construction of a new city hall for Napa, an addition to the county court house, and general street and sidewalk improvements.

St. Helena spokesmen said the city is in dire need of an increased water supply, which can be attained by increasing the

147

capacity of the present reservoir. They also stressed the need of street improvements and additional facilities at the high school.

The meeting brought out many phases of post-war planning that may easily lead to changes in state plans for aid to municipalities.

Another boy who is well known in Calistoga has given his life for his country. According to a telegram from the Secretary of War, Staff Sergeant William C. Richter of Lindsay, California, was killed in action over England on August 1 while serving as a mechanic and gunner on a Flying Fortress.

The news reached *The Calistogan* in a letter from Bill's sister, Haidie, with a clipping from a Lindsay newspaper. She said Bill lived in Calistoga for 11 years and attended grade school here. Their father, Frank Richter, owned the People's Meat Market for a time. In 1930, the family moved to Lindsay, where Mr. Richter purchased a hotel.

The Lindsay newspaper has the following to say about Bill.

"Sergeant Richter had been in England since the first part of July. On July 27, he wrote in a V-mail letter, the last the family received, that there had been 'nothing exciting' as yet, so it is presumed his crew had not at that time been on a bombing mission. Since the above letter, however, information received indicates he later had been on several missions over Germany.

"Entering the service December 31, 1942, Sergeant Richter had first studied radio, then took training at the gunner and mechanics school at San Antonio, Texas. His duties consisted of testing the radio and equipment just before each flight. When the flight started, he took his place as a gunner.

"Sergeant Richter was 28. He is survived by his mother, one sister, two daughters, and a grandmother."

Due to the lack of harvest help, the Calistoga School Board decided Monday to set back the elementary and high schools' opening date from September 25 to October 2. The full-time schedule of classes will start then. Classes at the high school will start at 9 a.m. in order to coincide with the starting hour of the elementary school.

The school bus run will be extended this year to include Mount St. Helena, where six children will be picked up daily.

The board appointed Charles O. Fink as custodian for the high school and named Mrs. Ward Taylor as secretary of the unified school district.

City officials and local law enforcement officers were considerably shocked Monday when Herman A. Buckner, field representative of the Federal Security Agency, Division of Social Protection, visited Calistoga to investigate reports from military enlisted men that they received venereal infections during visits here.

Armed with documentary evidence to support his investigation, Buckner gave Calistoga authorities full information regarding the sources of those cases.

Buckner said his agency seeks to work with communities in protecting servicemen. Whenever possible, officers and officials of those communities are given all available data as to when, where, and from whom the infection was received.

Buckner went on to say that some 300,000 servicemen are now confined to hospitals due to venereal diseases, a number that represents 20 divisions. Each of these men is incapacitated for a minimum of 30 days. "It is obvious," said Buckner, "that only by education can this appalling situation be remedied. The individual soldier must be educated in the matter of prophylactic protection, and communities must be educated to protect the servicemen within their gates by controlling prostitution and the 'pick-up' girls that prey upon these servicemen."

Royce Lathrop, 15-year-old son of Mr. and Mrs. Homer Lathrop of Calistoga, may have impaired sight for the rest of his life following an accident last Friday night in which a shot from a BB gun in the hands of his brother, Vernon, hit Royce in the eye.

It is not known just how the incident occurred, as it was just one of those things which so often happen when youngsters "fool" with guns.

Royce was first rushed to the St. Helena Sanitarium by his parents, who were advised to take the boy to an eye specialist. They took him next morning to a specialist in Santa Rosa and, later in the day, to Stanford Hospital in San Francisco. There, a specialist removed the BB shot from the eye. There is no information available at the present time as to the extent of the injury to the eye. Since the shot entered the eyeball below the pupil and the cornea, it is hoped that his sight will not be lost.

After six years in Calistoga, L.S. Mitchell, owner of Mitchell's Market and Mitchell's Feed Store, is closing his cash-and-carry market tomorrow night. He will continue the feed store here. A large portion of the unsold stock of the market has been taken to Mitchell's store in Middletown.

Mitchell said he plans to open a grocery store in Calistoga after the war. The exact location has not yet been chosen.

Note: Mitchell eventually opened a store at Highway 29 and Tubbs Lane. The name remains though ownership has changed.

Meeting at Healdsburg Tuesday, members of the Grape Growers' Association from Napa, Sonoma, and Mendocino counties agreed to minimum prices of $150 per ton for standard whites and $135 per ton for standard black wine grapes.

Dewey Baldocchi, president of the association, presided at the meeting, which was called following conflicting and ambiguous ceiling prices announced by the Office of Price Administration (OPA).

"The prices agreed upon by the growers' organization will be submitted to vintners and considered by them," Baldocchi said.

Mr. and Mrs. H.C. Staub of Calistoga have received the news that their son, Stanley Harry Staub, RM 2/c, USN, has been reported missing in action since August 30. While the younger Mr. Staub has never lived in Calistoga, the news that he is missing is received here with sincere regret. Sympathy is extended to his parents, who now live here.

When he was last heard from, young Staub had been in action at Guam and in the Elice Islands. Previously, he had been stationed in and near Honolulu. He made his home in San Francisco before entering the service some 15 month ago. A brother, Mortimer Staub, also is in the Navy.

Army PFC Riley C. McEuen, has been cited for heroic action on February 3, 1944, according to the information received by McEuen's mother in Calistoga, Mrs. Clara McEuen.

"Private First Class McEuen, after taking an automatic rifle from a wounded man, rushed forward to a position from which he could place effective fire on the enemy. In so doing, he exposed himself to heavy small arms fire which had already mortally wounded two of his comrades. McEuen's initiative and aggressiveness aided materially in repelling the enemy attack and were an inspiration to every member of his platoon."

Note: The article did not say where the action took place.

Plans of the local American Legion post to stage a rodeo here on Armistice Day are approaching completion, members were told Monday night. Larry Duff, chairman of the rodeo committee, said he is about to sign up with J.H. Rowell, Hayward rodeo impresario, for the staging of the show. Final details will be released next week.

Note: Armistice Day was a national holiday celebrating the end of World War I on November 11, 1918. 11/11 is still a holiday, but it is called Veterans Day.

A fire burning since last weekend has blackened some 20,000 acres in Lake County, destroyed two resorts, threatened several others, and swept to the outskirts of Middletown.

Fire fighting equipment from as far away as San Mateo County was called in to help control the blaze. Ashes from the fire fell in Calistoga on Saturday and Sunday in sufficient quantities to form a gray film on streets and sidewalks. Since then, the fall was lighter but noticeable.

The blaze originated at Pine Flat. Houdd Gibson Resort, recently remodeled, was destroyed, as was Mira Vista Resort on Cobb Mountain. Backfiring by fire crews saved other resorts and summer home areas. In Middletown, a large percentage of the population hurriedly packed belongings to be able to make a fast escape.

Volunteers from the Calistoga branch of American Red Cross served on a mobile canteen. Mrs. Frank Pocai, head of the branch's emergency canteen service, enlisted the aid of six members: Mrs. Harry Coulter, Mrs. Bill Cavagnaro, Mrs. L.E. Light, Mrs. D.N. Dixon, Mrs. Mazie Lawson, and Mrs. Glenn Rodgers.

Rotarians this week heard a recuperating Marine private describe his experiences fighting in the South Pacific. It was one of the best talks heard at Rotary for some time.

The club was meeting in a new place, the club rooms of the Civic Club. Due to circumstances beyond their control, the Rotarians were recently forced to give up their meeting place at the Hotel Calistoga, a move which is regretted by the members, as they had been meeting there for many years. Present plans call for the Civic Club room to be the permanent meeting place, with catering to be handled by Rotarian Ross Reeder and his staff from Reeder's Creamery.

Calistoga 1944

For the first time, military training will be offered as a part of the curriculum at Napa Junior College during the fall semester, according to an announcement by Principal H.M. McPherson.

Youths in the 11th, 12th, and 13th grades are eligible for the classes, to be held twice weekly. They will consist of instruction in the manual of arms, close and open order drill, marksmanship, and lectures on "how to get along in the armed services."

Retired Marine Corps Major G.W. Walker has been retained to instruct the classes. Major Walker has recently completed training designed to fit him for this work.

The new "A" gasoline ration book now being issued to California motorists for use beginning September 22 has new safety features. "A" coupons will have serial numbers, useful in spotting stolen coupons. When issuing the new books, War Price and Rationing Boards record the serial numbers of the coupons along with the name of the person to whom they are issued. The new coupons are printed on a special kind of safety paper which responds to a secret test known only to government identification experts. Counterfeit coupons on imitation paper may look the same to the untrained eye, but will show up the minute this secret test is applied.

A third safety feature, not new, is the endorsement of the motorist. The cover of the "A" book reminds motorists to write or stamp the car license number and state of registration immediately on the face of each coupon – otherwise, the coupons are invalid and may be revoked.

As long as it is necessary to ration gasoline, it is important to guard against the misuse or counterfeiting of the currency that assures each citizen a fair share.

Skies may be blue, but not ration tokens after October 1, the Office of Price Administration (OPA) announces. After that date, blue tokens will be discontinued and blue ration stamps alone will be needed for the purchase of canned fruits and juices, canned tomatoes, catsup, and chili sauce. Food point values will be set up in such a way that most items remaining under rationing will be worth 10, 20, or 30 points, enabling housewives to use their 10-point blue stamps without change being needed. The points to keep in mind are these:

1. You may use blue tokens, just as you've been using them, until September 17.

2. After that time, you will receive no blue tokens in change.

3. And use all your blue tokens by the last day of September, because they are no good after that date.

4. September 17-30, we can spend our blue points only in groups of ten. In fact, no fewer than ten tokens can be used; if you don't have ten, you can pool your seven with a neighbor's three to make the required number.

The substitution of cotton for leather in the gun slings of Army rifles accounts for one of the many uses G.I. Joe makes of the same source material that goes into his wife's dresses or his baby's rompers. The taxpayers have saved $5 million on the switch-over since August, 1942, states the San Jacinto Ordnance Depot, Houston, Texas, which has placed 13.3 million orders for web slings in the past two years. The slings are treated for protection against moisture, mold, and general jungle conditions.

page 4

Editorial: A State Senate committee on motor vehicles is reported to be considering a proposal to charge one dollar for each automobile operator's permit issued.

For years, these permits have been issued free of charge. Why should any charge, however small, now be made for them? Certainly, the highway users of this state are paying out plenty in gasoline, personal property, and license taxes, and taxes on virtually everything they use in connection with their cars.

Even under gasoline rationing, Californians are putting out approximately $4 million monthly in gasoline taxes. Of course, not all of this is paid by individual motorists. A large part is paid by commercial vehicles, such as buses and trucks, which also pay many millions in other forms of taxes not imposed on individual car owners.

Over the years, automotive taxes have been steadily rising. From the start of the gasoline tax in 1919, the various governmental bodies have found the motoring field a most lucrative one for tax returns. In 1942, for example, special taxes on trucks totaled more than $539 million. In 1927, such taxes amounted to $144 million. Even as between 1942 and 1943, special taxes on commercial motor vehicle operators increased 12.8 percent.

No one is likely to be financially depleted by paying one dollar every four years when his driver's permit is renewed or when a new one is issued. But it is high time for the lawmakers to give thought to reducing, not increasing, taxes on highway users.

Calistoga 1944

Calistoga Community Church is launching a drive for funds to renovate the Presbyterian Church building at Third and Washington streets. It has been estimated that $10,000 will be needed. Because of the present national emergency, the actual construction of the new building will not be undertaken at the present time, but it is hoped that the relocation of part of the current building can begin quite soon, as very little in the way of materials will be needed to accomplish this first step.

It is hoped that all residents of Calistoga who are interested in developing the town's best assets – its schools and churches – will take a part in helping this building program.

Mrs. Mitto Blodgett, chairman of the building committee, is receiving contributions. Her phone number is 26. Other committee members are Mrs. C. Ingalls, secretary; Mrs. Gordon Hunt, financial secretary; and Mrs. Ray Oxford, treasurer.

Governor Thomas E. Dewey
(Photo, public domain)

Governor Thomas E. Dewey of New York will make a major address in his campaign for the presidency from Seals Stadium in San Francisco next Thursday. The Republican standard bearer will be introduced by Governor Earl Warren.

That Dewey will bring his heaviest guns to bear on the New Deal in his San Francisco address is considered certain in view of the importance of carrying California, a pivotal state in the November election. California, now third state in the Union in population, is considered more than likely to swing to the Republican side.

A son was born to Mr. and Mrs. Arthur Leoni in San Diego on September 5. Arthur, a Calistogan, is in the Navy. The baby's grandparents are Mr. and Mrs. Joseph Leoni of the Bennett district.

Note: Arthur and two classmates quit Calistoga High School in January 1941 to join the Navy. He retired after 30 years and three wars, with the rank of master chief of aircraft maintenance. He lives in Chula Visa.

Local News Briefs:

Einor Berg, whose wife is the former Evangeline Carlson of Calistoga, has been wounded in action and is now somewhere in France in an American hospital. Mrs. Berg is making her home in San Francisco.

Her brother, Wilbur Carlson, now in the merchant marine, recently returned from eight months of service in the New Guinea area. He is on a 30-day furlough with his family. His wife is the former Catherine Nolasco of Calistoga.

Note: Evangeline, Wilbur, and Catherine were graduates of Calistoga High School in 1934, 1936, and 1937, respectively.

After spending a few days with family in Calistoga, Bretta Lundell of the U.S. Waves has returned to her station in San Diego. Miss Lundell is the only daughter of the H. Lundells of the Tucker district.

Note: Bretta, a 1928 graduate of Calistoga High School, returned to town after the war and worked at Bank of America. She died in 2000.

page 8

War Food Facts bulletins received by the local Civil Defense office this week give the following information:

Bread and milk – Non-fat milk solids are in good domestic supply now, so the War Food Administration has amended War Food Order No. 1 to remove all restrictions on their use in the manufacture of bread, effective August 22. This will enable bakers to return to the pre-war standards, averaging about six parts of milk to 100 parts of flour.

Olive oil – American consumers may soon be seeing more imported olive oil on their grocers' shelves. The WFA has made arrangements with the government of Spain for the export of 3,000 tons of olive oil to the United States. Olive oil was among the several oils returned to private trade by the WFA several months ago, and no permit is necessary to import it.

Butter – Homemakers will be able to buy four out of every five pounds of butter manufactured in September. In other words, 20 percent of the butter will be set aside by manufacturers for war uses.

Chapter 21

September 17-23

The War: Allied troops capture Brest, France, an important English Channel port. Russia and Finland sign an armistice. Russia takes Tallinn, Estonia. U.S. troops capture Ulithi Atoll in the Pacific, which will become an important naval base.

Politics: The second Dumbarton Oaks Conference begins; it will set guidelines for the United Nations.

Weekly Calistogan of September 22, 1944

page 1

City officials, led by Mayor Edward J. Stevens, said a thorough investigation has shown there is absolutely no indication of the existence of any house of ill-repute here, nor is the town harboring any known prostitutes.

They said Herman A. Buckner, representative of the Federal Security Agency, who visited Calistoga last week, failed to inform anyone in authority here as to specific cases of prostitution and that he bordered on misrepresenting the few facts in his possession.

Buckner replied, in a statement to the press, that he had fully informed authorities here of specific instances where servicemen received venereal infections from prostitutes.

Calistoga receives regular visits from the office of the FBI in Santa Rosa, and the investigator who covers this territory has been familiar with conditions here for the past two years. He states that he has always been able to give Calistoga a clean bill of health and considers it one of the cleanest towns, morally, in his territory.

Mr. and Mrs. N. Montelli of Tucker district have received the news that their son, John, who is overseas with the U.S. Army, has been awarded the Bronze Star, with the following citation:

"Corporal John P. Montelli, 20908935, Army Corps of Engineers. For his heroic achievement in connection with a counterattack by the enemy on February 4, 1944, during the Kwajalein operation. Corporal Montelli became separated from his unit during the heavy counterattack, in which the enemy infiltrated in large groups. Disregarding the fact that he was in an occupied area infested with the enemy and often exposed to heavy fire, Corporal Montelli occupied a position near a wooden shack which seemed to be the operating headquarters for the enemy. Through his extremely accurate rifle fire, he was responsible for killing or wounding eight of the enemy who were causing considerable casualties among the troops. Corporal Montelli's actions, without regard for his own safety, undoubtedly saved the lives of many friendly troops and were in keeping with the highest traditions of the military service."

John, who has been in the Army about a year and a half, is well known in Calistoga. He attended the local high school with the class of 1941 before entering the service. He has a brother, Vito, who is in the Navy. Another brother, Louis, expects to enter Navy service soon; and a sister, Mary, is a 1941 graduate of Calistoga High School.

Note: John returned to Calistoga after the war and worked as a building contractor. He died in 1987. Many of his kids and grand-kids have attended Calistoga schools.

Some of the huskiest bucks seen in town since the opening of the hunting season were brought in Monday night by Nieman Sledge and Jesse Manuel, returning home from a hunt in Modoc and Shasta counties. Their three mule deer weighed 175, 187, and 235 pounds, dressed out. The big buck boasted four points; the others, three points.

Angelo Demattei and Laurence Demattei, sons of Mr. and Mrs. Lory Demattei, are moving up the ladder of promotion in the Army. Both now wear the two stripes of a corporal.

Angelo, after intensive training in radar at various Army schools, is on his way overseas. Rated as a crew chief, he also has charge of all athletic equipment used by his outfit.

Laurence received his corporal's stripes at the completion of training at a Texas air base. He is stationed in Colorado. Already rated as an aerial gunner, Laurence will undoubtedly be sent to an action front after completion of his present course.

Both boys recently spent short furloughs with their parents. They were prominent in athletics at Calistoga High School with the classes of 1940 and 1943, respectively.

Note: Both returned to Calistoga and participated in town team sports.

Another "unloaded gun" came close to bringing tragedy to a local family Tuesday when a rifle was accidentally fired by the youngster handling it.

Charley Mariani, returning from a hunting trip, left his .300 Savage in one of the bedrooms in his home. The gun was left with the chamber empty, but the magazine was full of shells.

Mariani's boys, Norman and Elvin, entered the house and went into the bedroom, where Elvin busied himself with a slingshot he was making, while Norman picked up the rifle.

As the shades were drawn in the bedroom, Norman went into the next room, where there was more light, and proceeded to examine the gun. Throwing back the bolt, he found that there was no shell in the chamber, and then closed the breech. Not aware of the fact that a shell had been brought into the chamber when he closed the bolt, the youngster pulled the trigger to lower the hammer.

The shell exploded and the bullet nicked off the lobe of Elvin's ear. A few inches to the left and the boy would have been killed. As it is, he will carry a nicked lobe for the rest of his life as a reminder that improperly handled guns are dangerous.

Note: Elvin (nickname: Buster) says details of the incident aren't correct. But the bottom line is the same. The bullet scratched his temple and tore his ear in half. Dr. McGreane sewed it up with 23 stitches. "The good Lord had something else for me to do," he says. He is a retired teacher and a great-grandfather.

Organizations preparing Calistoga's Christmas gift boxes for local servicemen and women are hard at work assembling the contents and making preparations for mailing them at the earliest possible date.

Mrs. Jack Matthews, in charge of the project, said the boxes will contain more gift items than in past years, although there will be no cigarettes or chewing gum. This is brought about by the shortage of both items. It has been ascertained, however, that both cigarettes and gum are available to those in the service, and the items being substituted for them will be more welcome.

The gift packages cannot be delivered unless they contain the full name, rank, and military address. Check with "Mickey" Mercer at his jewelry store on Lincoln Avenue and make sure that he has all the necessary current data. A gift box will be exhibited in Mercer's window today.

Donations for the gift fund have been coming in, but more is needed. Contributions may be made to Frank Piner or Edmund Molinari at Bank of America.

Mr. and Mrs. Arthur Emerick of Napa, formerly of Tucker district, have received word from the War Department that their son, Pfc. Milton Revere Emerick, was killed in action in France on August 3.

Young Emerick was born near Calistoga. He attended Napa schools and, before entering the service, was employed at Mare Island. His father for many years has been the superintendent of the Napa County Mosquito Abatement District.

Registration for pupils at Calistoga High School will take place at the school next Friday, September 29, from 1 to 5 p.m. and 7 to 9 p.m. and Saturday, September 30, from 1 to 5 p.m.

All students are required to register, even those who registered last spring. This is because several changes have been made in the classes offered, according to the new principal, Jack Rannells.

There will be eight periods each day. New classes include current history, public speaking, mechanical drawing for girls, orientation for all freshmen, and driver education.

Girls' P.E. will be held in the seventh period instead of the eighth, as in the past. Another change is the dropping of Spanish classes for the coming year. Chemistry and physics will be taught only in alternate years. The school day will start at 9 a.m., with a 50-minute lunch period, and classes dismissed at 3:36 p.m.

Andrew J. Higgins, formerly of Calistoga, has recently been employed at Sierra Ordnance Depot at Herlong, California. It is a key Army depot for the shipping of supplies and ammunition to fighting men in the Pacific battle zone.

Higgins is the son of Mrs. Rhoda Higgins of Calistoga.

Men and women of prominence in the fields of literature, education, and art have given enthusiastic response to the request that their names be included in the membership of the committee dedicated to raising funds to be devoted to the purchase of property for the proposed Robert Louis Stevenson Memorial Park on Mount St. Helena.

Even before the fund-raising campaign has started, almost half of the goal has been deposited in the bank account, which is being handled by Jack Behrens, treasurer of the committee.

The committee, under the leadership of chairman Ralph P. Winston, is ready to send out letters with an illustrated pamphlet showing views of the mountain and describing the memorial project.

All of the parlors of the Native Daughters and the Native Sons organizations in California are giving support to the park.

Stevenson, the noted Scottish author, and his bride spent a two-month honeymoon in an abandoned mining camp on Mount St. Helena. He wrote a book, *Silverado Squatters*, about their time in the Calistoga area.

Note: Winston, the de facto *editor of the* Weekly Calistogan, *gave extensive news coverage to creation of the park.*

The California State Railroad Commission this week approved the merger of the Vallejo Express Company and the Vallejo, Napa, and Calistoga Transportation Company. The merger calls for pooling of equipment and the assigning of specific routes to each carrier, thus, effecting a conservation of fuel, equipment, and manpower.

page 2

Dear Editor: Some of us who have called Calistoga home were amazed after reading the article by Mr. Garrison in the September 8 paper. It was in Calistoga that we learned the necessity for equal opportunity for everyone, tolerance for our fellow men, and respect for the rights of all citizens of our country. In our town, we would expect to find put into effect these principles which we have been taught. But, apparently Calistoga has forgotten how to use these principles. Instead, citizens have been denied equal opportunity, their rights have been ignored, and intolerance IS the order of the day.

Calistoga has overlooked or rejected the whole principle of democracy upon which our country is based, not realizing that every part of the United States is on trial in the eyes of our Allies, who are looking for practical applications of these ideals.

Our boys are overseas fighting for the greatest of our ideals – life, liberty and the pursuit of happiness. Will they want to come back to a town which has within it the nucleus for another and greater war? What good does it do to make noble gestures toward the war effort if the basic principles for which we are fighting are forgotten in the problems at home.

We do not believe that this situation is due entirely to the active will of a few, but to the lethargy of the community which has allowed such a condition to arise.

In order to have a better world after the war, there are many problems to overcome. One of them is racial discrimination, which must be solved in every section of the country before we ever lay the foundations for an enduring peace.

Lois Jean Power
Rosemary Senter
Corinne Westbay
University of California, Berkeley

Chapter 22

> ## September 24-30
> **The War:** British forces pull out of Arnhem, the Netherlands. Hopes of an early end of the war are lost.

𝔚eekly 𝔠alistogan of September 29, 1944

page 1

The following are excerpts from letters written by Lieutenant Emily Musante, who is serving as an Army nurse with the American invasion forces in France. They were received recently by her parents in Calistoga, Mr. and Mrs. Giuseppe Musante. The letters, written between August 28 and September 3, contain these interesting comments:

"I feel it is time for me to write a long letter to my dear family – mail means so much to us, and I know that it means the same to you.

"When we are working, there is little time to do anything; and this has been our first rest period since June. The first day of rest, one is in no mood to do anything; the second day, we wash clothes and get things in order to move, as one never knows. 3 a.m. seems to be the good hour, and you should see us rolling our bedrolls in darkness.

"The French neighbors walk through our area with eggs, and then the bartering starts. We give soap, cigarettes, and our old shoes. They are more than happy, as they need clothes. Our French is poor, but they know enough English; and, of course, sign language is always convenient.

"At present, two little boys are in our tent, and my tentmates have given them shirts and shoes. You should see how happy they are. I will take their picture.

"Yesterday, a lady brought us a dozen eggs and some flowers, so this morning we had breakfast in bed. Such a luxury! One of the girls had the eggs fried in the kitchen tent and served us.

"Today, we did well – two chickens for two pairs of shoes, soap, and cigarettes – our first chicken in France. Money these days has

162

no value, as there are no stores in the sections we inhabit. Therefore, exchange is the popular thing.

"There are many rumors as to our next stop. One never knows. Sorry, but we cannot send cables. We have not received mail for many days, and all are looking forward to a good amount, including packages.

"The countryside is pretty. Many apple trees, but the fruit is not ripe. The natives apparently make cider. While we were in the previous area, we had some very good wine, which was bought for $12 per bottle. We have had some cognac, which was very good; but a small taste was sufficient. Champagne – we have not seen any.

"Don't worry about us, as we do have good times in between times. We make our fun – little occasions are what keep us in good spirits.

"Yesterday is a day I shall long remember – my first visit to Paris. It surpassed all expectations. Never have I seen such a beautiful city. (Of course, considering that for so long we have seen only ruins, this was heavenly.) The streets lined with trees, parks, flowers in bloom. All so clean and neat. The women so smart, very stylish, fancy hair styles, pretty clothes. The stores with so many lovely things. It was indeed a surprise – the excellent condition of all, considering the long period of war. Bus lines and street cars are not in operation, nor the lights at night.

"Bicycles and horse carriages are the main methods of transportation, but one also sees automobiles. Yes, and the ice wagons and frozen ice carts are still there – and the sidewalk cafes, just like you see in the movies. We had some very good beer, and some champagne, too!

"I could not get over the modern buildings, apparently apartment houses. We were there only a few hours and did not have time to visit the cathedrals. I do want to go back. It was truly a thrilling experience – crossing the Seine and viewing the panorama of the city, seeing the American flag waving over the Eiffel Tower, riding down the Champs Elysees. Truly, I don't know when I have been so thrilled, and so proud of being an American. The French people appeared so friendly, all saying how glad they were to see us. Yes, most of them speak English.

Versailles, too, is such a lovely place. The palace grounds are breathtaking. Again, I want to go back. One never knows these days if and when we will see the famous places again, but I always feel I will return in peacetime. If there is a will, there is a way. God is so good to us."

Calistoga 1944

The Calistoga High School band is honored again this year by an invitation to its director and six members to play with the Santa Rosa Symphony Orchestra.

The students are Norman Piner, trumpet; Verna Nicchia, French horn; Mary Bardes, clarinet; Pat Shoemaker, cymbals; Jean Evans, bassoon; Angelo Demetroff, violin. They will be joined by Clifford Anderson, musical director for the Calistoga schools, who will play the violin, and Alvin Kuster, principal of Calistoga Elementary School, who will play the bass viol.

Demetroff, a sophomore, is a newcomer who Anderson says has all the indications of a musical genius. He will appear as a guest artist at a symphony concert this season. He is the son of Mr. and Mrs. P.E. Demetroff of Rosedale Farm.

George Trombley, director of the symphony, said it will give five concerts during the year. Dates have not been set.

News of another of Calistoga's fighting men came from the South Pacific this week, when the *Weekly Calistogan* received a Marine Corps press release containing word of Blaine Huston.

"Somewhere in the South Pacific – Marine Private First Class Blaine Huston of Calistoga, California, is a member of the quintet which recently captured the basketball championship of a veteran leatherneck combat outfit here.

"The 19-year-old is a veteran of the attack on Cape Glouster, New Britain, in which he served as a machine gunner with the assault contingent.

"He is a former student of Calistoga High School, and captained the basketball team during two of the four seasons he played on the varsity squad."

Blaine's many friends will be glad to get news that he is quite evidently in good shape if he is playing basketball. He is the son of Mrs. Ida Huston of Calistoga.

Our police made two arrests this week that may lead to interesting developments because both men seem to be draft dodgers, very much on the loose, financially and otherwise.

During the early part of the week, Night Officer Otto Bohn observed that Frederick C. Barker was acting in a suspicious manner and took the pains to listen to a conversation between Barker and his companion.

Feeling that what he heard was sufficient to warrant further investigation, Bohn called Acting Chief of Police Lee S. Roberts, who came downtown at once. They took Barker to the police station for questioning. Barker produced a 2-A draft card – issued to essential war workers; but so garbled was his story as to why he was in Calistoga and not engaged in war work, that Roberts held him for investigation.

A call to the FBI in Sacramento brought out the fact Barker has been jailed for vagrancy in several of the major cities of the United States, and has served short terms on almost every charge. Appearing before Judge J.B. Winkelman, Barker was given 10 days in county jail. In the meantime, the Detroit draft board is being contacted to determine whether Barker is entitled to his 2-A card.

The second arrest which led to inquiries as to draft status occurred late Wednesday night, when Paul M. Huffman, 29, was arrested on Lincoln Avenue by Officer Bohn for being intoxicated. Telling conflicted stories as to why he did not have a draft card and as to his reasons for being here, Huffman was held until Roberts called Sacramento. Two hours later, the FBI phoned Roberts and told him to hold Huffman for investigation.

Members of the local post of American Legion voted Monday night to abandon the idea of holding a rodeo here on Armistice Day (November 11). The decision came after a lengthy discussion regarding costs, uncertain weather conditions, and the obvious disinterest of the town in general. It was suggested that next Labor Day would be a better time to stage a rodeo.

Despite an early-season threat of a labor shortage in the valley, the prune crop is off the trees, and grape picking is well under way. Most of the county is sufficiently supplied with help, except in areas where tomatoes and walnuts are major crops.

Joe Oleata, manager of the Calistoga Farm Labor office, says that he has been able to fill all orders for workers, and vineyardists can count on getting their crops off the vines right on schedule.

County agricultural officials estimate that the prune crop this year was approximately 60 percent of the 1943 crop. The fruit is of better quality than that of last year, and growers probably will have as great, or greater, returns this year.

The local farm labor office will be taken over by C.B. Corkett on Monday, as Oleata returns to his duties as a teacher at Calistoga Elementary School. Corkett has served as secretary for the office. He will do both jobs until the office closes November 1.

Calistoga 1944

Calistoga's schools will open for the fall semester next Monday.

The high school faculty members and their classes are as follows: Jack Rannells – principal, freshman mathematics, applied English, and physical education; Claude A. Bryner – vice principal, chemistry, advanced mathematics, geometry, and mechanical drawing; William Manford – world problems, senior problems, orientation, United States history, civics, physical education, and coaching; Mrs. Edith Baptie – English; Clifford Anderson – band, instrumental music, and drum corps; Steve Searcy – agriculture, biology, and farm mechanics; Mrs. Rozellen Salladay – home management, foods, sewing, and girls' physical education; Miss Lamona Johnson – typing, shorthand, bookkeeping, and girls' physical education.

Between noon and 12:30 Monday, there will be a high school student body meeting, with President Milton Petersen presiding. The meeting will feature the introduction of new teachers and a brief resumé of planned activities for the school year.

Two new teachers will join the faculty of the elementary school – Miss Margaret Grauss and Mrs. Helen L. Dixon. Both are experienced in their profession. Mrs. Conrad Weil and Mrs. Howard Butler, who have frequently substituted in times past, have been added to the regular faculty.

Friends in Calistoga were grieved to hear of the passing in Mill Valley last Saturday of H.J. Hendrick, local Southern Pacific station agent for eight years until last February.

Mr. Hendrick, 65, died following a heart attack. He gave up his position in Calistoga due to health problems, and retired from company service on June 4. He was born in Roseville on June 5, 1879. Practically all of his working life was with Southern Pacific in various parts of the state. He is survived by his wife, Maude; two daughters; seven grandchildren; and a brother, Milton Hendrick of Calistoga.

Calistoga received $93 and Napa County $1,317 in the apportionment of vehicle license fees collected by the state during the quarter ending June 30.

Gordon H. Garland, Director of Motor Vehicles, said a total of $1,105,231 was collected. Twenty percent of that went to the state's general fund for the retirement of highway bonds. The remainder went to cities and counties on the basis of population.

Vehicle license fees formerly were collected by cities and counties as personal property taxes. Vehicle owners will pay the same license fees next year as this, despite the current upward trend in market values of used cars, because of a special law sponsored by the Department of Motor Vehicles and signed by Governor Earl Warren.

Chester E. Wallace sustained a broken leg Wednesday morning in a fall at the walnut plant on Washington Street. The accident occurred while Wallace was on a ladder installing new bins.

Taken to the Calistoga Hospital, Wallace was found to have a compound fracture above the left ankle and possible broken bones in the ankle itself. He was taken to San Francisco that afternoon for the services of an orthopedic surgeon.

Calistoga property owners are reminded that city taxes are due and payable at City Hall on and after Monday, October 2. They will become delinquent if not paid on or before November 6 at 5 p.m. Persons who allow their taxes to become delinquent will be subject to a penalty, according to Tax Collector Ed E. Light.

Chapter 23

October 1-7

The War: Russian troops enter Yugoslavia. German troops put down the Warsaw Uprising. Allied forces land on Crete in the Mediterranean. Canadian troops cross into the Netherlands. Russian and German troops clash in eastern Hungary.

𝔚eekly 𝔊alistogan of October 6, 1944

page 1

Calistoga, ever mindful of the fact that her sons and daughters will be returning from their service with their country, is making plans to render all possible aid to those who will be re-entering civilian life and making their way again in a world that will seem new to them after the life they have led under the rigors of the service.

Many adjustments will have to be made, not only by those who are returning but also by those who have remained at home. To that end, the various organizations of Calistoga, under the leadership of the Calistoga Rotary Club, have met and agreed upon a general plan of action that they hope will be a satisfactory solution to the many problems that will arise.

Sometime over a year ago, the Rotary Club conceived the idea of a "Work Pile," which, when first suggested, seemed to offer a means of providing jobs for all of those who would be coming home to Calistoga. As time went on, it became quite evident that it would be impossible to promise definitely that there would be a job for every man and woman who returned to their home town. It was also obvious that it would be unfair to let those men and women think that such would be the case.

At a recent Rotary meeting, it was decided that the best service that could be rendered to members of the armed forces would be to assure them that, once they are returned, they will be given sincere, honest, and helpful consideration. The club is even now gathering complete information as to opportunities in various fields of endeavor, in Calistoga, the county, and the state.

Rotary intends to invite returning service personnel to sit with the directors of the club and discuss their desires in the matter of work, and to plan with the Rotary directors regarding the future, either in the matter of jobs or returning to school for completion of an education interrupted by war.

Calistoga Post No. 231, American Legion, has agreed to lend all aid possible. It will work with the Napa County Veteran's Employment Council, a group organized for the sole purpose of helping to solve the problems of the returning service personnel.

Officials of the council and Post 231 met last night. Manager Roy Portman outlined the aims of the council and asked that Post 231 appoint members to attend all meetings.

The Calistoga parlors of Native Sons and Native Daughters have passed resolutions to cooperate with Rotary in the work to be done. The Chamber of Commerce is behind the movement, as are the Odd Fellow, Rebekah, Mason, and Eastern Star lodges.

A.L. Hawke of Calistoga, president of the Napa County Farm Bureau, states that his organization will aid in finding jobs for those who wish farm work, as will officers of Bennett and Tucker Farm Center. Twelve farmers have been appointed to act as advisers to any servicemen interested in taking up farming, or returning to it.

Calistoga's schools opened Monday.

The high school has 103 students (53 girls, 50 boys). They had 15-minute introductory classes during the morning and then a student body assembly. Angelo Demetroff, a new member of the sophomore class, played two selections on the violin. Freshmen and new students introduced themselves.

New students, outside of freshmen, are Irving and Camile Twight, sophomores from Livermore; Demetroff, from South San Francisco; Frances Tedeschi and Marilyn Moran, transfers from the Ursuline Academy at St. Helena; Virginia Warren, sophomore from Napa; and Barbara Tedeschi, who returns to Calistoga High after a serious illness that forced her to leave school last spring.

There are 24 freshmen, 32 sophomores, 19 juniors, and 28 seniors.

Calistoga 1944

The elementary school has 227 students. The first day there was devoted to getting classes settled and the students acquainted with their teachers and the school routine.

Calistoga Elementary School

Due to unforeseen circumstances, there is a definite shortage of labor to pick the local grape crop, reports Charles Corkett, head of the local Farm Labor Office.

Grape growers of the Calistoga area will face crop losses unless sufficient help is available at the earliest possible moment. Corkett said anyone who wishes to devote the weekend, or even part of it, to picking should go to his office on Washington Street, or telephone Calistoga 116.

Armistice Day – November 11 – in Calistoga will feature a barbecue during the afternoon and a dance and other entertainment during the evening, according to plans being made by the Last Man's Club, an organization of World War I veterans.

As in 1942, when the Last Man's Club held its annual convention here, guests of the day will be veterans from Letterman General Hospital in the Presidio of San Francisco and the Mare Island Hospital. It is hoped to have at least 25 veterans in attendance, with all branches of the service represented.

The barbecue will be prepared at Pioneer Park, under the direction of Joe Forni. If the weather permits, the food will be served at the park. Otherwise, tables will be set up in the Recreation Center. Calistoga High School Band, under the direction of Clifford Anderson, will provide entertainment.

The charge for tickets has not been set. It will cover supplies for the barbecue, transportation for the guest veterans, and other expenses.

Volunteer help toward making the day a success will be most welcome to the committee in charge. Club president Lee Roberts can furnish full information.

Raymond E. Fechter Jr. of Calistoga has been awarded a Certificate of Honorable Service by Rear Admiral William K. Furlong, commandant of Pearl Harbor Navy Yard, in recognition of his faithful work and contribution to the war effort while in the islands as a civilian employee.

Word was received this week that Lieutenant William J. Young, husband of Mrs. Evelyn Young and son-in-law of Mr. and Mrs. Frank Zeek of Ukiah, has been reported missing in action over Germany. Mrs. Young was a 1933 graduate of Calistoga High School, having lived here when her father was principal of the local elementary school.

Mrs. Mitto Blodgett spent Wednesday in San Francisco at a luncheon of the Republican women of the Northern California. As chairman of the Napa County Council of Republican Women, Mrs. Blodgett gathered much information to use in furthering the candidacies of Dewey and Bricker for the Presidency and Vice Presidency.

Next Friday marks the opening of the 1944 drive for funds for the California War Chest. In 1943, the state quota was $18 million, with funds distributed between 17 agencies. This year, the state goal is $20 million, with 22 agencies sharing in the funds.

The national goal is $250 million, to be collected from over 10,000 communities.

Last year, Calistoga's quota for the drive was $2,400, with $2,000 of that to go toward the state's share of the national goal, and the balance held for Boy Scout Troop 18 and other local needs. At the close of the drive, Calistogans had donated $2,602, with everything over $2,000 remaining here.

This year, the local committee will seek $2,800. Again, there will be $2,000 earmarked for the state quota, and Calistoga will retain the balance for local needs.

Over half of the money collected throughout the nation will be allocated to the USO, an organization that provides the largest volume of service of any of the 22 agencies receiving funds. There are 1,980 USO clubs in operation at the present time – all but 130 in the continental United States. There are 220 in California alone.

In addition to the USO, Community Chest and other home-front welfare agencies will benefit from the War Chest. Another agency, the War Prisoners' Aid, will be allocated funds to purchase textbooks, recreational materials, and musical instruments for American prisoners held in enemy prison camps.

Another very important agency is the United Seamen's Service, which is to the merchant marine what the USO is to the men of the armed forces. There are rest and recreation homes maintained for these men in more than 120 ports scattered over six continents.

In spite of the fact that Christmas boxes to be sent to the men and women of Calistoga who are in the armed forces are ready to be assembled and mailed, there is a sad lack of response to the request that names and current addresses be turned in to Mickey Mercer to assure that every hometown member of the armed forces gets a box.

The Christmas box addresses must be current. The program cannot rely on lists like those covering subscriptions to the *Weekly Calistogan* or the lists submitted for the memorial plaque erected by the American Legion.

The final shipment of gifts to be included in the boxes arrived this week. Starting tomorrow, the boxes will be wrapped, addressed and mailed. It would be unfortunate if any service personnel from Calistoga do not receive gifts from their home town.

"Unless the American people wake up, right now, our fighting men will return to find out that the principles for which they have fought and died have been lost here at home," Lieutenant Governor Frederick F. Houser declared in an address in Napa last Friday.

Houser, campaigning for election to the U.S. Senate, spoke at a luncheon at the Plaza Hotel, attended by Republicans and Democrats alike, all interested in returning America to the constitutional government from which she has parted.

The lieutenant governor was unable to remain long in the county as he had been called to take over the position of acting governor. He made a hurried trip as far north as the Veterans' Home, and then returned to Sacramento to take over the duties of

Governor Earl Warren, while the latter started East to make a series of talks in support of Thomas E. Dewey's presidential campaign.

Houser made an excellent impression on his Napa audience. His talk was forceful, well organized, and entirely devoid of the too usual mud-slinging campaign oratory. He spoke very briefly of his opponent, incumbent Sheridan Downey, choosing only one point on which to attack Downey's record in the Senate – his perennial absence from his Senate seat and his continuous failure to vote when important issues are at stake.

News was received this week that former Calistogan Staff Sergeant B. H. (Harry) Clark, son of Mrs. B.H. Clark and the late Ben H. Clark, has been decorated for "meritorious achievement in connection with military operations against the enemy near Gorissi and Iboki Plantation, New Britain, in the South Pacific on February 22 and 24, 1944.

The letter of commendation, signed by Colonel Allen L. Keyes, is now in the hands of Harry's wife. It reads: "Your comrades, the officers, and men of the 592nd Engineer Boat and Shore Regiment, are proud of your courage, initiative, and energy which have won for you the award of the Bronze Medal. We salute you."

In commenting on the award in a letter to his wife, Harry said, "The credit really belongs to the men in my boat. I just happened to be the one that led them on the mission."

Note: Harry Clark graduated from Calistoga Elementary School in 1928.

Theta Rho girls met Tuesday night, initiating a new member and planning for the installation of officers on Wednesday night, October 11. Marjorie Fisher is president.

Napa-Lake Pomona Grange met at the Rutherford Grange Hall last Saturday night, with Overseer D. Lindebeck presiding in the absence of Worthy Master H.L. Bounsall.

There was a good crowd considering the gas situation.

page 4

Staff Sergeant Loring Tomasini, son of Mrs. and Mrs. Walter Tomasini of Knights Valley, has been awarded the Bronze Star medal for outstanding and meritorious service against the Japs during the three-week battle for Attu a year ago.

The presentation by Major General A.V. Arnold took place at a Central Pacific base.

Loring is a veteran of two campaigns in the Pacific war. After the Aleutian action, he participated with the Seventh Division in the assault upon, and the capture of, Kwajalein Atoll in the Marshall Islands.

In addition to the Bronze Star, Loring wears the Asiatic-Pacific Theatre ribbon, with two battle stars; the American Defense Service ribbon; the Good Conduct Medal: and the Combat Infantryman's Badge.

Editorial: Smell It? There must be SOME reason why the Democratic candidate for the Presidency is receiving the wholehearted and all-out support of three of the most corrupt political machines in the United States.

There must be SOME reason why Sidney Hillman and his PAC are behind the Democratic candidate for the Presidency of the United States.

There must be SOME reason why the intelligent majority of the Democratic Party are turning to the Republican candidate as the man who can keep this country from being eased into a National Socialist regime.

When men like Hague of New Jersey, Kelly and Nash of Chicago, and Tom Pendergast of Kansas City swing in behind a candidate, there must be a reason for it; and that reason, in this election year of 1944, is that the re-election of Franklin D. Roosevelt assures them of four more years of unlimited power – power that has been and will be given to them from Washington in payment for their work in perpetuating Mr. Roosevelt in office.

Hague, Kelly, Nash, Pendergast, and Sidney Hillman. What a sweet-scented group of supporters. All of them have been flirting with federal indictment for years.

In the case of Pendergast, the law did take its course, and Big Tom did his little stretch in a federal prison. One of the conditions of his parole was that he abstain from any activities along political lines. Can you believe that Pendergast had nothing to do with the nomination of Harry Truman for the Vice Presidency? Pendergast took Harry Truman into the fold in an attempt to give a slight odor of sanctity to the stinking political cesspool in Kansas City, and he boosted Truman on up and into the Senate. And do you think that Pendergast has forgotten Truman? And do you doubt that Pendergast pulled the wires that put Truman into his present spot?

Vice President Henry Wallace was dumped, and better men than Truman were suggested for the post. Did they get a chance at Chicago? They did not. Whatever chance they did have was wiped out when Franklin D. Roosevelt, three times president and avid for a fourth term, talked with his national chairman when the presidential special stopped in Chicago, en route to the West Coast, and agreed to the program set up by Kelly-Nash-Hague-Hillman.

Remember his parting words to Hannegan? They were: "Clear everything with Sidney."

In other words, the Democratic Party stooped so low after votes that it put the second highest office in the United States into the hands of a labor racketeer and allowed him to name the candidate.

Private Kenneth Moran of the Army Medical Corps left for Camp Barkley, Texas, Tuesday after spending a 10-day furlough in Calistoga with his parents, Mr. and Mrs. Frank Moran. Kenneth is an X-ray technician and has been at the Texas camp for some time following a many-month assignment at Camp Lewis, Washington.

Note: Moran was a 1937 graduate of Calistoga High School.

The Friendly Circle met Tuesday evening in the social hall of the Methodist Church, with 20 members and five visitors present. Features of the meeting were the presentation of baby gifts to Marcella Cole and Peggy Schuman, and a farewell gift to Dorothy Swearinger, who will leave soon for the state of Washington. A birthday cake was cut for Mrs. A.E. Lucas. The club will stage a Halloween Party for its next gathering, at the home of Mrs. Thomas Elder.

Don Simpkins, who has been in the U.S. Army for about two years, was at home during the week with his parents, Mr. and Mrs. Don Simpkins Sr. Don is stationed at Camp Beale, near Marysville, but he expects a new assignment.

The Women's Association of the Community Church will hear a missionary recently returned from the Asiatic fields at its meeting in the Methodist social hall Tuesday afternoon. Other features of the afternoon will be a report by Mrs. J.S. Black on a recent interdenominational missionary conference in Vallejo, and a "Dollar Day", when each member will explain her way of earning the dollar she is giving to the collection.

Chapter 24

𝔚eekly 𝔠alistogan of October 13, 1944

page 1

Calistoga was shocked Friday morning when the news reached the streets that Blaine Huston had been reported killed in action with the Marines in the South Pacific.

The news reached here in the form of a telegram from the War Department to Blaine's mother, Mrs. Ida Huston, and his sister, Mrs. Jack Pacheteau.

Blaine Huston

Masses were held at the Calistoga Catholic Church on Tuesday and Thursday of this week. Another will be held Monday.

The high school held an assembly in front of the main building and lowered the American flag to half mast while senior Norman Piner played Taps. The "Back to School" dance scheduled that evening was canceled in respect for Blaine.

Born in Calistoga on June 7, 1925, Blaine was just past his 19th birthday at the time of his death. A graduate of the local elementary and high schools, he was widely known here and among the most popular boys of his class at the high school.

Entering the service prior to the graduation of his class, he was granted his diploma at the annual commencement exercises in 1943.

Blaine was active in many high school sports and noted for his prowess as a basketball player. A news release from the Marine Corps, received here two weeks ago, told of Blaine's having been an outstanding player on his outfit's championship basketball team. It described him as a veteran of the attack on Cape Glouster on New Britain island, north of New Guinea.

Although only in the service for 18 months – a year of which was spent in the South Pacific – Blaine is known to have seen much action, as the First Marines participated in many of the attacks and landings on Japanese-held islands.

Surviving are his mother; his father, John R. Huston; two sisters, Mrs. Pacheteau and Mrs. Sally Ware; and a half-brother, Rowden Huston.

Note: The sports field at the fairgrounds in Calistoga is named in honor of Blaine.

Calistoga was thrown into a dither Tuesday afternoon at 4:45 p.m. when a Navy Grumann Hellcat plane crashed into the mountainous terrain four miles east of town.

First news of the crash came from Ted Tamagni, who, visiting a vineyard south of town, had idly watched two planes as they circled over the valley. Suddenly, one went out of control, spiraled steeply, and disappeared behind the ridge of mountains. A sudden sweep of smoke indicated that the plane had crashed.

Tamagni called Chief of Police Ed E. Light and, not having identified the type of planes, informed him that a P-38 had cracked up. The chief, assuming that an Army plane was down, immediately called the Santa Rosa Army Air Base. The Army responded by dispatching an ambulance, a jeep, and a "recon" wagon.

Arriving in Calistoga and stopping for further information from authorities, the Army contingent was informed that their headquarters had telephoned orders they should not proceed to the scene of the wreck because it was a Navy plane that had crashed; the Army could not use time, gasoline, nor effort in an attempt to get to the scene of the crash in spite of the fact there was a remote chance of the pilot still being alive.

The Navy, belatedly notified of the accident – due to no fault of theirs – had their rescue crew in Calistoga approximately one hour after the alarm went out. Bill Martin volunteered to guide the crew, and they shoved off for the scene of the wreck, going by the Oat Hill Road and stopping at the summit behind the High Rocks, where the road ended.

Taking part of the Navy crew with him, Bill led off toward the place where the plane had crashed. Equipped with a "walkie-talkie," the rescue crew kept in touch with the ambulance, jeep, and "recon" car by radio. At 10:45 Tuesday night, Martin and the Navy crew arrived on the crash scene. They found others already there: a fire suppression crew from the St. Helena unit of the State Division of Forestry, three Calistoga High School students – Norman Piner, Bob MacDonald, and Frank Saviez; and another Calistoga group – police officers Ed E. Light and Otto Bohn and "Babe" Ames, Harry Cohen, and "Red" Redly.

The body of the pilot, badly smashed up, was found 50 feet away from the plane wreck. The rescue groups brought the body out of the hills, passing through Calistoga in mid-morning.

Note: The Army objected to this story. See Chapter 25.

Warren H. Atherton, past national commander of the American Legion and chairman of the Republican War Veteran's Division of the Dewey-Bricker presidential campaign, is now in New York City to establish headquarters.

Atherton broadcast a vital message to war veterans and their families from New York last night over the Mutual Radio Network.

In accepting the chairmanship of the war veteran's division from Herbert Brownell, chairman of the Republican National Committee, Atherton declared:

"The nation will have a stronger national offense and defense in the future if Governor Thomas E. Dewey is elected President. The crucial demobilization period will be made easier for men and women now in the service if the present administration is defeated in November. That is what the veterans of all wars are saying and thinking.

"They remember the President's Economy Act, which severely cut allotments to disabled men. They remember the suicides which followed. They have in mind Mr. Roosevelt's veto of the act to remedy this injustice.

"Soldiers of every war recall the refusal to allow any form of military training in Civilian Conservation Corps camps. They know that the woeful pre-war helplessness of this country invited the Pearl Harbor disaster.

"They remember, too, the President's failure to create stockpiles of rubber and other critical material – a failure that almost lost the war. They have in mind the need for an after-war executive who will work to create real jobs and business opportunities. They know that a President sympathetic to the needs of service men and women should be in office.

"In 1942, thousands of veterans disabled in Africa and the Pacific were discharged. No provision was made for helping them or their dependents. Men and women badly wounded and wholly unable to make a living were left waiting for months for compensation, vocational training."

December 15 is the date of the annual Firemen's card party in the Masonic Auditorium. Funds will be used toward the purchase of another truck chassis, to be equipped with pumper and tank, states F.W. (Bill) Martin, who heads the organizing committee.

Volunteer firemen, dressed for a social event in the late 1940s, include: left to right, front row – Bill Whitney, Charles Nolasco, Rigby Tuttle, Rico Birleffi, Harry Drake, Shorty Spain and Joe Flynn.

Middle row – Sig Light, Peter Molinari, Babe Ames, Eugene Tedeschi, Tony Cardoza, John Ghisolfo, Gino Birleffi, Fred Lerner, Laurel Switzer, and George Butler.

Back row – Louie Carlenzoli, Joe Scholl, Bill Cavagnaro, Frank Piner, Linus Smith, Bill Thomas, Lawrence Locey, Vincent Archuletta, Charles Case, Peter Marciano, Al Stanton, and Clarence Thom.

Once a year, the firemen give a party, with funds derived always directed to a worthy cause. Remember that the boys volunteer their services, and that this is the only opportunity townspeople have for expressing their appreciation.

Note: Calistoga's fire department was an all-volunteer force until the late 1990s.

Staff Sergeant Buron B. Camp, home after many months of fighting with the Marines in the Pacific war zone, visited his parents, Mr. and Mrs. W.A. Camp, in Calistoga last Saturday and Sunday. He had to return to Oakland, but will no doubt be back.

Sergeant Camp is suffering a rather serious malarial infection, which has kept him in and out of hospitals for some time. He will undergo treatment in this country, and then he expects to return overseas.

Sergeant Camp has been in the Marine Corps for three-and-a-half years, two of them in the thick of battle on various islands – Guadalcanal, Tarawa, Tinian, Saipan – that will go down in history as major engagements in the war with Japan.

Meanwhile, his wife, an Australian girl, and their six-month-old daughter are in New Zealand. They will probably come to this country before long.

Buron has two brothers, Dariel and Lloyd, who are still serving overseas and a third brother, Don, who was discharged following injuries received in the Pacific area. Dariel, a corporal in the Marine Corps, is somewhere in the South Pacific. Lloyd is in the Army in the European theater.

Note: Don was a 1942 graduate and Lloyd a 1943 graduate of Calistoga High School. Buron and Dariel graduated from the elementary school here in 1939. Dariel returned after the war and ran a rock, sand, and gravel pit at Middletown for several years before taking over a readymix plant at Cupertino. He died in 1988.

With more than a hundred packages already in the mail, the committee in charge of sending Christmas boxes to every Calistoga man and woman in the armed forces is more than busy getting the balance of the boxes ready for the post.

Mrs. Dorothy Matthews, chairman of the committee, advises that the following boys are eligible for gift boxes, but the committee does not have their latest addresses: Bert Sorth, William Spencer, Richard White, Howard Pearson, W.W. MacArthur, D.W. Newton, Robert Love, Gerald Clifford, Bruce Gammon, Roy Brown, James Dunlap, Clarence Proaps, and George Reinicke. It is earnestly requested that the addresses of these men be sent in to Mickey Mercer at once. Tomorrow is the last day.

Recipients of the boxes will get a "lift" far beyond the dollar value of the gifts. The fact that their home town, Calistoga, remembered them at Christmas time will have an astonishing result in building up morale.

A large percentage of those who will receive the boxes are in the South Pacific. That phase of the war is going to last a long time.

Duggelin Brothers, who have been operating James' Coffee Shop on Lincoln Avenue for the past several months, announced this week that they have sold it to W.G. Walker.

Walker, an experienced restaurant owner who formerly operated in Portland, Oregon, said he will specialize in American home-cooked meals. Mrs. Walker will assist her husband in conducting the business.

The first fall meeting of Calistoga's Troop 18 of the Boy Scouts of America will be held in the old auditorium of the high school Monday night, with Scoutmaster Bill Connolly presiding and Assistant Scoutmaster George Locey helping. Also attending will be John Opman, counselor, and the principals of the local schools, Alvin Kuster and Jack Rannells.

H.J. Baade, county agent for the U.S. Department of Agriculture, offered these thoughts for Fire Prevention Week (October 8-14, inclusive). "It would be well for all of us to consider the seriousness of the annual loss due to fires. It would be well for all organizations to devote a few minutes to the discussion of fire prevention, the removal of fire hazards, and being careful not to let fire get beyond control. The annual loss due to fires is too high. It is reflected in great loss of property and lives, and in high insurance rates."

Byron Karcher, home from Camp Robinson, near Little Rock, Arkansas, following six months of service with the Army Corps of Engineers, spent part of a recent furlough in Calistoga with his parents, Mr. and Mrs. Charles E. Karcher.

Byron ranks as an expert rifleman. He is being transferred to the 42nd (Rainbow) Division and will be at Camp Burley, Oklahoma, for a time.

His sister, Mrs. Jane Johnson of Richmond, and brother, Westal Karcher, joined the family for a luncheon. Westal is employed as an electrician – a trouble shooter – at the Hunter's Point Naval Shipyard in San Francisco. Due to a stiff arm caused by a fall from a bicycle many years ago, he was not been able to get into the armed services.

Note: Jane and Westal were 1933 graduates of Calistoga High School.

Calistoga 1944

Getting off to a flying start Monday, the annual drive of the Calistoga War Chest gives promise of following the pattern of other Calistoga money-raising campaigns and going well over the top. Calistoga's quota is $2,575.

Leading the local committee is James Albright. Other members are Ray Oxford, vice chairman; Mabel Mangus, organizations; Mary Parsons, high school; Alvin Kuster, elementary school; Edmund Molinari, treasurer; L.P. (Babe) Ames; and George Locey.

A booth will be maintained at the Bank of America here under the charge of Mrs. Mangus. Donations may be made at the booth, or directly to Molinari, a cashier at the bank.

Mrs. J.E. Scott was hostess to the Sunnyside Club last Thursday afternoon at her home in the Tucker district. The ladies devoted the session to sewing and knitting and making plans for the birthday luncheon at the next meeting. The "spring lambs" will entertain the "fall nuts" at the home of Mrs. Olaf Hansen.

Napa County has reached a new high in the number of registered voters, County Clerk R.A. Dollarhide announced. There are 17,709 registered voters – about 1,000 more than in 1940, the previous high mark.

Party affiliations are as follows: Democrats, 9,701; Republicans, 7,671; other parties, 41; declined to state, 296.

These figures do not include members of the armed forces who have already been mailed ballots for the November 7 general election.

page 2

Recent promotions have advanced the Enderlin brothers, sons of Mr. and Mrs. George J. Enderlin, in the ranks they hold in their respective branches of the service.

Arnold, the elder of the two, has been advanced to the rank of sergeant in the supply department of the Army Air Corps. He is stationed at Kingman, Arizona.

Roy, who entered the service more recently, holds the rank of petty officer third class in the Navy. He has been taking gunnery training at Corpus Christi, Texas.

Note: Arnold and Roy are 1940 and 1943 graduates of Calistoga High School. Roy saw action as a seaplane tender in the Philippine Sea. Both returned to Calistoga after the war and still live here.

Arnold worked as an electrician and, in retirement, has gotten into wood carving. Roy has been a grape grower and handyman.

John W. Bricker, Republican vice presidential nominee, will be in the spotlight of the western political stage this week. He will arrive in Sacramento tomorrow by train. Governor Earl Warren will accompany him on a round of appearances, including San Francisco, Santa Barbara, Santa Ana, Los Angeles, Long Beach, San Diego, San Bernardino, Bakersfield, and Fresno.

page 4

Elementary School Notes: Tuesday was the school year's second stamp and bond day. The total sales for the two days were $428. Bonds were bought by Eddie Tedeschi, Joe Tyme, Tom McGreane, Wayne Merry, and Pete Marciano.

Fourth graders had a bat in their room and used it as a subject for nature study. It was a baby bat, caught by Emile Wall. Many children in the various grades saw a bat for the first time.

Seventh graders elected the following officers: Joyce Jackson, president; Delores Stanley, vice president; Barbara Salmina, secretary; and Frances Snow, treasurer. They are planning an exhibit of rocks, shells, spearheads, and feathers.

Eighth graders elected Clarence Brown, president; Philip Snow, vice president; Frances Kelley, secretary; Chuck Howard, treasurer.

Sewing for seventh and eighth grade girls will start next week. The boys of both grades will start shop.

Army Air Force Staff Sergeant Walter Hays returned to Southern California Tuesday to his new assignment as a gunnery instructor at March Field, Riverside. Sergeant Hays has 62 completed missions in the Southwest Pacific to his credit. He will be joined later by his bride, who for the present is remaining in Calistoga.

Staff Sergeant John A. Ghisolfo and his wife spent a three-day visit with his parents here during the week. His mother-in-law, Mrs. Mary Cummings, joined them. They returned to Modesto today.

Note: Ghisolfo was a 1932 graduate of Calistoga High School.

The City Council indicated at its meeting last Friday that it would be open to proposals for construction of a bandstand in Pioneer

Park, providing plans for a suitable structure are presented for consideration.

At the same meeting, the City Clerk was instructed to arrange for construction of a suitable dog pound on a portion of the Feige Canyon reservoir property. Councilman Howard Butler was authorized to select and employ a poundmaster.

page 5

Henry Carlenzoli has completed advanced pilot training at Corpus Christi, Texas, and was commissioned an ensign in the Navy on October 4.

Following his home leave here, Henry will report to an operational base for three months of further training before being assigned to active duty.

Note: Carlenzoli was a 1935 graduate of Calistoga High School.

page 8

High School Notes: Senior class officers for the first semester are Al Boland, president; Barbara Tedeschi, vice president; Lucille McFall, secretary; Ann Tamagni, treasurer; and Earl Evans, representative. The class is making plans for the Senior Hop, October 27.

Junior class officers: Allan Ballard, president; Shirley Longmire, vice president; Barbara Fechter, secretary; Marie Pocai, treasurer; Jim Ingalls, representative.

Sophomore class officers: Anne Richey, president; Mary Parsons, vice president; Henrietta Leoni, secretary; Geniel Tuttle, treasurer; Bruce Piner, representative. The class's main interest at present is initiating the freshmen.

Freshman class has named temporary officers: Ed Greer, president, and Stanley Locey, vice president.

This year, girls' sports are under the direction of Mrs. Rozellen Salladay and Miss Lamona Johnson. Sports available: tennis, volleyball, basketball, tumbling, ballroom dancing, and, possibly, swimming.

Chapter 25

October 15-21

The War: Russian troops and Yugoslav partisans liberate Belgrade. Hitler orders a call-up of all men ages 16-60 for Home Guard duties. U.S. troops occupy Aachen, the first major German city to be captured.

𝕎eekly 𝕮alistogan of October 20, 1944

page 1

As the presidential campaign enters its final stage, it becomes more and more evident that the Republican candidate, New York Governor Thomas E. Dewey, is gaining ground throughout the nation. Borderline states are swinging to his support, and several of the states that the Democrats had considered as "being in the bag" are showing signs of revolt against the domination of the New Deal.

Replying to attacks based on the assumption that the Republican party had no definite foreign policy, Dewey swung into action with his outstanding speech of the campaign when he addressed the *New York Herald-Tribune* Forum Wednesday night.

Dewey assailed President Roosevelt's handling of the international situation as regards Poland, Italy, France, and Romania. He went on to cite the inexcusable blunders made by the administration in attempting to plan for the occupation of Germany.

One of the most telling blows delivered by Dewey was his citing of the fact that Roosevelt took Secretary of the Treasury Henry Morgenthau Jr. to the Quebec conference rather than Cordell Hull, Secretary of State. Dewey brought out the fact that Morenthau's plan for the de-industrializing of Germany, given wide publicity by the Democrats, had resulted in giving Propaganda Minister Goebbels a weapon with which to terrify the German people and whip them into a state of frenzied despair. A situation that nullified, in large part, any chances of an uprising against the Nazi regime within Germany proper. Although the Morgenthau plan was scrapped, the damage was done.

Dewey touched upon the fact that Roosevelt, in attending the Cairo and Teheran conferences, took with him Harry Hopkins rather than Cordell Hull, or any other man of experience from the State Department. In Dewey's words, "All that Hopkins knows about international affairs is what he learned running the WPA."

Bringing out fact after fact dealing with the secret, personal diplomacy of the President, Dewey stated that, for the first time, a president took upon himself the dual role of President and Secretary of State.

Note: This was presented as headlined news rather than what it was – an editorial.

Staff Sergeant Lloyd Decker arrived home in Calistoga this week on furlough from duties in Britain. He will remain here with his parents, Mr. and Mrs. Les Decker, until the first part of November.

On hand to greet Lloyd were his wife, Auben, and his baby daughter, Lloydell, whom he had not seen. Lloyd had service on several fronts during the African and Italian campaigns before reassignment to England.

Note: See Chapter 3 for more on Decker's war and post-war careers.

Seaman Second Class Doyle Rose left for his station at Farragut, Idaho, this week following a 15-day furlough in Calistoga with his parents, Mr. and Mrs. Albert Rose, and other relatives. He expects to be reassigned, either to another Navy base or active duty at sea. Prior to joining the Navy, Doyle was employed at Mare Island Naval Shipyard. He has a brother, Albert, who is in the Army.

Enjoying a two-week furlough from his Navy duties, John Lucas has spent the past week in Calistoga with his parents, Rev. and Mrs. A.E. Lucas. He expects a new assignment upon his return to the Navy base at Farragut, Idaho.

Note: John was a 1943 graduate of Calistoga High School.

With only a few hours' pass from his Navy duties, Dale Barber was able to make a short visit home Monday evening to spend time with his mother, Mrs. Berwin Barber, and sister and brother,

Florence and Raburn Barber. Dale has been training at Norman, Oklahoma.

Note: Dale was a 1942 graduate of Calistoga High School.

Army officials have asked for a correction of *The Calistogan's* article last week regarding the crash of a Navy plane near the High Rocks. They asked that the people be advised that the Army ambulance which came as far as Calistoga and then was called back to Santa Rosa was not called back due to any reluctance on the part of the Army to go to the scene.

They said that the statement in *The Calistogan* to the effect that the Army "could not use the time, gasoline, nor effort in an attempt to get to the scene of the wreck" was not true and it had been misinterpreted by many who read it.,

The Army ambulance, according to the officer, was stopped here after it was found that the Navy had an ambulance on the way. It was felt there was no necessity for two outfits to go into the hills to the scene of the crash. They further stated that there is no friction between the two branches of the service.

The Calistoga School Board decided Wednesday night to offer the long unused Franz Valley School property for sale to the highest bidder.

In other matters, the board voted to submit a proposal for release time for religious education to the parents of all students now in school. The results of that poll will govern the future action of the board.

The board also approved the establishment of a student store at the high school.

Thomas Kenny pleaded guilty Wednesday morning to a charge of stealing gasoline from a Greyhound bus that was parked in Calistoga overnight.

He was arrested by Police Officer Otto Bohn during the night of October 11. Bohn told the court that he found spilled gasoline on the ground under the tank of the bus, a trail of spilled gasoline from the bus to the tank of Kenny's car, and a five-gallon can in the back of Kenny's car.

Kenny was fined $100 and sentenced to 60 days in county jail by Judge Louis Vasconi of St. Helena, sitting in place of Judge J.B. Winkelman, who is on vacation. Judge Vasconi suspended the jail sentence on the condition that Kenny avoid any further law violations.

On Monday of last week, the Napa County Tuberculosis Association patch-tested 29 first grade students in Calistoga Elementary School, and skin-tested 33 in the third grade and 25 in the seventh grade. At the high school, 20 tenth graders were skin-tested.

The project was under the supervision of Dr. Frank McGreane of Calistoga; Mrs. Marie Boden, supervisor of health for Napa County rural schools; and Mrs. Margaret Whitney, field worker for the tuberculosis association.

American Legion Post 231 plans a card party on the night of February 10 to help raise funds to erect its own building in Calistoga. The event will be held in the Odd Fellows' Hall. There will be a door prize and valuable prizes for high score winners.

Note: Post 231 built quarters out near the cemetery. It is long gone.

page 4

Storekeeper Second Class Janet E. Wall, daughter of Alonia Wall of Calistoga, recently was selected WAVE of the Week by the *Hoist* newspaper of the U.S. Naval Training Center at San Diego.

Janet is a member of a four-star family, with two brothers and a sister in the service.

Albert Wall, an engineer in the Maritime Service, is in the South Pacific; Navy Gunner's Mate Second Class John Wall is stationed at Port Chicago in the East Bay; and WAVE Second Class Seaman Mary Wall is on duty at the Naval Mine Warfare Test Station, Solomons, Maryland.

Note: Albert was a 1931 graduate of Calistoga Elementary School.

Hopes for an inter-city bus line went a-glimmering yesterday when word was received from Congressman Leroy Johnson that Washington officials have refused to grant a permit for the proposed line. They said a survey did not show any need for transportation of war workers to their jobs.

Calistoga High School's first evening program of the school year, a "Navy Day broadcast," will take place next Thursday at 8 p.m. in the gymnasium. The program will feature the high school band, under the direction of Clifford Anderson.

The program is in the form of a broadcast from Station N-A-V-Y, with band members saluting each of the representatives of the Navy, Marine Corps, and the Coast Guard, as well as our allies.

Students of the Applied English class who will take an active part in the dialogue are: Andy Richey, LeNora Ulmer, Norman Piner, Mary Bardes, Colleen Kelley, Milton Petersen, Virginia Caras, Stratton Wiggins, Verna Nicchia, Barbara Tedeschi, and Pat Shoemaker.

Editorial: Proposition 11, the Townsend-sponsored $60-at-60 pension scheme on the November ballot, proposes an expenditure by the State which will cost the people about a billion dollars a year in a gross income or transactions tax.

Do you know how much a billion is?

To live a billion minutes, you would have to out-Methuselah the oldest man on record. With 60 minutes to an hour, 24 hours to a day, and 365 days to a year, you'd have to live 1,903 years to be a billion minutes old.

At $1 an hour, 4 million Californians would have to work eight hours a day, six days a week more than five weeks out of every year, and turn their entire earnings into the state treasury, to pay the pensions that Proposition 11 would freeze into the state constitution.

Note: Voters soundly rejected Prop. 11.

Editorial: There is one thing that we KNOW about the coming national election – the next President and Vice President of the United States will be members of the Masonic fraternity.

President Roosevelt is a 32nd degree Mason and a member of the Mystic Shrine. His vice presidential running mate, Senator Truman, is a 32nd degree Mason and a past grand master of the State of Missouri. He is also a York Rite Mason and a Shriner. On the Republican slate, Governor Thomas Dewey is a 32nd degree Mason and a member of the Shrine, and Governor Bricker is a 33rd degree Mason and a Shriner.

Chapter 26

October 22-28

The War: Battle of Leyte Gulf in the Philippines begins; it will be the largest sea battle in history. Japan starts suicidal "kamikaze" aircraft attacks. U.S. B-29s based at Tinian Island bomb Japan. Romania is fully liberated by Russian and Romanian troops.

𝔚eekly Calistogan of October 27, 1944

page 1

Editorial: A front-page editorial opposes the re-election of Franklin Delano Roosevelt as President in the November 7 national election. It expresses a "deep conviction that America must turn her back to the New Deal and its fourth-term candidate." The editorial lists seven reasons for its stand.

First, Americans have known since the days of Washington and Jefferson that "danger lurks where power is entrusted too long to any one man. So do the people of Germany, Italy, and, yes, even Japan." Second, "it is sometimes necessary, and wise, to swap horses in the middle of the stream." The editorial cited the example of Winston Churchill replacing Neville Chamberlain as Prime Minister of England in May 1940, early in World War II. Third, "we do not believe that Mr. Roosevelt's presence in the White House is necessary to winning the war." What the military commanders need is "a united, productive home front, which they have not always had under Mr. Roosevelt."

Fourth, "the New Deal has no plan for rapid demobilization of the armed forces when peace comes. We DO NOT want our boys to remain in the armed forces longer than is necessary. Nor do we want them to come home to soup kitchens and leaf raking under the New Deal." Fifth, "the record shows that in peace time the New Deal was not able to produce jobs, and we have no reason to believe that it could do better during the peace that is to come. It took a

190

war to bring employment and prosperity back to America, but we do not want to face a future in which prosperity must be purchased with the blood of Americans."

Sixth, "Mr. Roosevelt is history's most lavish spender, and yet, with all his gross extravagance, he was unable to bring prosperity to America without war. Mr. Roosevelt is NOT a business man, and he is leading America to bankruptcy." Finally, Harry Truman, "who will be the Vice President, and perhaps the President, if Roosevelt is re-elected, is a protégé of Thomas J. Pendergast, notorious Kansas City political boss."

Note: Weekly Calistogan *followed up the next week with its reasons for endorsing Thomas E. Dewey. How did Calistogans vote? See the November 10 issue, Chapter 28. Historically, today's editorial was correct in suggesting that Roosevelt would not complete another four-year term. He died on April 12, 1945 – only months after starting his fourth term as President.*

Polling places and election officials in the Calistoga township for the November 7 elections include:

Calistoga No. 1 – polling place: Full Gospel Tabernacle, Washington Street; officials: Sara Kenny, Adele Light, Gertrude Conner, Maggie Turner, Frank Pocai, and Theresa Cavagnaro.

Calistoga No. 2 – polling place: library building; officials: Felix L. Grauss Sr., Lou Davis, Evalyn Wolleson, Auben Decker, Isabelle Multer, Shirley Nance.

Hot Springs – polling place: Tucker Farm Center; officials: Harry L. Bounsall, Chester E. Boland, Ella Light, Katie Morosoli, Thelma Tamagni, Berwin Barber.

Silverado – polling place: Bennett Farm Center; officials: F.E. Williams, Jessie Mangis, Thelma Hand, Ethel Bentley, Samuel W. Kellett, Clara L. Butler.

Kellogg – polling place: Knights Valley Club House; officials: Idelle Kettlewell, Vernon M. Smith, Amelia Fisher, Mary Corkett, Pearl Cornwell, Delma Gallaher.

Tarwater – polling place: John McCann residence, Porter Creek; officials: McCann, Herbert Moors, Mary Adams, Mildred Fechter, Vera Willson. E.H. Martin.

The walnut plant has received only 200 tons of nuts to process so far this year – about one-fifth of what it handled during the same period last year. Deliveries have been increasing, and Manager A.

E. Gilbert expects to have the plant operating at full capacity next week. There are 36 persons on the payroll.

The county's prune crop was only 9,070 tons – less than half the 1943 crop – due mainly to an unstable growing season. However, the quality of the crop was better than last year. With prices at a high level, growers are getting their orchards in better condition. More fertilizer is being used than in any previous year, and pruning is receiving close attention.

Police Chief Ed E. Light issued a warning against Halloween pranks that damage property. He cited two seemingly harmless actions that can cause permanent damage – using candles to mark windows and/or screens and throwing tomatoes against motor vehicles. Candle wax leaves a permanent mark. And tomato juice ruins paint if the smear is not washed off immediately, he said.

Walter Butler, an Army Air Force radio operator and mechanic, has been promoted to sergeant. He is stationed "somewhere" in the Netherlands East Indies after serving some months in New Guinea. Get his new address from his mother, Aurelia Butler of Calistoga.

Note: Butler was a 1938 graduate of Calistoga High School. The Netherlands East Indies now is known as Indonesia.

George Hoberg was elected president of the Redwood Empire Association at a two-day meeting at his Lake County resort, attended by more than 500 delegates.

Committee meetings dealt with important phases of post-war development, including highways and other plans for an expected surge in tourists once wartime travel restrictions are lifted.

Calistogans at the meeting included County Supervisor Charles Tamagni, City Councilman Frank Piner, Police Chief Ed E. Light, Councilman John B. Ghisolfo, Judge J.B. Winkleman, L.P. (Babe) Ames, James F. Albright, Ed Federspiel, Charles Corwin White, and Ralph P. Winston.

Rotary Club members heard a blind man, John Capelli of St. Helena, describe how he has overcome his handicap. He was blinded six years ago. The Rotary and 20-30 clubs of St. Helena provided him with a seeing-eye dog that helps him get around. He raises chickens, travels around town without hesitation, and picks an average of 50 boxes of grapes a day during that season.

The Navy issued an urgent appeal for men 17 to 26 years old to serve as gunners, technicians, and radio operators on its bombers and fighter planes. Enlistees will be trained for a year at the Navy facility at Jacksonville, Florida. Applicants must be single and have perfect vision. They will be eligible, under the GI Bill of Rights, to continue their education with government subsidies after the war. There are numerous other benefits under the bill.

Angelo Demetroff, a brilliant violinist and Calistoga High School student, will be a guest artist at a concert of the Santa Rosa Symphony in February.

Boy Scout Troop 18 will camp tonight at Calistoga's reservoir at the base of Mount St. Helena. The boys will hike to the site, cook outdoors, and engage in various Boy Scout rituals. Bill Connolly is Scoutmaster.

The U.S. Maritime Service is seeking 1,000 Bay Area recruits between ages 17 and 50 during the month of November. "MacArthur's invasion of the Philippines is just the beginning of the gigantic job ahead for our merchant marine. It will take every merchant seaman we can muster to keep up," said Lieutenant Commander C.L. Mosher, Pacific Coast enrolling officer for the service.

The Citizens' Service Corps office is distributing free recipe pamphlets aimed at coping with wartime rationing. They include tomato dishes, egg dishes, and pickles and relishes.

Mrs. Lauren Brown Jr. returned to her home in the Tucker District after spending several weeks near her husband, Bud, in Alexandria, Louisiana. He expects Army duty to take him overseas.

page 2

The following letter about racism in Calistoga, written from "somewhere in the Pacific" and dated October 17, has been received from Corporal James E. Campbell of the Marine Corps. Jim, a grandson of Mrs. Ella Campbell of Calistoga, attended high school here. Since going overseas, he has been in many major engagements, including Saipan, Tinian, Roi-Namur.

His letter reads: "I read Mr. Garrison's article in the September 8 edition of the *Calistogan* and was shocked to learn what has been going on back in Calistoga. I failed to write and voice my opinion on the subject, but as I read the 'Open Letter' in the September 22 edition I see that someone else has.

"I want to state that I heartily agree with those three girls' ideas on democracy, and I believe that the people of Calistoga should take heed and find out what is going on in the community.

"If democracy can't be practiced in the smaller units of our government, how can the federal government practice it? Also, what am I, and others in the same position, doing over here, if the people at home can't hold their end up?

"Maybe it would help if these people who were responsible for this breach of democracy would drop in at the library and read the Constitution of the United States. If they follow the laws laid down by this great document, the victory at home will be won, and when we boys come home, we will find that we have not spent our time in vain."

"The great struggle of the Greek people, which began four years ago, when Mussolini's forces attacked October 28, 1940, is still far from ended, despite the liberation of the country," Oscar Broneer, executive vice president of the Greek War Relief Association, said in a statement to the press this week.

"Today the Greek people begin their long and difficult period of reconstruction, with at least 1,300 of their villages and towns destroyed, their supplies exhausted, their clothing in rags, and their health impaired.

"Courage and resistance during the past four years give Greece a claim to the honor and assistance of this country," Mr. Broneer said. "The Greek War Relief Association will continue to supplement the aid being provided Greece by government agencies."

In Calistoga, information concerning donations of clothing or money to help the Greek people may be secured from Mrs. Louis Bardes at the Green Café.

Chapter 27

October 29-November 4

The War: British forces take Salonika in northern Greece.
Canadian troops complete the liberation of Belgium by
taking Zeebrugge.

𝔚eekly Calistogan of November 3, 1944

page 1

Editorial: The following front page editorial offers a different
perspective than the one published on October 27 (Chapter 26),
explaining why the *Weekly Calistogan* is supporting Republican
candidate Thomas E. Dewey, the governor of New York, against incumbent Franklin D. Roosevelt in next week's presidential election.

"We think Dewey has fully demonstrated his ability to handle
the reins of government during the trying years that will face us
until the peace is declared; during the long period of establishing a
world unity; and, most important, to handle the problem of bringing
these United States back to normalcy, through an intelligent
understanding of the needs of the nation during the period when
our men are returning from the fighting fronts, and when there
will be a need of 'jobs for everyone.' "

The editorial lists six things Dewey offers: "A national
government composed of three equal branches, with no fear of
federal dictatorship threatening the freedom of the individual
states of the union...Our courts shall once again be inviolate...The
conflict between the President and the Congress will cease...Class
prejudice will be a thing of the past, and our government will once
again be a government of, for, and by the people...Private enterprise, the very thing that brought our nation to its full bloom, will
have the hampering bonds of government domination removed...
Diplomatic agreements – the terms of peace, the results of conferences
of international representatives, tentative agreements as to the
conduct of the war...the results of meetings between the heads of

nations – all these things will be made public. There will be no more of the 'hush hush' that has kept the nation, and the world at large, in doubt as to just what occurs behind the closed doors so beloved by the present administration."

Note: The editorial also recites Dewey's 11-point program. A front page editorial October 27 criticized Roosevelt and his vice presidential candidate, Senator Harry Truman.

Voters are reminded that they may cast their ballots for either of the two Presidential candidates in the November 7 election, regardless of the party with which they are registered. Only in primary elections must a voter follow party lines.

Louis M. Caramella, 63, was found murdered last Friday morning on the back porch of his house at 217 Bale Lane. He had suffered repeated blows to the head – his skull "crushed like an egg shell." The body was found by friend Harry Tucker.

Law enforcement officers spent the night questioning neighbors. They placed the time of the killing as Thursday night or early Friday morning. One of Caramella's fingers was broken – evidence that he fought for his life.

Wednesday, Sheriff's Deputy Andy Johnson arrested George James for questioning. James was described as an American Indian who lived in the hobo jungle near Caramella's ranch and had been working in the area in recent times. He was being held for questioning at Napa County Jail.

Note: Police released James after he convinced them he had no connection to the killing.

Halloween Eve turned into a wild riot in downtown Napa Tuesday night that Chief of Police Riordan characterized as the worst in the history of the town.

Several gangs engaged in throwing eggs and tomatoes at passing cars. Even a police prowl car was hit. Police rounded up gang after gang and took them to the corridors of the county court house. Several of the youths escaped through rear windows. They joined others who had left the community party at Napa Pavilion and put property at serious risk.

Ringleaders attempted to storm the police station, where some 20 rioters were being held. Dispersal of the gangs was accomplished only after the fire department brought fire hoses into play. Three water trucks went into action at main intersections, and the drenching given the youths soon discouraged them from further activities.

Lieutenant (j.g.) P. E. Sigmon recently left Calistoga for assignment to the office of Admiral King, top man of the Navy, in Washington, D.C. He is the son-in-law of Mrs. H. Thorburn of the Tucker District. His wife, the former Helen Thorburn, plans to join him in Washington as soon as he can find accommodations.

page 8

Former Calistogan Evelyn Zeek Young has received word that her husband, Army Air Force Lieutenant William Young, is a prisoner of war in Germany. He had been reported missing in action in late September.

"I feel very fortunate to have heard so soon," Mrs. Young said. "Others have waited so long, or never heard."

Lieutenant Young had completed 43 missions over Germany when he was taken prisoner. Mrs. Young, a 1933 graduate of Calistoga High School, and her three-year-old daughter are now in Ukiah with her parents, Mr. and Mrs. Frank Zeek, former residents here.

The Jesse Garrison family is comfortably settled in Athens, Ga., according to a note received by friends. Mr. Garrison is employed in a state normal school nearby.

Mr. Garrison says that he is about to get a church started. In closing, he says, "We are not making quite as much as we made in Calistoga, but the family is happy, and that is what counts. It's not the money that makes the home, but the happiness in the home."

Note: Garrison's complaints about racism in Calistoga appeared in Chapter 19. Readers responded in chapters 21 and 26.

Chapter 28

𝖂eekly Calistogan of November 10, 1944

page 1

The Calistoga area did not follow the nation in the Presidential election, but stayed on the bandwagon of Governor Thomas E. Dewey and gave the Republican candidate a vote of 506, against incumbent Democrat Franklin D. Roosevelt's 400. In the town itself, Roosevelt carried by three votes – 269 to 266.

In the U.S. senatorial race, challenger Frederick Houser got

President Franklin D. Roosevelt
(Photo, public domain)

490 votes in the Calistoga area, against incumbent Sheridan Downey's 350. In town, Houser led 269 to 227.

Tarwater and Knights Valley precincts, lying in Sonoma County but with a population that considers Calistoga its shopping center, both swung to Dewey, giving him 120 votes to Roosevelt's 49. Those precincts, too, favored Houser over Downey, 118 to 44.

Unapposed incumbents Congressman Leroy Johnson,

State Senator Frank Gordon, and Assemblyman Ernest Crowley were returned to office with a large complimentary vote.

B. Rey Schauer was elected associate justice of the State Supreme Court, and Paul Peek was elected associate justice of the Third District Court of Appeal.

As of yesterday, President Roosevelt had a total of 23,437,274 votes nationwide, against Dewey's 20,628,446. Roosevelt apparently has 413 electoral votes, Dewey 181. In 1940, Roosevelt beat Wendell Willkie by nearly 500,000 votes. Dewey received more votes in the "Solid South" than Willkie did.

In California, Roosevelt garnered 1,657,051 to Dewey's 1,234,602. In the Senate race, Downey received 1,435,075 votes, Houser 1,302,737.

Totals quoted here are not final, as several states have not yet completed their counts, and the soldier vote is yet to be tallied.

Note: When all votes were counted, FDR had 25.6 million to Dewey's 22 million. An editorial on page four concedes: "We, along with the rest of the nation, accept the election of President Roosevelt to his fourth term with good grace. Despite the fact that we fought for the election of Thomas E. Dewey and attacked the manner in which the President has conducted his office, we have felt that many of his reforms have been of definite good to the country. It is to be hoped that Mr. Roosevelt will eschew any attempts of his backers to put into effect any of the crack-brained ideas that have discredited them in the past. It is our hope, and trust, that the election just past has brought about a national unity that will lead us all to give the administration an all-out support that will show every other nation on the globe that we, as Americans, will stand by our choice, undivided and unafraid."

California voters approved ballot propositions 1,2,3,4,5,7,9, and 10. Calistoga area voters were with the majority on all except 3 and 4. Here are the measures:

No. 1 – A $30 million bond issue to assist California veterans in acquiring farms or homes.

No. 2 – Constitutional amendment extending the benefits of tax exemption, up to $1,000 worth of property, to World War II veterans. World War I veterans already have this privilege.

No. 3 – Giving jurisdiction to the Legislature over salaries paid to the lieutenant governor, secretary of state, superintendent of public instruction, and treasurer. Their salaries are now frozen in the constitution. In several instances, their deputies are paid more than they are.

No. 4 – Exempting religious, hospital, and charitable organizations from property taxes.

No. 5 – Constitutional amendment authorizing the reinstatement of public officers and employees who resign to serve in the military.

No. 6 – Providing for an annual 60-day session of the Legislature and an annual budget. Both are now on a semi-annual basis.

No. 7 – Providing expense accounts for members of the Legislature.

No. 8 – Validating deeds to property sold for delinquent taxes.

No. 9 – Raising the state's ADA (average daily attendance) subvention to school districts from $60 to $80.

No. 10 – Authorizing increases of salaries of county, township, and municipal officers during the war.

No. 11 – Providing a $60 monthly payment to all persons over 60 years old not gainfully employed, and repealing the sales and use tax and substituting a gross transactions tax.

No 12 – The "right to work" amendment.

Earl C. Lander's selfless heroism as a Navy gun captain is cited in a letter from Admiral Louis P. Hayes, commander of fleet operations in the Mediterranean. The letter was sent to Earl's parents but forwarded to his grandparents, Mr. and Mrs. C.O. Fink, with whom he lived while attending Calistoga Elementary School.

Lander "was serving on board the USS *Kaweak*, which participated in the North Africa, Sicily, and southern France invasions," Admiral Hayes' letter says. "He was in charge of an anti-aircraft gun. Though wounded twice in action, he refused the Purple Heart.

"In the invasion of southern France, his ship was constantly under enemy fire. When returning to a port on the southern coast of France, his ship was sunk after a fierce battle. Your (grand)son's gun was responsible for knocking down a plane, but three of his men were killed by a near hit. With only four of his men left, he kept the gun firing, until it was hit, throwing him over the side. It took great courage to keep his gun in action faced by overwhelming odds.

"He was recommended for the Navy Cross by his commanding officer for conspicuous gallantry in performing his duties above and beyond the call of duty. He refused this award for what he said was what anyone would have done in his place. He was placed in a hospital overseas and was released to be sent back to the States for six months of limited shore duty. What your (grand)son has done for his country should make you very proud."

Note: Lander graduated from Calistoga Elementary School in 1940.

Community Chest may come into being in the near future, following a suggestion made by Frank Piner at the Calistoga War Finance Committee meeting last night.

Piner, noting the multiplicity of demands made on Calistoga by various fund-raising drives, suggested that the community might be better served by a single agency to collect and allocate funds.

At this time, the town is faced with requests by the War Chest, Salvation Army, Boy Scouts, Girl Scouts, the Christmas package fund, and sundry necessary amounts for local relief. Other donations frequently are requested through the City Council.

The Community Chest would have a board of directors empowered to act upon every request for funds. Needs of the numerous organizations would have to be anticipated, and a drive held to collect the needed funds. Just two drives would remain outside its jurisdiction – War Loan drives and the Red Cross.

Piner emphasized that the plan would require much thinking by all concerned, and that it will be some time before concrete plans can be presented for final action.

Note: In 2012, Calistoga had the only surviving Community Chest organization in California. Other places had shifted to the United Fund.

Some 300 Farm Bureau members from five North Coast counties gathered in Napa Saturday to discuss the post-war outlook for agriculture in California.

The keynote speaker, Dr. H.R. Wellman, director of the Giannini Foundation at University of California, said that government action in the farm price program should be limited. With continued farm prosperity, the law of supply and demand should operate freely through the competitive market, with a minimum of governmental support, except in a regulatory way to avoid the piling up of too great a surplus.

He said there is some danger that post-war demobilization may bring a break in farm prices, as after World War I, with a resulting danger that farmers may be caught between falling farm prices and rising production costs. In this event, farmers will have a definite stake in price controls, particularly of industrial products.

In the event of farm distress, government assistance could take several forms, depending on the extent and seriousness of the deflation, he said. Wellman said that subsidized food consumption programs, like the food stamp plan, would be of great value, both to feed low-income groups and to dispose of vast quantities of farm products. He said deferment of farm mortgage payments could be undertaken, and in the event of a protracted period of depression, certain income payments could be made to growers. He said these payments could be in the form of outright grants to inject money into the national income stream and, at the same time, keep the farmers solvent.

He concluded by pointing out that the crucial issue for a farmer in the post-war period will be whether he wants security of income through government assistance in some form or another, or free enterprise and strict market competition. The security trend is growing, he said.

O.B. Earle, a former resident of Calistoga and the owner of property here, has been promoted to the rank of captain in the Navy. He is head of an ordinance department at Mare Island Naval Shipyard. Captain Earle has many years of Navy service. He retired from command of the USS *Montgomery* in 1935, but he returned to active duty in 1939.

One of the largest real estate deals to be consummated in Calistoga for some time was closed this week when L.P. (Babe) Ames sold his home on Greenwood Avenue, off Myrtledale Road north of town, to George H. Hanvy, San Francisco advertising man.

Long a show place of Calistoga, the property goes into good hands. Mr. Hanvy plans on making his home here in the near future. Mr. and Mrs. Ames will move into town and will occupy the Hoover home on Berry Street, now the property of Mrs. Alice Hoover Papandre of Oakland. Babe's not-too-good health brought about the change. He felt the Greenwood property demanded too much time and effort.

Postmistress Josie Ratto announced that Christmas packages may be sent to Rome, Naples, Palermo, and Vatican City under a limited parcel post service. Packages must not weigh more than four pounds, nor measure more than 36 inches in length and girth combined. The value of each gift is limited to $25.

Calistoga's new Hospitality House is winning praise in letters received by Mrs. John Mingus.

"It was very thoughtful of you to include the Mare Island Navy Yard enlisted personnel in your list of invited guests for the Halloween dance on October 28," Lieutenant Commander S.M. Higgins, assistant enlisted personnel officer at Mare Island, wrote. "I will personally see that the information given in your letter has the widest publicity.

"Believe me, the efforts put forth by activities such as yours do not go unappreciated by either the enlisted personnel or officers who are charged with the responsibility of maintaining high morale."

Another letter signed by a sailor, a soldier, and their girl-friends says: "We want to express our appreciation for your kindness last Tuesday when we were in your city. You were very sweet to us, and we can't begin to thank you enough."

page 4

Stanley M. Jessen, a Navy aviation chief machinist mate, has been advanced to pay grade one – the highest war-time non-commissioned officer rate. He is a veteran of nine years in the Navy. He currently is assigned to the Naval Air Station at Glenview, Illinois, where he is in charge of the maintenance of synthetic training devices. He previously was attached to the fleet air wing at San Diego.

Chief Jessen graduated from Calistoga High School in 1934. He was employed by Pan American Airways before enlisting in the Navy. His wife, Nancy, and son, Stanley, reside with him in Chicago. His mother, Rosa, now lives in Oakland.

Note: Jessen, a retired airline maintenance director, died in 2005 in Grass Valley.

News briefs: Delbert Pearl, who is in Navy training in San Diego, has written his parents, the A.M. Pearls, that his life is satisfactory so far. He has run across Jack Scott, another 1944 graduate of Calistoga High School.

Army Sergeant Robert Whatford recently spent a short furlough in Calistoga with his wife and other relatives. He has returned to his station at Camp Lewis, Washington.

Most stores in Calistoga will be closed tomorrow, Armistice Day.

Chapter 29

November 19-25

The War: The first B-29 bombers originating from Tinian raid Tokyo. U.S. ships in the North Pacific are heavily damaged by suicidal Kamakazis. Hitler moves to Berlin from his wartime headquarters at Rastenberg, East Prussia. Metz and Strasbourg in eastern France are liberated.

𝔚eekly 𝔗alistogan of November 24, 1944

page 1

Another local boy has distinguished himself on the battle front. He is Army Private Ed "Willkie" LaSalle, the rather long-geared boy who in his two years at Calistoga High School distinguished himself in basketball, tennis, and in first aid. He admired Wendell Willkie so sincerely that forever after the 1940 presidential campaign he carried the nickname.

His mother, Mrs. Gertrude LaSalle of San Francisco, this week forwarded a clipping about him to James F. Albright of Calistoga, with whom Willkie lived in Franz Valley while attending high school with the class of 1942. It was taken from the newspaper published by the Army regiment to which Willkie is assigned. Here it is, verbatim:

Edmond "Wilkie" LaSalle

"Nice goin', pard. You really showed those b------- that it is foolish for them to survive. Private Edmond C. LaSalle of Calistoga, California, a capable aide-man, gave them a bit of hokum that turned the tables.

"One dark night in No Man's Land, Ed was administering first aid to a wounded soldier. During the operation, three mental midgets – Nazis to you, Bud – pulled a fast sneakeroo and captured Ed. They led the medic to their makeshift headquarters that housed six additional E-flats and an officer. Technically, Ed was a prisoner of war; actually, the West Coaster thought differently. Although he could not speak German, his spirited gestures during the night convinced them that surrender was their only salvation. The following morning, our boy marched them back to the unit, where they became the regiment's prisoners.

"LaSalle was asked by Major Robert H. Townley, regimental surgeon, to take a much-needed rest. Said Ed, 'Hell no, Sir! I wanna get back in the thick of it.'"

Willkie has received a Bronze Medal and a citation for bravery as a result of his presence of mind while he was very much behind the "8 ball" and in the hands of the enemy. He is serving with old "Blood and Guts" Patton in the Third Army in France.

The thought has been expressed that residents of Calistoga might do well to remember the exploits of Willkie and a hundred other Calistoga boys during the Sixth War Loan Drive.

With three days of the Sixth War Loan Drive passed, Calistoga has made a fair start toward the $200,000 quota, having already subscribed $40,000.

Slowly gaining the upper hand in Germany, and edging closer to the homeland of Japan, the arms of the United Nations face what is perhaps the most critical period of World War II.

It is a basic fact that neither this war, nor any other, can be won by the use of inferior arms. To supply quality arms, there must be billions of dollars available; and in the United States, it is up to the citizens to supply those billions.

In every preceding drive, the nation met the quota, and Calistoga oversubscribed.

The government, aware that farmers have enjoyed one of the most prosperous seasons in recent years, has issued an appeal to farmers to lend part of their harvest profits.

Frank Piner, chairman of the Calistoga War Finance Committee, said, "Calistoga occupies a peculiar position insofar as business incomes are concerned. The resort owners enjoy summer prosperity. Then the farmers reap the benefit of their harvest. Now it is up to the growers of the area to take up the slack and buy bonds to the full limit of their capacity. The money is earning interest for the buyer of bonds and, at the same time, is serving the primary purpose of helping to win the war."

Calistoga 1944

Clifford Anderson, director of music for Calistoga schools, has sent out a rehearsal call for persons who want to be in the chorus at the community Christmas concert on Wednesday evening, December 20. They will sing the background music for a one-act play.

The first rehearsal will be held at the high school on the night of Tuesday, November 28. This year's Christmas program will be the most ambitious ever undertaken. The first part will be Christmas selections by the high school band. The second half will be a one-act play, "Why the Chimes Rang." Admission will be free.

Mrs. Marvin McCormick of Napa has been named chairman of the 1944 Christmas Seal campaign of the County Tuberculosis and Health Association, which will open on Monday, November 27.

"Seventy-nine cents of every dollar received stays in this county for case-finding projects," Mrs. McCormick states, "while sixteen cents goes to the state organization and five cents to the national organization."

There was rejoicing at the Robert Sylvester home in Franz Valley Monday night, when the family received a telegram from Washington, D.C., saying that Corporal Bertram Washabaugh, the son of Mrs. Sylvester, who was reported missing in action early in September, is safe and is a prisoner of war in Germany.

Landing in France on the third day of the D-Day invasion, Bert went into action with his anti-tank division. He was reported missing on August 17.

Washabaugh was a graduate of Franz Valley Elementary School. He attended high school and business college in Santa Rosa. He worked for Pacific Gas & Electric Company in the San Joaquin and Sacramento valleys until he entered the service.

Note: The September 8 Weekly Calistogan (Chapter 19) carried the report that Bert was missing.

Approaching the end of the 1944 processing season, the Calistoga walnut plant is working at capacity, with 70 persons employed.

Up to Tuesday night, the plant had processed 1,075 tons of walnuts; and 23 carloads had been shipped by rail.

In common with the rest of the state, walnuts in this area are far below normal quality this year. The unusual hot spell that came just before harvest is blamed. Nuts from the higher altitudes in Lake County are better than those coming from the valley, but those too are not up to the usual standard.

Note: The walnut processing plant on Washington Street was a hub of fall harvest activity from 1939 until 2000.

A letter from Charles (Chuck) Schmitt, who is on active duty with the U.S. Navy Reserve, tells his mother, Mrs. Mary Schmitt, that he is now in a hospital "somewhere in the South Pacific" recovering from injuries received during the invasion of the Philippines.

Chuck could not disclose the exact nature of his injuries, nor where he is. He was able to write the letter himself, so he evidently is recovering satisfactorily.

Note: Schmitt was a 1937 graduate of Calistoga High School.

Public response to the Post Office Department's "Shop Now! Mail in November" campaign is good, but it needs to be better, according to Postmaster General Frank C. Walker's recent letter to Postmistress Josie Ratto of Calistoga.

"Extraordinary wartime conditions face us," Mr. Walker said. "Unless more people buy and mail this month, the postal service cannot do its job of delivering all Christmas gifts on time.

"Unprecedented shortages of manpower and transportation facilities growing out of the war compel early mailing. The postal service has given 50,000 experienced employees to the armed forces, and 300,000 railroad workers have gone to war.

"Equally serious is the fact that rail and other transportation facilities are taxed to the limit with the great burden of war traffic, which all of us know must take precedence.

"We urge everyone to buy now, mail in November, and mark the gifts 'Do not open until Christmas.'"

The sale of Maplewood, home of Mr. and Mrs. Curtis Wright, to Charles B. Forni of St. Helena was announced this week. The estate consists of some 25 buildings scattered over 270 acres. It has long been a show place of the upper valley. To old-timers, it is known as the Holje place.

Forni, having also purchased the Brown property, across the highway from Maplewood, plans on planting much of the two sites to grapes – creating one of the largest vineyards in this area.

Calistoga 1944

Next Thursday, November 30, citizens of the upper valley will again be given the opportunity to donate blood to the Red Cross Mobile Blood Bank, which will be in St. Helena that day.

Setting a quota of 200 pints of blood, those in charge of the bank hope to see St. Helena and Calistoga exceed that amount by a very substantial margin. Over 70 Calistogans journeyed to St. Helena the last time the Red Cross unit was there.

Mrs. Mitto Blodgett, head of the Calistoga Red Cross, urges donors to get in touch with her at the earliest possible moment so she can arrange transportation.

The vital importance of blood plasma becomes more and more apparent as news stories and pictures reach the public press from the battle fronts. It is an extreme case when blood plasma does not save a wounded man's life. Donors realize, or should realize, that the very blood they give will save the life of a soldier.

Don E. Cole, son of Calistoga barber Howard Cole, is a student at the U.S. Naval Reserve Midshipmen's School on the campus of Notre Dame University in Indiana.

After a one-month indoctrination course, Don will be commissioned a midshipman. At the end of the four-month course, he will emerge with the stripe of an ensign.

Don has two brothers in the service of Uncle Sam. Jack is a prisoner of the Japs at a camp on the Japanese mainland after having been captured at the fall of Corregidor in the Philippines. Fred, the second brother, is in the Navy and on duty "somewhere in the Pacific."

Note: Jack and Fred Cole returned to Calistoga after the war. Fred worked with his dad, and Jack ran a beauty shop.

Calistoga residents are again asked to gather all of the scrap metal lying around loose and unused in the back yard, the farm yard, the wood shed, and the attic. It is being collected for the war effort by Calistoga Post 231, American Legion. Any metal but aluminum is wanted. Bring it to the Schuman-Tamagni garage on Main Street.

Note: Main Street now is Foothill Boulevard.

Chapter 30

November 26 – December 2

The War: Japanese attacks threaten Kunming in south-western China, an important Allied air base.

Weekly Calistogan of December 1, 1944

page 1

E.A. (Buck) Erickson of the State Division of Forestry calls attention to the fact that it is unlawful for anyone to remove Christmas trees growing on land not his own without a written permit from the owner, signed by him or his authorized agent.

Any person who knowingly sells, offers or exposes for sale, or transports for sale Christmas trees from land not his own without the written permit of the owner is guilty of a misdemeanor.

Anyone transporting more than two Christmas trees must have a shipping permit that can be obtained at the Division of Forestry headquarters in St. Helena.

Mrs. Phoebe Janet Tyler, 82, a resident of this area much of the time since 1877, died Sunday at a nursing home near the St. Helena Sanitarium. She was the last member of her family.

Mrs. Tyler was born near Elmira, Solano County, December 23, 1862. With her parents, Mr. and Mrs. Harry L. Lincoln, and other family members, she came to Calistoga in 1877 and spent most of the rest of her life here. She was in the first graduating class of the Calistoga Grammar School, finishing her work in 1883 under Principal G.W. Weeks.

She united with the Seventh-Day Adventist Church in Calistoga in 1887 – she and her mother being among its charter members.

Her funeral, held from Simic Funeral Home in Calistoga Tuesday afternoon, was followed by burial in the Calistoga cemetery.

Calistoga 1944

The following are excerpts from letters received by Mr. and Mrs. W.E. Tomasini of Knights Valley from their son, Staff Sergeant Loring Tomasini, who is now in the Philippines:

October 31, 1944: "I am on Leyte and am fine. A coconut just fell off a tree and almost beaned me, but this is my closest shave so far.

"I have not been dry for days, because it rains every night and I sweat all day. However, both the country and the operations are very interesting, and there is nothing monotonous or boring about this kind of life.

"There are a lot of things I could tell you, but want to be sure that this letter reaches you intact, so you will know I am OK. Don't worry about me: the sailing has been smooth enough so far, and probably will remain the same."

November 1, 1944: "The most striking thing about the Philippines so far is the display of pyrotechnics. It is a continual Fourth of July. At night, the tracers, flares, and ack-ack light up the sky. When Uncle Sam is not providing us this entertainment, nature takes over. The fireflies here are incandescent and can be seen 100 yards away. They tend to swarm around a few trees, and such a tree, with 100 or so fireflies around it, is as decorative as a Christmas tree.

"The situation for me is quiet and restful now. Things are much better organized than they were on Attu. We are not suffering from the hardships and privation we had there. An amusing similarity between the two operations is that we have been harassed by birds both places. On Attu, there was a relative of the killdeer that flew close to our positions. At night we thought their calls were Jap signals, as we had heard that they used bird calls. There were so many of them that we thought we were surrounded. Here there is a bird that whistles like a bullet, and every time that he calls we all duck."

November 7, 1944: "Made a trip into the hills yesterday and saw a lot of natives who were anxious to trade for cigarettes and food. The trouble is that they have nothing to offer but Japanese currency and a very few bananas. The country is covered with banana palms, but there is no fruit on them. I was in a group of three who hit the jackpot, because we found a boy who had a bottle of beer. He had no idea of the value of it, because we got it for eight cigarettes and a few matches. He had traded a Jap soldier a few bananas for it.

"I saw two natives riding a water buffalo. They twist its tail when they want it to start moving. It did not have to be coaxed to stop."

November 11, 1944: "We have moved away from our river, with its bathing and laundering facilities, to a beautiful beach, where I am sitting under the shade of a palm grove, watching the natives build grass houses for the soldiers to live in. I watched sunrise while taking my morning dip in the surf. Our principal commodities for barter with the natives are undershirts, rations, and cigarettes. In return, they will build a shelter out of bamboo, leaves, and telephone wire. We have pesos to pay them with, but there is nothing they can buy as yet, so they want goods.

"There seems to be a great shortage of cloth, so I wish you would send me about three small packages of cotton print goods. Used things will be OK, like waists or shirts or just the material, so they can make their own. Sox are worthless, as they all go bare-foot. Heavy materials are not necessary, since clothes are worn for decoration or modesty, not for warmth. An undershirt is good for half a day's work."

The $30 million taxable value of property in Napa County for 1944-45 is up 25 percent from the $24.1 million assessed value in 1940-41, the California Taxpayers' Association announced this week in an analysis of changes since the United States entered the war.

Property values in the county this year are as follows: land, $11 million; improvements on land, $13.2 million; personal property and money, $6 million. Exemptions, which have been deducted from these valuations, total $686,670.

The total taxable value of property in California for 1944-45 is $8.3 billion, an increase of 16 percent over the $7 billion valuation for 1940-41.

Note: In 2010, the assessed valuation for property in Napa County was $27.1 billion. For Calistoga, it was $651.5 million.

After more than a year in the South Pacific, Navy Chief Gunner's Mate Ephraim "Barney" Light returned home on Thanksgiving Day and is spending a 30-day furlough here with his family.

His homecoming was highlighted by his meeting, for the first time, his young son, Ronald, who was born some five months ago. And, too, there was the pleasure of getting re-acquainted with Sally

Joan, who is now just past two years old. Returning to Calistoga with him was Mrs. Light, who had been with him since his ship tied up in the home port.

This is the longest furlough Barney has enjoyed in a long time. He is the son of Mr and Mrs. L.E. Light of Calistoga.

Note: Barney was a 1936 graduate of Calistoga High School.

Calistoga's newest industry, the production of bees-wax and honey, is growing steadily through the energy of Starr C. Cahill, who recently purchased the F.A. Wright property south of town and immediately started improvements and the installation of the equipment necessary for the commercial production of honey and its byproducts.

A new 30 x 50 shed houses the equipment used in the extraction of honey and the processing of wax. The shop also provides room for the building of hives and the preparation of the frames upon which the bees build their combs.

At the present time, Cahill has some 300 hives set out, and he will add a considerable number during the early spring. Stocked with Caucasian bees, noted as being tame and hard workers, the Cahills produced a little over two tons of honey during the past season.

During 1945, Cahill will also propagate queen bees on a commercial scale, and he expects to find a wide market for them throughout the state.

With over 350 different uses for bees-wax in the armed forces alone, the government is lending every aid to apiarists who will process and sell wax to it. The wax is used for everything from waxing bullets to waterproofing machinery and coverings.

Another valuable use of bees is in the pollenizing of orchards. Hives are set up in the orchards where the bees are to work, and the grower is assured that his trees will be pollinated through the honey-gathering effort of the bees. Cahill already has contracts signed and will move his hives to the orchards when the blossoms come out in the spring.

Young men of Calistoga and vicinity will be able to obtain complete information about opportunities for enlistment in the U.S. Navy when Jack Balin, recruiter based in Santa Rosa, visits here next Wednesday, December 13.

Headquarters will be at the hardware store of Alm and Ames. A boys' assembly at the local high school will be a part of the program.

Of particular interest, Balin says, are opportunities to qualify for special training as radio technicians or air crewmen.

Friends of Lieutenant Commander Arnold F. Schade were pleasantly surprised last Sunday when they opened a supplement of the *San Francisco Examiner* and found the commander's picture included in a group of pencil portraits of outstanding fighting officers of World War II.

The caption under Schade's portrait said: "Rated youngest submarine commander for 1943 is Lieutenant Commander Arnold F. Schade, who also has been decorated with a Navy Cross with Silver Star. His unrelenting destruction of Japanese ships since the Pearl Harbor attack gives Nippon more reason than ever to fear deadly warfare dealt out by U.S. submarines."

Schade is the son-in-law of Captain C.N. Fiske, USN (retired), of Calistoga.

Note: His daughter Helen attended Calistoga Elementary School.

page 4

Editorial: Strikes have been such a common occurrence during the war that, unpardonable as they are, they no longer shock some people, except in cases where the abuse is most glaring.

A recent strike in Detroit was of the latter type. A jurisdictional dispute tied up work in 24 vital war plants. It is not hard to imagine the bitterness that this uncalled-for action must have aroused in the hearts of millions with members of their families serving in the armed forces and dependent upon the products of these Detroit plants to carry on the war. They cannot be blamed for wondering what in the world has happened to the souls of workmen who sanction these strikes, knowing full well, as they do, the consequences to our fighting men.

Corporal Lawrence G. Demattei, son of Mr. and Mrs. Lory Demattei of Calistoga, is completing his training on a Liberator bomber at the Pueblo Air Base, according to a news item received directly from the Colorado base this week. Lawrence is the engineer on his crew. He entered the service in July, 1943, shortly after graduating from Calistoga High School.

Note: Larry and his brother Angelo returned to Calistoga after their war service. They were stars on Calistoga's baseball town team.

High School Notes: The Junior Prom is to be held in the new gym on December 9. A 16-piece Army Air Corps band has been engaged. Bids may be secured from members of the junior class.

The war bond quota for the high school has been set at $2,081. That's an $18.75 bond for each student and teacher. Sales by class so far are: freshmen, $95; sophomores, $203; juniors, $728; and seniors, $40.

The student store has now been functioning for two weeks. The total of sales for that time is $74. Approximately half of this is profit, which will be split between the four classes.

Taxpayers are reminded for the last time that the first installment of county property taxes will become delinquent on December 5. A penalty will be added after that date. Taxes may be paid in Calistoga at Bank of America or in Napa at the office of Tax Collector A.H. Shepard in the County Court House.

Nick Bardes, who is training with the Army Air Corps at Merced, visited his parents, Mr. and Mrs. Jim Bardes, over the weekend.

Patients fill the Calistoga Hospital. However, most of them are either permanent residents or are hospitalized for more or less minor ailments. Recent arrivals include Mrs. Edmund Molinari, Mrs. Alex Bardenotis, Jack Snyder, and Mrs. Ben Schuman and small daughter Sally Bernice. Mrs. Schuman transferred to the hospital following the birth of her baby in the St. Helena Sanitarium on November 18.

page 8

Elementary School Notes: War bond and stamp sales have totaled $1,473 since October 3. Pupils who have purchased bonds are Mary Edna Stevens, Nancy Tamagni, Kenneth Lindsey, Jackie Grauss, Teddy Tamagni, Monte Gorman, Tommy Albright, Joe Tymn, Ernest Bjorkland, Eva Marie Lindsey, Eleanor Federspiel, Tom McGreane, and Patsy Anderson.

Chapter 31

December 3-9
The War: The U.S. begins pre-invasion bombardment of
Iwo Jima.

𝔚eekly 𝔠alistogan of December 8, 1944

page 1

Calistoga's Sixth War Loan Drive went booming over its
$200,000 goal yesterday. The week's sale of bonds topped $100,000,
pushing the drive total to $205,746 with another week to go.

It was the heaviest six days' sales in the history of local War
Loan drives. Again, the community has demonstrated its willingness
and ability to meet the financial demands made upon it by the war.

As in previous drives, two local wine companies helped Calistoga by
making substantial bond purchases. Larkmead Vineyards, through
Elmer and Felix Salmina, bought a large block of bonds, as did
C. Mondavi & Sons, through Chapin F. Tubbs, manager of the
Mondavi interests in the Calistoga area.

Other firms and corporations that bought bonds here, through
their representatives, are: Safeway Stores; Sonoma County
Farmers' Mutual Fire Insurance Company, represented by Mrs.
Lee Pressey; Golden Gate Bridge and Highway District, through
Director Nathan F. Coombs; Standard Oil Company of California,
represented by Roy Thorsen and Everett Giugni; Greyhound Bus,
though Owen Kenney; Texas Company; Shell Oil Company, by Ray
Oxford; Hammond Lumber Company, by Pete Molinari; Pacific Gas
and Electric Company, through Lee Wise; and State of California.

The drive does not officially close until a week from tomorrow.
With bond sales falling far below normal all over the United States,
Calistoga has reason to be proud of being among the first communities
to meet, and pass, its quota.

More than 150 persons gathered at the Plaza Hotel in Napa
Saturday night to do homage to Robert Louis Stevenson and to

hear Flodden W. Heron of San Francisco, internationally known authority on Stevenson, tell about the famous author's life.

Joseph R. Knowland, chairman of the State Park Commission and owner of the *Oakland Tribune*, assured those present that the proposed Robert Louis Stevenson Memorial Park on Mount St. Helena has the unqualified support of the commission.

Senator Frank L. Gordon assured the crowd he will present the memorial park bill at the next session of the State Legislature and he has been assured it will pass without opposition.

Norman B. Livermore confirmed his offer of land which will be added to the park.

Mrs. Maggie Turner of Calistoga, who knew Stevenson during his stay in Calistoga and on Mount St. Helena in 1883, told of her memories of the author. She mentioned in particular his visits to her childhood home, the hotel in Knights Valley owned by her father, Frank McDonald. Mrs. Gertrude Stratton, a child in Calistoga when Stevenson lived here, told of making daily deliveries of milk to the Stevenson home and of the games of "mumbley-peg" that she and Stevenson frequently played.

George Hoberg, president of the Redwood Empire Association, spoke of the park's value as an added attraction to the area.

Ralph P. Winston, chairman of the Robert Louis Stevenson Park Committee, expressed its appreciation for the efforts of Miss Edith Livermore, who, single-handed, has raised some $4,000 toward the sponsor's fund. Winston said the largest part of the credit for raising the necessary funds for the park must be given to her.

Climax of the evening came when Heron placed his world-famous collection of Stevensoniana on the cleared speaker's table and launched into his talk on Stevenson's life, career, and place in the world of literature. Time after time, the speaker brought Stevenson closer to the audience through his use of a manuscript, a first edition, or a picture, to illustrate the anecdote, or fact, he was telling at the moment.

Many of those who attended the banquet journeyed to Calistoga the next day and visited places associated with Stevenson, including the site of the proposed park on the slopes of Mount St. Helena.

Some 30 people climbed the narrow trail that leads to the Stevenson monument, erected on the site of the Stevenson honeymoon cabin in 1911. Author Anne Roller Issler described the terrain as it existed when Stevenson lived there and touched on his description of it.

Miss Ivy Loeber, representing the Napa County Federation of Women's Clubs, laid a wreath upon the monument, spoke briefly of its history, and described the work of her organization in placing the tablet in 1911.

Flodden W. Heron asked: "I wonder if all of you realize the importance of today's ceremony? Many monuments have been erected to Robert Louis Stevenson; there are streets, bridges, buildings, and recently a vessel, named in his honor.

"The news of this memorial park dedication will pass across the cable lines of the world — from Edinburgh to Australia, and from New York to Capetown, because wherever the English language is spoken, people will learn with pleasure of this latest honor to a beloved author. This dedication — this park — will eventually bring to Napa Valley more publicity and advertising than do its famous wines.

"I am going to hope that when a building is erected on this site, where he spent many happy days, it will be a replica of the home that R.L.S. personally designed and lived in as his home in Samoa. And I would suggest that the side of one room contain a tier of bunks, just as they were in the miner's cabin here in which he lived.

"If and when the state erects the proper fire-proofed building, I propose to make some gifts to the Stevenson room, and I know other collectors of Stevensoniana who, I feel, will do likewise.

"Let us hope that the day is not long distant."

Note: See Chapter 1 for background on the Stevenson project.

"The Story of Dr. Wassell" will be the featured at the War Bond Show at the Ritz Theatre next Tuesday, December 12. Tickets can be secured only by purchasing a bond at the local Bank of America branch, the Post Office, or at the theatre's ticket booth on the night of the event.

"The Story of Dr. Wassell," about a Navy crew's survival in the Dutch East Indies, has been proclaimed among the best pictures dealing with the war. It was filmed in Technicolor. Gary Cooper turns in one of the best characterizations of his long career.

Heartbreaking news was received a few days ago by Staff Sergeant Buron Camp, Calistoga boy who recently came home after months of service with the Marine Corps in various major engagements in the South Pacific.

A cablegram informed him that his six-month-old daughter, Carolyn Joy, whom he had never seen, passed away at sea, enroute with her mother to join Buron in this country. She was buried at Noumea, New Caledonia. Many of the details are missing and will be supplied only when Mrs. Camp arrives here.

Sergeant Camp, son of the W.A. Camps of Calistoga, was married in New Zealand, but has not seen his wife for many months. He is in this country for rest and rehabilitation.

Odd Fellows Lodge 227 held a busy session Wednesday night, highlighted by the acceptance of 15 applications for membership and the decision to start a junior lodge in Calistoga, with Kenneth Brown as its first adviser. Further details will be released soon.

That the local lodge is fast expanding is evidenced by the fact that the second degree was conferred on four candidates.

Other business included a vote to make further purchases of War Bonds and to subscribe to the annual drive of the Napa County Tuberculosis Association.

Marine Sergeant Patricia Kelley, daughter of Mr. and Mrs. Jack Kelley, arrived home on a surprise visit last Friday. She is attached to the paymaster's section at Marine Corps headquarters in Washington, D.C.

Pat says she finds her work intensely interesting. Recently, she found an apartment, and has moved out of the barracks where she had been quartered for some time.

Note: Pat was a 1940 graduate of Calistoga High School.

Calistoga Rotarians were spellbound yesterday during an hour-long program with two war films.

Between reels, Petty Officer P.L. Newmeyer gave a very moving talk on what our fighting men are facing on the battle fronts and stressed the importance of keeping supplies of all kinds moving to the war fronts. He brought the war very close to his listeners as he described the conditions under which our men are fighting, and the bravery with which they carry on.

The first film, "Lifelines," covering the landing on Rendova and the subsequent fighting with the Japanese, showed the vital part that supplies play in the conduct of war.

The second reel, "Our Return to Guam," showed the rescue of Chief Radioman Tweed, the only American left on the island after the Japanese occupation, and then went on to show much of the action during the American landings. Several scenes give vivid pictures of the atrocities committed by the Japs on the natives of Guam.

Ornaments are very badly needed for decorating 10 Christmas trees in nearby hospitals where servicemen will be spending the holidays, states Mrs. John Mingus, chairman of the Camp and Hospital department of the Red Cross.

Full details of the sale of Napa Soda Springs were made public Wednesday following the recording of the agreement of sale. The resort was founded by Colonel John P. Jackson in pioneer times and had been in the hands of the Jackson family for over 80 years. It was hit by a disastrous fire in August.

New owners of the Napa Soda Company are A.D. McLean, Henry R. Pace, Edias Nasser, William Nasser, and Gordon W. Dennis. The group will form a corporation to take over the property, trade names, contracts, and all obligations.

Listed as sellers of the property are Hooper Jackson, San Francisco insurance broker and resident of Knights Valley, who signed as president of Napa Soda Company, and Stanley H. Jackson, secretary.

Chapter 32

December 10-16

The War: The Battle of the Bulge – the largest single land battle in U.S. history – begins as German forces attempt to a breakthrough in Ardennes Forest, Belgium. U.S. and Filipino troops land at Mindoro, the Philippines.

𝔚eekly 𝔠alistogan of December 15, 1944

page 1

On November 24, this paper carried a news story covering an exploit of a Calistoga boy, Ed "Willkie" LaSalle, that led to his being awarded a Bronze Medal and a citation for bravery, plus a promotion.

This week came the unhappy sequel.

A letter from his mother, Mrs. Gertrude LaSalle of San Francisco, says that Ed got back into the thick of it, and he is missing in action. Mrs. LaSalle was so informed in a telegram from the War Department.

The episode which brought Ed his medal took place on September 18-19. His last letter to his mother was dated November 4. The telegram stated that he had been missing since November 11, Armistice Day.

Those who knew Willkie during his days in Calistoga schools are holding the hope that he was captured and is now a prisoner. The fact that he is a member of the Medical Corps offers substance for such a hope. First aid men, technically non-combatants, are seldom fired upon deliberately. It is very probable that LaSalle, while attending the wounded, was caught in a counter-attack and taken prisoner.

Willkie's mother has been accepted in the Women's Army Corps and expects assignment during the latter part of this month.

Note: National Archives list LaSalle as "killed in action." He attended Calistoga High School his junior and senior years, with the class of 1942.

Nick Bardes and his 16-member Army Air Force band played at the high school's Junior Prom dance last Saturday night. They were honored before the dance with a turkey dinner at Hospitality House. The boys, based at Merced, were joined by several sailors who "happened in."

The dinner was served by Mrs. John Mingus, Mrs. W.C. Wiggins, Mrs. Kenneth Brown, Mrs. Myrtle Siemsen, Mrs. Tom Elder, and Miss Rosemary Senter, assisted by members of the Friendly Circle, who set tables and furnished hot rolls and salads. Lois Elder made the pumpkin pies, topped with real whipped cream.

Also helping were the Civic Club and various individuals who made cash donations to help pay for the 30-pound turkey, which was roasted by Ross Reeder. Jim Bardes, father of Nick, was on hand to do the carving.

The boys were guests for the night and for Sunday breakfast of Mr. and Mrs. James Bardes, Mr. and Mrs. Louis Bardes, Mr. and Mrs. John Ghisolfo, and Mr. and Mrs. John Mingus.

Note: Nick Bardes returned to Calistoga after the war and became a trumpet player/band leader. He served as secretary-treasurer of the Sonoma County Central Labor Council, 1983-91, and as leader of Musicians Union Local 6 in San Francisco until retirement in 1995. He died in 2004.

For the convenience of Calistoga residents who wish to get their Christmas packages into the mail, the local post office will be open tomorrow afternoon, Saturday, until 3 o'clock, states Postmistress Josie Ratto.

With the holiday season almost here, the mailing of packages becomes imperative if remembrances are to reach the recipients in time for the traditional Christmas morning opening of gifts.

John S. Butler, a pioneer of the Porter Creek district and long-time resident of Calistoga, died at the home of his son, Reed Butler, Sunday, December 10.

Born in Missouri on November 18, 1855, Mr. Butler came across the plains with his parents in an ox-driven wagon. The family settled in Santa Rosa, then moved to a ranch on the Mark West Creek Road, where John lived until his marriage to Miss Nancy Durham in 1875.

Taking up his own homestead on Porter Creek, near the Tarwater school, Mr. Butler followed ranching in that area until his family was grown. He then moved to Tubbs Lane in the Bennett district. He outlived two wives. He was a member of Calistoga Lodge of Masons and of Community Church.

Surviving are five children: Ella Teale, Edna Downer, Stella Ingalls, and Reed and Jesse Butler; nine grandchildren: Glenn Butler, Lloyd Butler, Martha Bimrod, Clarence Butler, Jack McLean, Bob Downer, Christie Teale, Kent Ingalls, and Lawrence Ingalls; and five great grandchildren: James Ingalls, Mel Ingalls, Lloyd Butler, Lynne Ingalls, and William Ingalls.

Funeral services were held Tuesday afternoon at the Simic Funeral Home, with Rev. A.E. Lucas officiating. Music was furnished by one of Mr. Butler's old friends, I.C. Adams. Pallbearers were all grandsons. Interment took place in the Calistoga Cemetery, with the graveside rites conducted by the Masons.

Despite the fact that a week ago yesterday saw Calistoga top its $200,000 goal in the Sixth War Loan drive, people continued buying bonds. At the close of business yesterday, the grand total for the town was $261,759.

In only one respect has the town fallen behind, and that is in the purchase of E bonds. The government, during the current drive, laid special emphasis on that type of bond and set comparatively high quotas for all localities. In Calistoga's case, the quota was $100,000. With the Sixth War Loan drive scheduled to close tomorrow, only $81,112 in E bonds have been purchased here. It could be the first time in the history of the six bond drives that the town has failed to make the grade.

Buyers still have time to purchase more E bonds, either at Bank of America or at the post office. If those who have already bought bonds will just strain a point and buy one more, Calistoga can still boast of an unblemished record.

Calistogans will present a free Christmas program of music and drama at 8:15 p.m. next Wednesday, December 20, in the high school gymnasium. The program has been arranged by Clifford Anderson, musical director for the Calistoga schools.

The high school band will open the program with five numbers: the National Anthem; Chenette's "Northern World Overture"; "Allegro Maestoso" from the "Water Music" of Handel; the ever-popular "On the Trail", from Groffe's "Grand Canyon Suite"; and "Christmas Rhapsody" by Long.

High school students will present a one-act Christmas play, "Why the Chimes Ring," by Elizabeth McFadden.

The cast: Holger – Jimmy Ingalls; Steen – Angelo Demetroff; the uncle – Norman Whatford; old lady – Marie Pocai; priest – Andy Richie; king – Harry Hawkins; courtier – Conrad Weil; sage – Bryan Putman; rich man – Bruce Piner; rich woman – Audrey Kelly; young girl – Camille Twight; and angel – Pat Shoemaker.

Teacher Mrs. Rozellen Salladay is the director. Incidental music will be furnished by the Calistoga Community Chorus.

Napa County and Calistoga city officials at a luncheon at the Mount View Hotel Tuesday discussed matters pertinent to the welfare of the county. Special emphasis was given to the part that Calistoga must play in the program that is being brought into shape for the betterment of the county and its communities once the war is over.

The luncheon featured talks by Thomas Maxwell, chairman of the Board of Supervisors; State Senator Frank L. Gordon; District Attorney Daniel K. York; Supervisor Charles Tamagni; County Surveyor Ed Ball, and others.

Calistoga has, indeed, been most fortunate in this relationship, in that the city has never failed to get the help of the county when it was needed.

Several enumerators are needed for the Census Bureau's upcoming agricultural census, according to Curtis Wright of Calistoga, who recently was named assistant supervisor for the area. A three-day training session will be held soon in Napa, with pay for each day's attendance. The Census Bureau does not furnish gasoline or tires, but it has arranged with local ration boards to furnish supplemental gas and tires for all enumerators, Wright said.

Calistoga Rotarians, their wives and guests, will gather at Bennett Farm Center hall tomorrow night for the club's annual Christmas Party and Ladies' Night. Over 120 are scheduled to be present.

The committee in charge of the evening's program, appointed by President Pete Molinari, is headed by George Locey. He is ably assisted by Charley Tamagni, Ed E. Light, George Leo Pease, Kent Ingalls, Alvin Kuster, and Frank Piner. The evening will hold many surprises in the way of entertainment.

Calistoga 1944

Meeting last Wednesday night, the Civic Club made plans for a future event, transacted a bit of business, and then held a stork shower honoring four members: Mrs. E.F. Palmer, Mrs. Alvin Kuster, Mrs. Edmund Molinari, and Mrs. Paul Alcouffe.

Planned for the future is a doll raffle. The doll, dressed by members of the club, will be displayed in the window of Johnston's Pharmacy.

With Noble Grand May Wallace presiding, Colfax Rebekah Lodge held a busy session Wednesday night, with election of officers holding the spotlight.

Mrs. Wallace was returned to the noble grand's chair, and Mabel Fisher was elected vice grand. Rosamond Hunt takes over the duties of recording secretary; Nona Wolleson, financial secretary; and Edith Fechter, treasurer.

It was made known that gifts which have been collected for soldiers will be sent to the Napa committee for distribution to men at Imola.

St. Helena and Calistoga Odd Fellows and Rebekahs will hold a joint New Year's Eve party on the night of Saturday, December 30, in St. Helena. It will be a box social, with bingo and cards. Proceeds will go to the war funds of the four lodges, evenly divided.

Following a tradition of many years' standing, the Calistoga Garden Club held its annual Christmas party Wednesday in the rooms of the Civic Club.

The program opened with a reading of "The Night After Christmas" by Mrs. J.E. Scott. Then the guests were shown a very fine collection of flower slides, in color, screened by Mr. and Mrs. Fred W. Rockhold.

Group singing of well-known carols formed the semi-windup of the affair, with refreshments and a real Santa Claus bearing gifts as the grand finale. Flower arrangement of the event consisted of a Christmas table decorated by Mrs. J.E. Scott and Mrs. W.T. Bentley.

For the next meeting, January 11, members are asked to bring a rock plant for exhibition.

page 4

Calistoga Troop, Girl Scouts of America, was officially recognized as a unit of the national organization in an impressive ceremony at the elementary school last Saturday. The ceremony was led by adult leaders and members of the Richmond Girl Scout troop.

The Calistoga troop members lit their candles from three candles which represented the three parts of the Girl Scout promise. Mrs. Carl Jursch was presented with a pin as leader of the local troop. Mrs. Ed Federspiel, local committee member, also received a pin.

Calistoga Native Daughters enjoyed their annual Christmas party and exchange of gifts following their regular parlor meeting Monday night. The meeting included the initiation of two new members. Business included a report on the Robert Louis Stevenson Memorial Park project and the acceptance of a gift – a lovely new Bear flag – from past president Elva Bettini.

Local News in Condensed Form: Bill Roberts, son of L.S. Roberts of Calistoga, has arrived overseas, according to word received by his parents. He is with the Marine Corps "somewhere" in the South Pacific.

Chief Machinist's Mate Jimmy Wolf, who has long been in the thick of the Pacific action with the Navy, has received his Christmas package from the City of Calistoga. He sent his thanks through relatives. Jimmy is the younger son of Mrs. Kate Wolf and a brother of Mrs. Pete Molinari.

Sergeant Robert Whatford, in a letter to his wife, who lives here, asked that his thanks be extended to Calistoga for the Christmas package he received from the city. Robert is now serving in the U.S. Army at Camp Lewis, Washington.

Mr. and Mrs. Richard V. Lee have returned from Napa, where they visited their daughters, including Mrs. DeForest Hamilton of Washington, D.C. Their son-in-law, Lieutenant DeForest Hamilton, U.S.N.R., was present for Thanksgiving. Mrs. Hamilton remained to visit her family. Lieutenant Hamilton has been on temporary duty with the U.S. Naval Photographic Supply Depot in Hollywood, but he will soon return to his post as educational consultant to the film branch of the Bureau of Aeronautics, Washington, D.C.

Staff Sergeant Ward Taylor, from somewhere in the European theater, has sent his thanks for the Christmas box sent from the City of Calistoga.

The Napa County Farm Bureau announces a meeting for all tomato growers at the Chamber of Commerce building in Napa at 7 p.m. Wednesday, December 20.

Calistoga 1944

Just back from 27 months of action in the South Pacific, Marine Private First Class Robert Cogan was a three-day visitor in Calistoga last week at the home of his uncle and aunt, Mr. and Mrs. George C. Locey, and his grandparents, the C.W. Nances.

Now only 20 years of age, young Cogan is a veteran of several major engagements. He is the son of Mrs. Irene Cogan of San Francisco, the former Miss Irene Nance of Calistoga.

After a 30-day furlough, part of which will be spent in Calistoga, Robert will report in South Carolina for further duty.

page 8

Elementary School Notes: Stamp and bond sales for this week were $253, bringing the total to $2,476. The amount for each grade was: first, $25; second, $59; third, $38; fourth, $19; fifth, $45; sixth, $30; seventh, $14; eighth, $24. Children receiving bonds were Eleanor Stevens, Myrel Moore, Milton Fechter, Monte Gorman, Charles Dixon, Jack Cary, Norman Wright, Warren Butler, George Hawkins, Frances Tedeschi, Billy Merry, Eugene Allen, Wayne Merry, and Albert Cravea.

Jimmy Rushing broke his arm and is absent from class.

Calistoga Rotary Club had two servicemen as guests at yesterday's luncheon meeting. They were Staff Sergeant Buron Camp, a Calistoga boy who recently returned from two years of action in the South and Central Pacific, and Chief Machinist's Mate John Knieling, who has over 14 years of service in the Navy, most recently three years in the South Pacific.

A.L. Plomgren, wholesale division manager for Shell Oil, gave a most convincing talk on the importance of aviation in the postwar world. He laid great emphasis on the need for communities to give immediate consideration to the development of airport facilities, even though construction of such facilities is something that may not become an actuality for several years to come.

Note: Calistoga got its first airport in 1947.

Births: In Stamford, Conn., November 6, to Mr. and Mrs. Jason Barthel, a son, John Norris Barthel. The baby's mother is the former Jacqueline Cole of Calistoga, and his grandparents are the Jack Coles of Richmond, also former Calistogan residents. His father, who returned to this country some time ago, miraculously escaped death in the Italian campaign (see Chapter 2 for details).

At St. Helena Sanitarium, November 24, to Staff Sergeant and Mrs. Revis E. Snodgrass, a son, Ernest Michael. The boy's father, a 1934 graduate of Calistoga High School, is a brother of June Snodgrass of Calistoga. He is stationed at the Benicia Arsenal.

In San Francisco, December 12, to Mr. and Mrs. Frank Losco, a daughter, Marcella. The mother is the former Marcella Musante, a 1933 graduate of Calistoga High School.

Calistoga High School's B basketball team (smaller, younger kids) began practices this month that led to a North Bay League championship early in 1945. The champs included, front row, left to right: Bruce Piner, Brian Putman, Ernie Zumwalt, Bob MacDonald, and Kenneth Westbay. Back row, l to r: Jack Fechter, Jim Ingalls, Conrad Weil, Allan Ballard, Gus Kelperis, Bob Johnson, and manager Norman Whatford.

Chapter 33

December 24-31
The War: U.S. troops begin their counter-attack at the "Bulge" and the German siege is broken. Churchill and his foreign secretary, Anthony Eden, try to reconcile warring factions in Greece. Russians free Budapest from German control, and Hungary declares war on Germany.

Weekly Calistogan of December 29, 1944

page 1

Mickel Harry Cohen, one of Calistoga's most respected businessmen and a veteran of the Spanish-American War, passed away at home Christmas morning following an illness of several months. He was 77.

Mr. Cohen and his wife have owned Piner's Hot Springs since 1926.

He was born in San Francisco on August 15, 1867. Entering the U. S. Army in April of 1887, he served with the Second U.S. Cavalry Troop at forts in Washington, New Mexico, and Arizona and then saw service in the Spanish-American War. He followed up his active service with a 17-year membership in the National Guard of California.

In 1909, he married Helen Frances Peterson of San Francisco, where he operated a men's furnishings business until 1911. The Cohens lived in semi-retirement in Lake County and then Calistoga before they bought Piner's Hot Springs. During the 18 years of their joint ownership of the resort, the Cohens built up a most enviable reputation as hosts. Friends say that his honesty, integrity, and kindness did more for Calistoga than can be measured in words.

Surviving him are his wife; a son, Harry Walter Cohen; a daughter, Mrs. Beatrice Davis of Long Beach; a granddaughter, Mrs. Aurelia Rosene of San Francisco; and two great grandchildren, Harold and Elaine Rosene.

The Rosary was said Wednesday night at the Simic Funeral Home, and the funeral mass was held at the Calistoga Catholic Church yesterday. Interment followed in the St. Helena Cemetery. *Note: Piner's now is Roman Spa.*

Calistoga sent out 197 Christmas boxes to Calistoga men and women with the armed forces, and presented Calistoga's Gold Star mothers with potted plants for Christmas.

The committee wishes to extend heartfelt thanks to all the ladies who made handkerchiefs for the packages, to Mrs. P. Oron for the roll of paper used for wrapping, to the *Weekly Calistogan* for the Christmas cards that went into the boxes, and, most of all, to those who made such generous cash donations for the projects.

Following several conferences with state officials and members of the State Park Commission, the Robert Louis Stevenson Memorial Park committee will endeavor to raise enough additional funds to purchase the acreage including the peaks of Mount St. Helena and, thus, create a state park with a double historical significance.

Back in the days before California was part of the United States, the Russians established Fort Ross on the coast of Sonoma County. The Commandant was Alexander Rotchef, a highly educated Russian famed for his translations into Russian of the works of Shakespeare, Schiller, and Victor Hugo. In later years, he wrote *Recollections of Travels Through India and California.* This California reference was based largely upon his experiences while at Fort Ross.

During June of 1841, Rotchef; I.G. Vosnesensky, zoologist of the Imperial Russian Academy of Sciences; and G. Tschernikh, an agriculturalist and amateur entomologist, climbed to the top of the then un-named mountain, the highest peak in sight from the fort. Once upon the north peak, they claimed all of the land in view in the name of their ruler, Czar Nicholas I, and planted wooden post with a bronze marker on it.

In 1853, after California became the 31st American state, the original plate was removed by Dr. T.A. Hyton of Petaluma and presented to the museum of the California Society of Pioneers in San Francisco. It was destroyed in the earthquake and fire of April, 1906.

Fortunately, H.L. Weston, also of Petaluma, had made a rubbing of the plate, which he presented to Miss Honora Tuomey. She, in turn, had a copy made in copper, and in 1912, the 100th anniversary of the founding of Fort Ross, the second plate was placed upon the summit.

V. Dobr, Calistoga resort owner and a student of the Russian occupation of California, says Rotchef named the mountain after Helena Pavlovna, sister of Czar Nicholas I.

In a letter to Mrs. Jack Matthews, head of the local unit of the British War Relief Association, Mrs. C.R. St. Aubyn, president of the organization's Northern California division, thanks the Calistoga unit for its outstanding effort. The letter follows:

"You have made it possible for us to send substantial relief to the victims of the robot bombs; you have contributed materially to the comfort of the sailors and airmen who have put in at this port, and, above all, by your loyal support you have helped us carry on the task we set ourselves to do in September, 1939.

"My committee joins me in wishing every blessing for you and the members of your group during the Christmas season. May we meet in peace soon after the start of the New Year!"

In 1943, the Calistoga unit shipped 48,000 dressings. In 1944, they will ship over 96,000.

After graduating as a second lieutenant in the Army Air Force last Friday, Laurel James Switzer Jr., son of Mr. and Mrs. Laurel Switzer of Calistoga, arrived home on a short leave during the early part of the week.

One of Jim's first calls was at the office of the *Weekly Calistogan*, where he left his thanks for the Christmas package sent to him by his home town.

Lieutenant Switzer leaves Monday for his new station at Liberal, Kansas, where he will start his training on B-24s.

Note: Jim was a 1942 graduate of Calistoga High School.

Jim Switzer

Christmas Notes: Small family gatherings characterized this holiday season in Calistoga, with only a few venturing far from their own firesides.

The minds and hearts of all went out to the men and women on the fighting fronts, and the homes of a few were gladdened by the presence of some member of the armed forces who was fortunate enough to be at home to enjoy the traditional festivities of the holiday season.

Some of the holiday activities enjoyed by local families follow:

Mr. and Mrs. F.L. Grauss Sr. enjoyed a family dinner at their home on Berry Street. Sharing the day's pleasures were their three daughters, Miss Margaret Grauss of Calistoga, Miss Muriel Grauss of Sacramento, and Mrs. Jack Root of Oakland. Also present was Mr. Root.

At the Frank Piner home, a small family gathering included their sons, Norman and Bruce, and Mrs. Piner's brother-in-law and sister, Mr. and Mrs. C.J. Schwarze of Napa.

After spending Christmas Eve with the Edmund Molinaris, the Pete Molinaris and their daughter, Marilyn, had dinner guests next day – Mrs. Kate Wolf; John Wolf; Mr. and Mrs. Tom Alexander and two daughters of Santa Rosa; and Mrs. James Wolf of Oakland.

Mr. and Mrs. Joseph A. Bagnasco entertained as their dinner guests on Christmas Day Mr. and Mrs. Tony Cardoza and his son Stevie; Mrs. Theresa Raynor of San Francisco; Mr. and Mrs. Joseph Bagnasco of Bennett district; and Mrs. Mazie Lawson and daughter Carol Lawson.

Mr. and Mrs. A.C. Bryant spent the holiday with relatives in the Bay Area.

The Ross Reeders shared a family dinner with three guests: Miss Flossie Delphy, Norman Flanagan of Napa, and Cecil Bryant. Also present were the Reeders' son, Harold; their daughter, Mrs. Lauren Procter; and their little grandson, Ross Procter. Like many families, they had a vacant chair at the table – that of Lauren Procter, who has been in the European theater for more than two years.

Dr. and Mrs. C.N. Fiske had their son and his wife, the Jack Fiskes of Colusa, and their niece, Dr. Stella Lovering of Los Angeles, as their guests.

Mrs. Mabelle Senter and son Eddie welcomed home several members of their family over the holiday, and had some other guests besides. Taking his family quite by surprise, Lieutenant Richard H. Senter, accompanied by two fellow Air Force officers, arrived in time to spend Christmas at home. Just back from the

Pacific area and awaiting re-assignment, Dick had as his guests Captain Joseph Huguini and Lieutenant John Gaiwenowski, both just returned from the European theater, where they served as pursuit pilots. Completing the family circle were Miss Rosemary Senter, a 1942 graduate of Calistoga High School who is attending the University of California, and her fiancé, Donald W. Wrinkle, now a teacher at Sutter Creek High School. Absent, but very much in mind, was Jerry Senter of the Navy Air Force, who was unable to get home from his base at Corpus Christi, Texas. Jerry, a 1941 graduate of Calistoga High School, is just finishing his advanced training.

The Charles Karchers entertained their son-in-law and daughter, the D.L. Johnsons of Richmond; their son, Westal Karcher of Hunter's Point; and their daughter-in-law, Mrs. Bryon Karcher of Berkeley. The vacant chair at the table was for Byron, whose army duties would not let him come home for Christmas.

The home of Mrs. A. Cavagnaro and Edith Cavagnaro was the scene of a large family gathering and dinner on Christmas Day. Guests included Mrs. Victor Canata and daughter Bernice, of San Francisco; Mrs. Aurelia Butler; Mr. and Mrs. Frank Pocai and daughters Betty and Marie; Mrs. Mary Pocai; Henry Pocai; Miss Lois Jean Power; and Mr. and Mrs. Bill Cavagnaro and son, Lester.

Realty transactions of the week include the sale of a 125-acre ranch on Mount St. Helena to some Eastern people, Mr. and Mrs. Charles Thorndike of Dover, Massachusetts. They plan to build a lovely home on the Lake County highway site, which has one of the finest views of the valley. The property formerly was owned by Claude Schroeder of Vallejo.

Mrs. Thorndike is the sister of Mrs. Carl Pisor, whose home, the former W.E. Harrington place, is also on the mountain.

During the past year, the combined parlors of the Native Daughters and the Native Sons have staged dances at regular two-week intervals. The dances have drawn large crowds and have added much to the social life of the town.

Tomorrow night, Saturday, the two parlors will wind up the 1944 season with a New Year's dance in the Masonic Auditorium. A four-piece orchestra will furnish the music.

Calistoga families, acting in response to an appeal by Hospitality House, hosted 25 visiting service men for Christmas dinners in their homes.

Civic Club was host at the house over the weekend. On Christmas Day, Myrtle Siemsen, Emma Wolleson, and Mrs. Ray Bascomb spent the day welcoming service men and sending them out to respond to the invitations by local residents.

Townspeople and service personnel alike complemented the directors of Hospitality House on the very beautiful Christmas tree that graced the center of the main room. J.E. Scott furnished the tree; Mrs. Neil Lindbloom and Mrs. John Mingus supplied the lights; Mrs. Frances loaned the decorations; and Mrs. W.C. Wiggins decorated the tree.

The community also has responded to a call for the donation of dishes and silverware to Hospitality House. It now is well supplied with the articles needed for food for service personnel who drop into town on short furloughs.

Middle front page display advertisement:

New Year Greetings to All
May Yours Be a Most Happy
and
Prosperous New Year

Mr. and Mrs. C.A. Carroll
Mr. and Mrs. Ralph P. Winston
Harry S. Osgood.

History, Memories, Perspectives

Calistoga is a jewel of a small town at the head of California's Napa Valley, north of San Francisco. That description fit it in 1944, too. Except that Calistoga was far smaller then, and it was caught in the lingering effects of Prohibition and the Great Depression in addition to World War II.

The town was founded as a health spa, featuring natural hot mineral water, in 1862 by entrepreneur Samuel Brannan. Brannan brought a railroad to town by 1868. Calistoga incorporated as a city in 1886. By the 1940 census, the town had a population of 1,124, and it was served by a daily Southern Pacific freight train. (The population reached 1,418 by 1950 and 5,155 by 2010.) But these numbers are for just the town itself. In 1944, the *Weekly Calistogan* focused – as it still does -- on the much greater area of Calistoga's school district. That stretches from Bale Lane on the south to Knights Valley, Franz Valley, and Porter Creek on the west; and up and over the shoulder of Mount St. Helena to the Lake County line on the north.

Communications

There was no television in Calistoga in 1944. No FM radio. No home computers. No internet. No cell phones. No CD or DVDs.

What many – but not all – families had was a telephone. Most had an AM radio. And some had a phonograph record player. People read about current events – including on-going World War II – in newspapers, or heard about them on radio newscasts. They could see some of the news events – including warfront scenes – a week or so after the fact in newsreels at the Ritz Theater.

Telephones

The telephone wasn't like today's. You cranked a handle to get the attention of an operator in the Pacific Telephone office by the Lincoln Avenue bridge downtown. She rang the telephone of the person you wanted to reach and then connected you. Did she listen to the call? We thought so, and imagined what a wonderful bag of gossip she came home with each day. That wasn't all. Most of us had multiparty telephone lines. Each customer on the line had a different ring – e.g., one long and two short. But any of them could pick up their phone and listen when others on the party line got calls.

Radio

Radios offered a wide variety of information and entertainment – usually in 15-minute bites during the day on weekdays and longer in the evenings and weekends.

Weekday daytime was a mix of newscasts; wake up shows like "Rise and Shine," "Breakfast Club," and "Breakfast at Sardi's"; soap operas like "Our Gal Sunday," "Ma Perkins," "Portia Faces Life," "Fibber McGee and Molly," "Just Plain Bill," "Stella Dallas," "Young Dr. Malone," and "Backstage Wife"; and shows featuring the recorded songs of specific singers: e.g., Kate Smith, Bing Crosby, and Frank Sinatra.

The late afternoon was geared to kids, with action dramas "Terry and the Pirates," "Jack Armstrong, the All-American Boy," and "Captain Midnight."

Big name newscasters – Gabriel Heater, Lowell Thomas, and Fulton Lewis Jr. – came on strong at dinnertime. Evenings had mixed programming, mostly 30-minute, once-a-week shows. Wednesdays, for example, had "Fred Waring Orchestra," "Kay Kyser and His Kollege of Musical Knowledge," "The Lone Ranger," "I Love a Mystery," "Bulldog Drummund," "Lum and Abner," and "Orson Welles."

Saturdays were big on music, ranging from classical to country, pop to exotic: "Metropolitan Opera," "Philadelphia Orchestra," "Boston Symphony," "Lawrence Welk and His Orchestra," "Swing," "Tommy Dorsey Orchestra," "Ink Spots," "Hawaii Calls," "Barn Dance," "Grand Ole Opry," and, last but far from least, "Your Hit Parade."

The hour-long "Hit Parade" presented the 15 most popular songs of the week in count-down style. The rankings were based on sales of sheet music and phonograph records and the songs most played on coin-operated juke boxes in restaurants and bars. In 1944, "I'll Be Seeing You," a wartime tearjerker, was the most popular song. It made "Hit Parade" 24 out of the 52 weeks. Other leaders included "Long Ago and Far Away," "Besame Mucho," "It's Love, Love, Love," "Praise the Lord and Pass the Ammunition," "I'll Walk Alone," "Don't Fence Me In," and "Mairzy Doats."

Other popular shows on Saturday included "Corliss Archer," "Groucho Marx," "Can You Top This" (a comedy panel), "Red Ryder," the "Truth or Consequences" quiz show, "Abie's Irish Rose," and "Inner Sanctum" mysteries.

Sundays had a variety of church services in the morning and early afternoon. But there was plenty else, by category: music – "Stradivari Orchestra," "New York Philharmonic," "Standard Symphony," "American Album," "Kings of Swing," "Bob Crosby and Orchestra," "World of Song;" comedy – "Jack Benny Show," "Edgar Bergen and Charlie McCarthy," "Fred Allen Show," "Life of Riley," "The Great Gildersleeve"; dramas – "The Whistler," "One Man's Family," "The Thin Man," "The Green Hornet"; and quiz shows – "Take It or Leave It" and "Quiz Kids."

Movies

The Ritz Theater was Calistoga's movie venue. The show usually included a main feature film, previews of coming attractions, a cartoon ("Mickey Mouse," "Donald Duck," "Woody Woodpecker"), and a newsreel. The news often included combat shots from one or more warfronts.

"Going My Way" ran away with 1944 Oscar honors: best film, best actor (Bing Crosby), best supporting actor (Barry Fitzgerald), and best director (Leo McCarey). Ingrid Bergman won best actress for her role in "Gaslight," and Ethel Barrymore best supporting actress in "None But the Lonely Heart." Other leading movies were "Meet Me In St. Louis," "Since You Went Away," "Thirty Seconds Over Tokyo," "Hollywood Canteen," "A Guy Named Joe," "The White Cliffs of Dover," and "Laura."

Post Office

The U.S. postal service was well established in Calistoga by 1944, but there was no home delivery in town. You rented a box in the post office lobby or picked up your mail from the general delivery window during business hours (8 a.m. to 5 p.m. on weekdays, 8 a.m. to noon on Saturdays). People outside the city had "rural free delivery." It cost three cents to send a letter, one cent for a postcard ("penny postcards," we called them).

Newspapers

Elementary school kids on bikes delivered at least seven daily newspapers in Calistoga during 1944. These included four from San Francisco – the *Chronicle* and the *Examiner* in the morning, the *News* and the *Call-Bulletin* in the afternoon – and the *Oakland Tribune, Santa Rosa Press Democrat,* and *Napa Register*. The *Weekly Calistogan* was distributed by mail and at newsstands.

Bus service

Greyhound offered six bus trips each way between Calistoga and San Francisco seven days a week in 1944. Its depot was in the lobby of historic Hotel Calistoga on Lincoln Avenue. The first bus left at 6:25 a.m., the last at 5:25 p.m. Catering to tourists, Greyhound offered two extra departures for The City – at 6:25 p.m. and 9:25 p.m. – on Sundays and holidays.

There were no freeways in those days. The City-bound buses wended their way through downtown Napa and Vallejo, across the Carquinez Bridge, along the winding road through Rodeo and Pinole, along San Pablo Boulevard from Richmond to Oakland, and then across the Bay Bridge. There were plenty of stops, and it took well over two hours.

Greyhound also offered daily buses to Lakeport/Ukiah/Eureka at 2:15 p.m. and to the Southern Pacific railroad terminal in Crockett at 3:45 p.m.

Miscellaneous

Auto traffic on Lincoln Avenue was stopped daily so the Southern Pacific train engine could chug to/from a turntable between First and Second streets.

Two major Calistoga streets have been renamed and renumbered since 1944. Main Street then is Foothill Boulevard now. Railroad Avenue then is Fair Way now.

Calistoga 1944

The shopping center era had not arrived. Stores were closed on Sunday. Some stores gave "S&H green stamps," which could be redeemed for items in a catalog full of household goods.

People had washing machines but not dryers. Most washing machines had wringers – like two rolling pins – that squeezed water out of the laundry before it was hung to dry on outdoor clothes lines. Many families had literal "ice boxes" instead of expensive refrigerators. The ice dispensing machine was adjacent to Reeder's Creamery.

In 1944, California's minimum wage was 45 cents an hour. The federal minimum wage was 30 cents an hour. The work week for many jobs was 44 hours – including four hours on Saturday.

"Kilroy was here," a graffiti scrawled by GIs around the world, got full play in Calistoga, too. It included the three words and a mischievous doodle of a bald-headed man with a big nose peeking over a wall, with the fingers of each hand clutching the wall. It is engraved on the World War II Memorial at Washington, D.C.

Popular graffiti, at home and abroad

What remains

Some Calistoga landmarks remain from 1944, although most of them have been remodeled or have new lives.

This list includes City Hall; the library; the elementary and high schools; Pioneer Park; the Tubbs building and auto race track at the fairgrounds; the Catholic and Presbyterian churches; the Odd Fellows lodge building; Mount View Hotel; several major resorts (Pacheteau's and Nance's – now combined as Indian Springs; Dr. Aalders – now Calistoga Spa; Piner's – now Roman Spa); a number of restaurants, including Fior D'Italia, Reeder's Creamery, and Village Green (now Calistoga Inn, Pacifico, and Sarafonia); the service stations at the west end of Lincoln Avenue; Pioneer Cemetery; and, outside of town, Lark-mead winery (now Frank Family Vineyards), Chateau Montelena winery; Myrtledale Hot Springs (now "Duffy's-Myrtledale" drug/alcohol rehab center); Old Faithful Geyser; and Petrified Forest.

New since 1944

We take what's here for granted, but much of it wasn't here in 1944.

Examples: stand-alone police and fire stations and post office; Community Center and the nearby Sharpsteen Museum; Logvy Park with its sports fields, community swimming pool, and veterans' memorial (178 World War II veterans are among the 438 men and women honored); Monhoff Center and its public tennis courts; the fairgrounds' golf course, campground, sports fields, and Butler and Cropp buildings; Tedeschi Field; youth sports programs; Calmart; Carlo Marchiori's vibrant murals on various building walls; the classic Musante metal sculpture on the Silverado Trail; four mobile home parks, numerous subdivisions, and all the resulting streets and homes; many new wineries, restaurants, and resorts; Copperfield's books; bicycle paths; a number of new churches – Baptist, Episcopal, Evangelical, Highlands Christian Fellowship, Jehovah's Witnesses, and Russian Orthodox; and year-around greetings from those Canadian honkers.

About the Author

So who is Jack Rannells?

Rolland Jackson Rannells was born in Chico, California, in 1933. He was raised in St. Helena, CA, through the fifth grade, then in nearby Calistoga from the sixth grade through high school. He graduated in 1951. His father was superintendent of the Calistoga Joint Union School District, high school principal, and football and track coach, 1944-52.

Jack attended Stanford University 1951-54 and then served two years in the Army, including a year as a clerk-typist at U.S. Army Europe headquarters in Heidelberg, Germany. He returned to Stanford and received a BA in journalism in 1958.

He played football and rugby for the Indians, as they were nick-named then.

Over the next quarter century, Jack worked as a reporter for four daily newspapers: *San Jose Mercury* (1958-59), *Santa Cruz Sentinel* (1959-63), *Palo Alto Times* (1963-69), and *San Francisco Chronicle,* (1969-84). He had married his Stanford sweetheart, Eve Ann Eunson, in 1958. They had one son, Buck Robert, in 1961 and one daughter, Nina, in 1963.

In 1984, with both kids out of the house, Jack joined Eve on a grand adventure. She took a job training librarians in the South Pacific country of Papua New Guinea. It was an 18-month job that stretched to 14 years. Jack, the dependent spouse, took on a number of volunteer writing and editing projects. He also created a 200-page mini-encyclopedia about Papua New Guinea for Oxford University Press. Jack has produced three editions of the book, which outlines the country's plants, animals, history, geography, provincial and national government systems, historic leaders, sports records, etc.

Eve contracted malaria and experienced other health problems, and they returned to the U.S. in 1998. They settled in Santa Rosa and then Calistoga. Eve died in 2001.

Jack married again in 2002. This time his wife is a full-blooded Calistogan. Virginia Lee (Beanie) Fisher was born here, schooled here, married here to Bill Thomas, raised four kids here, and was widowed here. She graduated from Calistoga Elementary School in 1944 (see Chapter 11) and is one of the many, many local names in this book.

Jack is blessed that Beanie has given him the free time to tell this story.

Thank You

For help researching the *Weekly Calistogan:* staff at the Calistoga Library

For help with background information: Catherine Wright Lerner, Betty Pocai Ballentine, Beanie Rannells, David Rannells

For help with photos: Sylvia Monfre Marciano (for the Sharpsteen Museum), Pam and Frank Brocco, Betty Pocai Ballentine, Jean Kelly

For help with editing and production: Stephanie Jackel of Printer's Ink

For her infinite patience: Beanie Rannells

About the 𝔚eekly 𝔚alistogan

The newspaper we know as the Weekly Calistogan was founded by J.L. Multer on December 12, 1877, just 15 years after the town was founded by Sam Brannan. The original name was The Independent Calistogian. Charles A. Carroll bought the paper on July 1, 1895, and was publisher until his death on December 7, 1946. Back in 1896, he married a local school teacher, Mertie E. Bennett.

By 1944, our focus year, much of the workload and responsibility for the newspaper were carried by their daughter, Lois, a 1917 graduate of Calistoga High, and her husband, Ralph (Scoop) Winston, an engineer turned journalist. Scoop died in 1955. Lois operated the business until November 1965, when she sold it to Ted J. Libby of Middletown. There have been several changes of ownership since then. Now, in 2012, it is owned by the *Napa Valley Register* (Lee Enterprises Inc.).